D0203038

Primo Levi and the Politics of Survival

Primo Levi and the Politics of Survival

FREDERIC D. HOMER

University of Missouri Press
Columbia and London

Library of Congress Cataloging-in-Publication Data

Homer, Frederic D.
    Primo Levi and the politics of survival / Frederic D. Homer.
        p.   cm.
    Includes bibliographical references and index.
    ISBN 0-8262-1338-3 (alk. paper)
    1. Levi, Primo—Political and social views.   2. Levi, Primo—Philosophy.
3. Politics and culture—Italy—History—20th century.   4. Holocaust, Jewish
(1939–1945) 5. Authors, Italian—20th century—Biography.   6. Holocaust
survivors—Italy—Biography.   7. Jews—Italy—Biography.   I. Title.

PQ4872.E8 Z69   2001
853'.914—dc21
[B]
                                                                    2001027168

Text design: Stephanie Foley
Jacket design: Susan Ferber
Typesetter: The Composing Room of Michigan, Inc.
Printer and binder: The Maple-Vail Book Manufacturing Group
Typefaces: Gill Sans and Sabon

Contents

Acknowledgments

I want to thank the faculty and students whose enthusiasm, discussion, and criticism were of great help to me as I worked on this book: Chris Williams, Steve Ropp, Ben Roth, Eli Isaacson, Derek Reiners, Zachary Rombakis, Jeannie Holland, Cliff Marks, Graham Baxendale, Eric Rasmussen, Luke Bowen, Sarah Talbott, Jennifer Cole, Nyla Bailey, Cynthia Reed, Jeff Williams, Gregg Cawley, Brian Farmer, Rodney Wambeam, Deena Weinstein, and James Stever. I am grateful to those who read and commented upon substantial sections of the manuscript and provided constructive criticism: Gail Simmonds, Larry Hubbell, and John Anderson.

I am indebted to all those at the University of Missouri Press for their intelligence and professionalism, and for making what can be a rough experience enjoyable. In particular, I would like to thank Managing Editor Jane Lago for the smooth and expeditious process, and acquisitions editor Maurice Manning for his excellent editorial suggestions, including the title for this work. I would also like to thank freelance editor Tim Fox, who handled the manuscript with sympathy and care.

Finally, I would like to thank my wife, Carole Homer, for those wonderful discussions about Primo Levi, her incisive reading of the manuscript, and her encouragement.

Primo Levi and the Politics of Survival

Introduction

Ever since my first book, *Se questo e un uomo*, I wanted my works—
though they appeared under my name—to be read as collective
works.

—Primo Levi
cited in Myrna Cicioni's *Primo Levi: Bridges of Knowledge*

It is common knowledge that nobody is born with a decalogue already formed, but that everyone builds his own either during his
life or at the end, on the basis of his own experiences, or of those
of others which can be assimilated to his own; so that everybody's
moral universe, suitably interpreted, comes to be identified with
the sum of his former experiences, and so represents an abridged
form of his biography.

—*The Reawakening*

Primo Levi was born in Turin, Italy, in 1919 and was trained as a chemist,
but he only briefly practiced his trade before World War II intruded. He
joined the anti-Fascist resistance and was immediately arrested by the Fascist Militia in December 1943 at the age of twenty-four. After a short in-
ternment in Fossoli, a camp where the Italians in charge assured him that
he would spend the rest of the war, the Germans took over. Levi left on a
train destined for Auschwitz in late February 1944. In late January 1945,
the Russians reached Auschwitz, and it took him until October 1945 to
reach his home in Turin. His experience at the death camp and his subsequent travels through Eastern Europe were the subjects of his memoirs,
Survival in Auschwitz (Italian title: *Se questo e un uomo*, "If this is a man")

1

and *The Truce*. Levi spent most of his working life as manager of a paint factory in Turin, retiring in 1977 to devote himself full-time to writing. His last completed work was *The Drowned and the Saved,* a retrospective look at the Holocaust. He died in Turin, Italy, in April 1987.[1]

The Holocaust and his work as a chemist were never far from Levi's thoughts. He expressed his ideas about them in short stories, poems, essays and in a novel, *If Not Now, When?* Levi also expanded on his ideas and recounted his experiences in extended interviews. Tulle Reggio's *Dialogo* finds Levi and Reggio in a dialogue about some of the current issues of science, and Ferdinando Camon's *Conversations with Primo Levi* is a far-ranging discussion touching on many aspects of Levi's life, but with an overall emphasis on Levi's political views. Other writers' fine work gives valuable information on Levi's life, literary career, and the literary merits of his writings. This work includes two intellectual biographies, Mirna Cicioni's *Primo Levi: Bridges of Knowledge* and Myriam Anissimov's *Primo Levi: The Tragedy of an Optimist,* and a collection of essays edited by Susan Tarrow, *Reason and Light.* The biographies can be read along with Philip Roth's probing interview that appears as an afterward in recent editions of Levi's *Survival in Auschwitz.*[2] Yet, to understand Levi, there is no substitute for his original works, for they are deliberate models of clarity.

This work is the elaboration of Primo Levi's political philosophy. Levi was a key witness to the Holocaust and an important literary figure of his era, but his arguments need to be inserted into contemporary debates about how we should live and work with others. Levi's political philosophy has been overlooked because prior to this volume, his insights on life and politics have not been gathered in one place. Although his thoughts are scattered in many volumes and in several different literary forms, and though he is drawn to the small naturalistic experiment and sharp observation rather than abstract speculation, Levi's work can be expressed as a consistent set of ideas about his life and circumstances.

Though Primo Levi expressed these ideas in a variety of literary genres, he consistently brought the wiles of a chemist—observation, detachment, and analysis—to his work. In *Survival in Auschwitz,* he writes: "My model (or, if you prefer, my style) was that of the 'weekly report' commonly

---

1. The words above are close to Levi's own in the stock autobiography he provided for his many works. The emphasis here will be on his ideas. While this book is not a biography, as Levi's ideas unfold, much of his life, in his own words, will become known. See for example, Levi, *The Drowned and the Saved.*
2. This book will generally use the English titles of Levi's works.

used in factories: it must be precise, concise, and written in a language comprehensible to everybody in the industrial hierarchy."[3] His naturalistic observations as a child, his formal chemistry training, and his relentless curiosity gave Levi the ability to analyze his life and public circumstances. His detached reporting was a matter of deliberate strategy, for when he began writing about the Holocaust, he felt that to be credible, he must limit himself to careful description. With the exception of his poetry and certain measured prose where he openly expresses his feelings, his writings are careful observational gems of the circumstances he and others faced and the strategies for dealing with them.

At first glance then, Levi is an "objective" reporter of facts who reserves his emotions and opinions for poetry. Yet Levi's objectivity and his modesty toward the complexities of existence distract us from his more ambitious attempt to comprehend life and politics. His understanding dictates many of his actions in Auschwitz, on his journey home, and for the remainder of what he calls "ordinary life."

Primo Levi brings three unique perspectives to his political philosophy. First, the Holocaust was horrible, and virtually inexpressible, but his nightmare there serves as a stark metaphor for the decisions we have to make in life. Levi invites us to ask ourselves whether we have the strength to stand up against the comparatively trivial problems of "ordinary life," whether our additional resources today are enough to make us a match for life. Levi gives us unique insights into the circumstances of the death camp and the circumscribed options chosen by those engulfed in the nightmare. He insists on using these experiences in thinking about ordinary life upon his return from Auschwitz.

Second, in his science fiction, Levi looks at the human species with a studied detachment and asks if we could have been constituted in a different manner. By what turn could we have become a better species? In one story, he asks what would happen if pain were pleasure and pleasure pain. In a second, he asks if we would go to planet earth if we knew in advance about life and existence there. In a third short story, a group of technicians make recommendations to God about constructing man before God has acted on his own in creating the world. These stories question our basic nature and ask whether a better job of constructing humans could have been done.

Third, Levi's work as a chemist brings a unique perspective to his po-

---

3. Levi, *Survival in Auschwitz*, 181.

litical philosophy. *The Monkey's Wrench* is a work about a rigger, Faussone, who serves as an alter ego to the thinly disguised narrator, who just happens to be a Holocaust survivor and chemist. In *The Periodic Table,* Levi sees life and work through the filter of a chemist. In this sense, his thought resembles that of Eric Hoffer, the American longshoreman who uses his work experiences to come to terms with his life. In sum, Levi's understanding of how people try to cope with circumstances when all the rules of life no longer apply, his habit of asking whether creation could have occurred in a better way, and his use of his work as a chemist as both method and meditation all create ideas that are a rich source for modern political thought.

Prior to World War II, Levi stood apart from his fellow students and tried to understand the world. He has admitted that he was filled with an assortment of inchoate and romantic views. The Holocaust taught him the urgency of understanding oneself as integrally connected with others, whether one wants to be or not. Given the brutal scarcity of Auschwitz, Levi was forced to confront the question of solidarity: First me, second me, why you? His political philosophy was forged of necessity and reflection on those terrible times. Political philosophy, as Michael Weinstein, our most pre-eminent life philosopher has us understand, is not a project for the bitterly disappointed among us reflecting on how we could have lived our lives after we have spent a lifetime of abstract speculation. Understanding our lives is a matter of understanding the needs of the flesh. Whether we are attacked by life as Levi was, or live lives of quiet contemplation as an ascetic, we are constantly faced with agonizing choices. Levi's work prepares us to think about possible futures as well as how to face the everyday trials of life—so ordinary to others and often so desperate to ourselves.

The introductory section of this book explores the question of whether we can ever completely overcome something terrible done to us, when we are crushed by other human beings and feel powerless to respond. This section foreshadows Levi's philosophy of "optimistic pessimism."

The second section of the book, "Optimistic Pessimism," examines Levi's assessment of how prisoners stood up to the brutalities in the death camp. He concludes that we are ill-constituted beings who often are not a match for life. Levi asks: Can we be better prepared as humans to contend with the tragedies of existence? In answer to this question, he critiques the postmodern, existential and intellectualist models of choice and gives us his "optimist pessimism" as the best option for the good life.

Levi's political ideas follow with his portrait of Auschwitz as the cynical construction of a synthetic state of nature that maximizes scarcity and terror—in Levi's own words, a "Hobbesian Hell." In his last days in Auschwitz, as the synthetic state of nature disintegrated, an actual social contract was forged between the eleven people left for dead in his infirmary barracks. This contract takes into consideration an understanding of our fragile natures and discloses Levi's minimalist expectations for politics, his "civilized liberalism" that rests on a firm Hobbesian base with no illusions about human nature. Levi's civilized liberalism provides a flesh-and-blood alternative to the contemporary liberalism of John Rawls.

The concluding section asks whether or not the manner in which Levi died should influence future assessment of his work. Several critics have tried to discount his work by suggesting that his apparent suicide negates his life and writings. In contrast, this work shows that his hedonism, optimistic pessimism, and civilized liberalism are consistent with the way he lived and the way he died.

For the most part, the story told is Levi's own, and as much as possible, in his own words. Other thinkers will remain for the most part in the background, except for the occasions where he mentions them or they help to strengthen his case. This book is an appreciative construction, for I am trying to cast Levi's incipient philosophy in terms that make it a comprehensive, viable alternative to other modern works of political philosophy. It would seem to be in the worst taste to construct a political philosophy, something that Primo Levi never asked for, and criticize him on grounds of its insufficiency. The reader, however, is free of such constraints and may judge Levi's works and my own interpretations against a close reading of Levi and those who have affinities and differences with him. The mistakes, I suspect, are for the most part, my own.

I have been teaching a course in political violence for more than twenty-five years, with a significant component on the Holocaust. When I introduced Levi's *Survival in Auschwitz* into the course, my interest in the Holocaust in general and Levi in particular increased. I began to use *The Drowned and the Saved* and some of his other writings in my Contemporary Political Philosophy course as an example of how someone with little formal tutoring in political philosophy can use courage, acute powers of attention, and a voracious appetite for ideas to understand his own life. Also drawing me to him were our similar early educational and religious backgrounds, a close affinity with his ideas, and the gnawing questions that people who read Levi ask of themselves: How would I have responded to such adversity? What are the physical and moral tools for survival? Do I have them? Is there any preparation for such evil? Can we prevent it from occurring again? As I wrote this book I found a sophisticated comprehensive political philosophy that answered many of my questions, questions that have intrigued me, as well as my students, for many years.

"To Lie on the Bottom"

The Origins of Levi's Philosophy

1

Force Majeure

The duel had not resembled its models: it had been unbalanced, unfair, dirty, and had dirtied him. The models, even the most violent,
are chivalrous; life is not. He set out for his appointment, knowing
that he would never be the same man as before.

— *"Force Majeure"*

In his short story *"Force Majeure,"* Primo Levi compresses his experience
of the Holocaust into a frightening confrontation between a citizen and a
sailor.[1] The story, a metaphor for the major tragedy of his life, brings Levi's
Holocaust experience closer to us as he presents a dangerous quandary, an
episode that could conceivably happen to us. The story opens with the protagonist, identified only as "M.," rushing to make an important appointment with the manager of a library. In an unfamiliar part of town, he asks
a passerby the quickest way to get to his appointment. The stranger points
to a long, narrow alleyway. It disturbs M. to see that there are no doorways or niches in the alley, and when he is halfway down the alley he sees
"a husky lad in a T-shirt, perhaps a sailor, come toward him." The sailor
whistles for a dog, and M. hears the panting dog come up behind him:
"They both advanced until they came face to face. M. moved close to the
wall to free the passage, but the other did not do the same: he stopped and
placed his hands on his hips, completely obstructing the path. He did not
have a threatening expression; he calmly seemed to be waiting, but M.
heard the dog let out a deep snarl: it must be a large animal."[2]

---

1. We are aware of the history of the term *Holocaust* and the arguments that follow as
to the proper use of the concept. Is the term to be appropriated by those describing other
events? It is used here for convenient reference and not to close down debate on the subject.

2. Levi, *"Force Majeure,"* in *"The Mirror Maker"*: *Stories and Essays by Primo Levi*,
62. Future references will be cited parenthetically in the text.

The man puts his hands against the walls, completely blocking M.'s path. M. asks, "'Why don't you let me through?' But the sailor answered by repeating the gesture. Perhaps he was mute, or deaf, or did not understand Italian: but he should have been able to understand, the question was not that complex" (63).

"Without warning, the sailor slipped off M.'s eyeglasses, stuffed them into M.'s pocket and delivered a punch to his stomach: not very hard, but M., taken by surprise, backed up several paces." M.'s situation is a first for him, even though he had come across it in modern literature; the moment for courage and defense would inevitably come, for it comes for every fictional character. "He tried to screw up his courage and answered with a straight punch but realized with astonishment that his arm was too short: he wasn't even able to graze the face of his opponent, who had kept him at a distance by propping his hands against M.'s shoulders." M. runs at the sailor with his head low: "The young man caught M.'s head between his hands, pushed him back, and repeated the gesture with the palms of his hands, which M. glimpsed through the haze of his myopia" (63).

M. then uses a tactic to get past the sailor that he also had read about in books—he hurls himself at his opponent's knees. Once again, he is easily rebuffed: "Meanwhile the dog had approached and was sniffing at M.'s pants with a menacing air. M. heard a sharp, resonant step behind him: it was a girl in gaudy clothes, perhaps a prostitute. She went past the dog, M., and the sailor as though she did not see them, and disappeared at the end of the alley" (64).

> The sailor beats him and toys with him some more. He straightened out his legs against the ground by pressing on the kneecaps. So that was the meaning of the gesture, M. thought: the sailor wanted him lying down, right away; he could not tolerate any sort of resistance. The man chased away the dog with a curt command, took off his sandals, and, holding them in his hands, prepared to walk along M.'s body as you walk down the balancing beam in the gym: slowly, arms outstretched, staring straight ahead. (65)

After walking across M.'s body, including stepping on his forehead, the sailor "slipped on his sandals and left, followed by the dog. . . . M., who until then had lived a normal life strewn with joys, irritations and sorrows, successes and failures, perceived a sensation he had never experienced before, that of persecution, *force majeure,* absolute impotence, without escape or remedy, to which one can react only by submission. Or with death: but was there any sense in dying just to pass through an alley-way?" (64).

For M., the "duel had not resembled its models: it had been unbalanced, unfair, dirty, and had dirtied him. The models, even the most violent, are chivalrous; life is not. He set out for his appointment, knowing that he would never be the same man as before" (65).

As I have suggested, this incident in *"Force Majeure"* is a distillation of Levi's confrontation with the Holocaust. The story's themes provide a convenient superstructure upon which we can sketch an outline of Levi's political philosophy.[3] In the beginning of the story, M. moves with the assurance that life has a purpose and there is meaningful work to do. Abruptly and involuntarily, his life is turned upside down due to circumstances beyond his control. Similarly, Auschwitz destroyed Levi's carefree, optimistic sentiments about life.

M. in the alley has few options available, and he quickly exhausts them. Levi goes into great detail, especially in *The Drowned and the Saved*, to explain to the reader that few options were available for the vast majority of concentration camp victims. Schoolchildren repeatedly asked him why he did not leave Europe in the wake of Hitler, or, once imprisoned in Auschwitz, why he did not cause a rebellion or escape from the camp (Lager). In his writing he shows great patience in trying to show why early flight, rebellion, and escape were not viable options for virtually anyone in the camps. Life for the prisoners resembled the narrow alley in *"Force Majeure,"* where few niches or doorways provide options.

The enemy came not as a monster with some great warning attached to his person or actions, but as an ordinary person playing a known role—a sailor, in the story—but acting in inexplicable ways. It was not possible to anticipate the awful confrontation or to know how to react to it. This occurred in civilized Europe. When the dog growls behind him or when the figure of the sailor appears, M. cannot gauge how powerful his adversary is. He quickly finds out that there is no reasoning with the new enemy. The young sailor's brutal actions and M.'s shock mirror the experiences of the deportees when they were ripped from their homes, thrown into ghettos, put on the dehumanizing trains, and beaten on the platforms as they got

3. The story mirrors Levi's experience, as a survivor, but as he emphasizes, his experience was quite unique in one respect; the vast majority of the people in the concentration camps never made it out of the "alley."

off. Ordinary experience has no framework for understanding such actions. In the Lager too, the intellectual tools prisoners brought to the confrontation were of little use—most often they were counterproductive. New understandings, however limited in usefulness—whether trying to understand a new language, or forgetting the "why" of why they were there and being treated badly—were necessary for even the smallest chance of survival.

M. has advantages that Levi never had in the Lager. Those who have read about the Holocaust or understood the modern messages in films like *Papillion* and *High Noon*—films Levi himself watched in the years after the Holocaust—might have at least imagined something like the encounter with the sailor. Since World War II, we have seen hundreds of films and been schooled in an ethos of resistance. Levi and his generation were not. Still, with all these modern advantages, M. has no proper response to the circumstances and is crushed. In contrast with M., in his novel, *If Not Now, When?*, Levi gives his hero a fighting chance because he has the time to convert what he reads about weapons into actual weapons he can use as a partisan. But the Holocaust, like the encounter in the alley, came upon the European Jews too suddenly and with no preparation for converting knowledge of resistance into tools of action. M. is more educated in self-defense and resistance than Levi, but these skills have no impact against the sailor's *force majeure*.

The prostitute makes M.'s persecution all the more puzzling. For Levi, being a member of a social category, a Jew, is no crime, no reason for guilt, and no basis for persecution. When the prostitute is let through, it violates any table of values that M. could have brought to the encounter. "Good" and "bad" mean something unfathomable in these circumstances. At the conclusion of *"Force Majeure,"* the sailor puts on his sandals and marches off just as the Germans left Levi and others in the Lager's infirmary (Ka-Be) to die. At their departure, the enemy does nothing to supply the "why" for their atrocities.

In M.'s world, everything is taken from him and he is left to ponder who he is when he hits bottom. Even though he picks up his life, he is never the same. All the models of life fail him, for "the models, even the most violent, are chivalrous; life is not." Levi spent his youth, as most of us do, in an Emersonian compensatory universe. His uneventful childhood supported a youthful optimism and naïveté toward existence, one in no need of a god for explanation. The boot came along and crushed his youthful outlook.

Philosophy is the compendium of systematic thoughts and actions that guide the individual in his or her response to the flux of existence. Life's not-so-gentle insistence provides the necessity for the individual to act before the answers to all of the philosopher's questions are in. The pragmatic philosopher would rather act on partial, though thoughtful, information than keep his head in the "intellectualist" tradition of knowledge for knowledge's sake. That tradition, today reinforced by the arbitrary truth of the separation of fact and value, is the basis of looking everywhere but in one's philosophy for principles of action. Life, flesh, and ideas were Levi's teachers, and they are worked into a philosophy through a keen ability to observe and synthesize the events of his life.

Levi's political philosophy is a way of viewing our lives and circumstances that may inform those who are trying to muddle their way through life with some specter of intelligence.[4] Unless we are engulfed like Isaac Bashevis Singer's "Spinosa of Market Street" in the ideas of another, philosophy only throws us hints about how we might conduct our lives in terms of our own individuality and the unique circumstances we face.[5] Examining the critical observations and ideas that guided Levi's life, a life not so favored by events, will present plenty of hints in Levi's philosophy that will be useful for our own lives.

"Force Majeure" and the Auschwitz horrors it symbolizes introduce the philosopher to two distinct but related problems. First, can we really comprehend the enormity and horror of Levi's story? Second, is there room to think of or act upon a set of orientations when someone is unexpectedly crushed by horrible events, forced to march to the cadence of others, and seems virtually incapable of recovery? How does this relate to our own lives where, in contrast, we have the potential for leisure to contemplate political philosophy, but we often end up with seemingly infinite discretion and no compass to guide us?

To address the first question, in *"Force Majeure,"* we are given a stark incident to ponder to bring us closer to Levi's experience of the Holocaust, but can we ever understand it? Can we imagine the unimaginable? For instance, he indicates in his writings that words like *cold* and *hungry* are not adequate to understand his experiences. He suggests that if imprisonment

---

4. Levi speaks of everyone developing a decalogue in life, and that life and how one lives it is one's biography. He is too modest, because he has gone further than most in the development of his life philosophy. This work simply gives him a nudge toward that end.

5. Adam Phillips, *The Beast in the Nursery*, 109, offers an interesting notion of how teaching ideas, no matter how dramatic or didactic, merely ends up as hints to others.

had gone on much longer, a vocabulary more adequate to the circumstances might have arisen. It was needed, because the experience of the Holocaust was sui generis.

In *"Force Majeure,"* Levi tries to make us understand the most unfathomable experiences—ones we have not seen before, ones where our world is turned upside down. We can understand selfishness, deprivation, brutality, and maybe even his hunger and thirst, but can we grasp these concepts *en extremis,* in a world where the laws of nature we have always assumed no longer apply? In this bewildering world, no prior experience helps us to understand what is going on, nor can the application of our reason to the baffling experiences make any impact.

In *The Drowned and the Saved,* Levi suggests that "the Lager was a cruel laboratory in which one could witness situations and behaviors never seen before or anywhere else." To draw us closer to his world, Levi suggests that the Lager is a useful metaphor for the human condition. Sooner or later we all face our own death: "Willingly or not we come to terms with power, forgetting that we are all in the ghetto, that the ghetto is walled in, that outside the ghetto reign the lords of death, and that close by the train is waiting."[6]

As much as Levi tries to narrow the distance between himself and the reader, the incommensurability of experiences remain. Levi acknowledges this when he replies to Ferdinando Camon's question in *Conversations with Primo Levi:*

> Camon: [Walter] Benjamin, however, said somewhere that the concentration camp is not an abnormal condition beyond comparison with the rest of the world. The concentration camp is nothing but the condensation of a condition common in the world. In short, the concentration camp itself mirrors the structures of every society: it too has its saved and its drowned, its oppressors and oppressed.
> Levi: I have two things to say about that. The first with repugnance: this comparison of the world with the concentration camp arouses revulsion in us, those of us who have been "marked," "tatooed." No, that's not the way it is, it's not true that the Fiat factory is a concentration camp, or that the psychiatric hospital is a concentration camp. There's no gas chamber at Fiat. You can be very badly off in the psychiatric hospital, but there's no oven, there's an exit, and your family can come to visit.[7]

6. Levi, *Drowned,* 95, 69.
7. Camon, *Conversations with Primo Levi,* 19–20.

Thus, though analogies can be useful, they must not be misused. For Levi, the Holocaust and the death camps are ultimately unique. We abuse our analogies if we allow them to convey more horror to another experience than the experience merits on its own grounds.

Still, if carefully used, the Holocaust can be instructive: Lager behavior can be generalized to other institutions and serve as a metaphor. Levi says to Camon:

> Nevertheless, and this is the second thing I have to say, they can be valid as a metaphor. I said so in *Survival in Auschwitz*, that the concentration camp is a mirror of the external situation, but a distorting mirror. For example, the automatic and inevitable establishment of a hierarchy among the victims is a fact that has not been sufficiently discussed, the fact that the prisoner who gets ahead on the backs of his comrades exists everywhere.[8]

The Holocaust can serve as a useful example, but it should not be trivialized by creating unworthy comparisons. Levi warns us not to forget other atrocities before and after the Holocaust, and states that "the Nazi concentration camp system still remains a *unicum,* both in its extent and its quality. At no other place or time has one seen a phenomenon so unexpected and so complex: never have so many human lives been extinguished in so short a time, and with so lucid a combination of technological ingenuity, fanaticism and cruelty.[9]

"Force Majeure" is one of the last attempts Levi made to enhance our understanding of what it was like reaching the bottom as a human being and never quite recovering. Perhaps there is this unbridgeable gulf between Levi and his audience: We may never comprehend, and even if we finally did, there still remains a gulf between us, because we can do something he could never do—walk away from the experience. According to Levi, because of the nature of existence and thought, we will never be capable of fully understanding others, and not just about the Holocaust. Nonetheless, we must make the effort. If we don't, then we do not know what to fear and how to confront our fears, whether real or imagined. Those who nurture doubt and do not act on what is available to them open the field of action to those who devoutly believe.

We will try to understand Levi's experience in the Holocaust without

8. Ibid., 20.
9. Levi, *Drowned,* 21.

diminishing its horror and minimizing the experience of the survivors. This respectful attitude will allow us to use Levi's philosophy as a metaphor with regard to experiences we face in our ordinary lives.

"Force Majeure" illustrates the second problem for a philosophy based on the Holocaust: No matter what action M. takes, life is destroyed by an irresistible force from which he cannot recover, and this defining experience leaves little room for action. Life is turned upside down, and none of the rules we know about its complexities apply any longer. M. is even better prepared for what happens to him than Levi was, since M. has been brought up on the ideologies of heroism and resistance and the testimonies of those few who lived to tell their Holocaust experiences. Yet, even for M., with all his advantages, there is no recovery from his experience. No useful preparation for disaster exists, nor does optimism for recovery after disaster.

Primo Levi, in writing about Auschwitz, describes the same *force majeure* when he asks what, if anything, is left of man when he reaches bottom.[10] "Then for the first time we became aware that our language lacks words to express this offense, the demotion of man." He goes on to describe this demoralization: "It is not possible to sink lower than this; no human condition is more miserable than this, nor could it conceivably be so. Nothing belongs to us anymore; they have taken away our clothes, our shoes, even our hair; if we speak, they will not listen to us, and if they listen, they will not understand. They will even take away our name."[11] To add to the offense, in the end the murderers walked away without guilt or material consequences, while the victims who survived never got over their experiences.

Here, at the bottom, there appears to be no room for a philosophy. This experience, emblematic of existence in many ways, ends in the destruction of man, an utterly pessimistic conclusion. Curiously, this conclusion rests side by side in Levi's works with his "optimistic pessimism," which calls for us to carry on in spite of the tragedies of existence, including our knowledge of the ultimate tragedy, our inevitable death. The prisoners in the Lager had choices to make, even though they were narrowly based upon upbringing and a limited and confined reason. Philosophy finds its way into the darkest confines. In addition, chance, reason, and will in the

10. The Italian title of *Survival in Auschwitz, Se questo e un uomo,* properly translated into English as "If this is a man," asks us what we are to make of the man who reaches bottom.

11. Levi, *Survival,* 26–27.

Lager serve up lessons for us in situations where reason is no longer confined. In sum, the apparent paradox in Levi is that he talks about the utter destruction of man at the bottom, and almost side by side with these passages, he speaks of how even in this cruel universe the survivors grasp shards of strategies to cope with overwhelming circumstances. He is destroyed and yet against this massive tragic betrayal he forges a "tragic optimism." He is betrayed by the circumstances of his own existence and our "ill-constituted" nature, yet he sees no other response than to proceed with life. This leap into practicality fringed by doubt is his honest reaction to the adversities of existence, and it shames those of us who might crumble under lesser pressures. Levi's philosophy begins with the recognition of its tragic base.

Levi and his fellow prisoners, who simply tried to survive the day, were confronted daily with restrictive ranges of choices about how to live.[12] Do we steal from one another? Do we collaborate with others for another piece of bread? Do we find a niche in the Lager? Levi's description of the limited, demeaning, and excruciating choices the prisoners were forced to make while being degraded on the way to extermination allows us to think about what our own responses to the Holocaust would have been. More humbling, do we respond honorably in life even when we face no such horror?

Levi's experience forces us to question ourselves: Are we prepared to understand an extreme situation where our world is turned upside down? Are we able to use the experiences of Levi and others to help us prepare ourselves? Once in the situation, how would we react? Levi suggests this last question is most difficult to answer, because few know their own breaking points: "Now nobody can know for how long and under what trials his soul can resist before yielding or breaking. Every human being possesses a reserve of strength whose extent is unknown to him, be it large, small or nonexistent, and only through extreme adversity can we evaluate it."[13] We probably do not know our limits, but given the trials in our lives, if we are honest, we know in what situations we are most vulnerable and where the flaws of character reside. If we try to answer these questions honestly, we might learn something about strengthening our own internal fortifications.

Force majeure is a penetrating concept. Although most of us do not go

12. Levi constantly reminds readers that most prisoners were marched immediately to their death; choice did not enter into their lives.
13. Levi, *Drowned*, 60.

through the terrors of a Holocaust, we have faced overwhelming force and feelings of humiliation at various times in our lives.[14] *Force majeure* is a limit situation, the penetration of the social into the existential; there is nothing more profound for us to reflect on. Do we submit? Do we fight back? Does the terror engendered necessitate that we go through life in fear and prevention of such future events? Our thoughts inevitably turn to such questions when we think of Levi's brilliant concept of *force majeure*.

For Levi then, the Holocaust is a unique event, yet he does not put it out of the reach of understanding. He also lays out side by side the seemingly contradictory ideas that those who came under the heel were utterly destroyed, yet many resolved to press on with life, optimistically pessimistic. The pessimistic part of the equation is not only based on the idea that something awful happened to those in the Lager, but that life is full of tragedy. Most importantly, we are ill-constituted beings who must deal with life, but we do not have the requisite tools. The section "Ill-Constituted Beings" concentrates on the foundations of his pessimism.

In *"Force Majeure,"* M. is inalterably crushed, but the question that haunts Levi, even in his earliest writings, is whether man can overcome such destruction. The third section, "Optimistic Pessimism," will focus on the pessimism that stems from Levi's views of human nature, and on the optimism that leavens it: the imperative of responding to the adversities of existence. Levi's efforts at overcoming begin when he is at the bottom and continue throughout his life. Compelled to witness and fortified by his optimistic pessimism, Levi surges forward to make a place for himself in this life and for others with whom he shares this world.[15] As he does so, he questions the role of luck, will and education in the attempt to respond to the adversities of existence in his own life and in public life.

This section on "Optimistic Pessimism" will also explore the strategies of survival Levi used in his Holocaust and post-Holocaust experiences. It will examine the actions Levi took to insure his continued existence, but his is not merely an empirical quest for the live options. Surviving also refers to doing it in a manner that involves a quest for the good, but more important for Levi, avoidance of the bad. Even when he chooses from a restricted set of alternatives, he tries to minimize debasement by refusing to live on stored moral capital.

14. We have to go no further than to think of the bully in ordinary life.
15. "To make a life for oneself and for others," the definition of the modern project of politics, describes Levi's efforts.

As he fights a losing battle with the crushing forces of life, whether in the Lager or in "ordinary life," he asks himself whether virtue need play any role. What might these virtues be? The relief from pain? The preservation of dignity? Survival at all costs? Reaching out to others? Is virtue crowded out by the sheer necessity of a "Hobbesian Hell"? If we choose to forgo martyrdom and live another day, what essential needs do we have to fill, and how do we treat others in the struggle to fill them? Do we have any choice? We encounter Levi's brutal honesty in answering these questions; he forgoes the temptation of any personal justification of his behavior.

The third section, "A Defense of Modernism," shows Levi returning from Auschwitz the way he went in, a firm believer in modernism. Although upon his return from Auschwitz he no longer believed in "progress"—he returned as an optimistic pessimist—Levi still believed in modern civilized liberalism, which the Nazis tried to destroy. His experience in Auschwitz led him to a sophisticated defense of civilized liberalism based on the idea that we are ill-constituted beings who must maintain an optimistic pessimism in the face of existence. Although our flawed beings are incapable of any kind of sustained progress, we are best served by modernism. We will explore his ideas about how we can, in our individualistic age, live and maintain an expedient accommodation with others.

Choices we make today come under different structures and circumstances than those that Levi had to make in the Lager. Saul Bellow helps us tack through modern society by reminding us that a crucial task is to separate out the important from the inessential.[16] Modern society implies that having time for thought is not a problem, for we have the leisure to make choices. What we lack is the will or direction to guide our behavior.

In a modern capitalist democracy, people are free to tell us what we should believe and how we should act, and they often do so in subtle ways. Many forces distract us from the essential needs of the flesh. We have the time, but there are distractions and we are distractible. Jean Jacques Rousseau, when he is providing the ideal education for his fictive pupil, Émile, sees the same difficulties as Bellow in separating the essential needs from the frivolous, even in the much simpler world of the eighteenth century. The only book to be found in Émile's library is *Robinson Crusoe*. That book will teach him one important lesson: "He [Émile] will want to know all that is useful, and he will want to know only that." The star pupil

16. For Bellow, see James Wood, "Essences Rising," 41.

will live his life in accordance with this lesson. "This is the true 'castle in Spain' of this happy age when one knows no other happiness than the necessities and freedom."[17] In other words, in Rousseau's times and in ours as well, so much is superfluous to a good life. In modern societies, we have to do a mental experiment to decide what is essential, and freedom simply means distancing ourselves from the dominant objects and opinions that the society has created. Society maintains subtle coercion, but we should be capable of recapturing our own existence.

This picture of modern society contrasts with the circumstances in the Lager. There, needs were clear and the moral consequences of choice were obvious. Utterly lacking in the death camps were circumstances that can lead to time and distance from the problems and an atmosphere free of duress in which to make choices. Finally, even if the slave could overcome exhaustion, the "proper" alternatives may come at the cost of his or her life. In this massive understatement, we can see the problems Levi and others faced. Choices were restricted, made under extreme duress, and driven by cruel necessity. In the Lager, each isolated monad foraged alone, and rarely could he scrounge enough to sustain himself for more than the day. His needs were clear: food, sleep, water, and protection from the cold. Isolated incidents of cooperation occasionally could yield Levi and the other prisoners more, but the most pressing impulse was to provide first for me, second for me, and to ask: Why you? The prisoners scrambled to fill the insistent needs, bartered for needs not initially fulfilled, and protected what they could scrounge, beg for, or steal. The lesson is "learnt not to let myself be robbed, and in fact if I find a spoon lying around, a piece of string, a button which I can acquire without danger of punishment, I pocket them and consider them mine by full right."[18]

Despite the differences between the nature of choices that faced Levi in "ordinary life" and the choices he faced in the Lager, Levi's ideas about how to confront life significantly changed only once in his lifetime, when his youthful optimism was driven away. His captivity in Auschwitz was decisive in the development of his political philosophy, and for the rest of his life he used and expanded upon principles he learned there, in addition to principles forged by his early family life and scientific training. In the Lager, the only choice was to put up as much resistance, however feeble, under the heel of the boot. During the rest of his life, where the major prob-

17. Rousseau, *Émile; or, On Education*, 185.
18. Levi, *Survival*, 37.

lem was to act upon the tragic, confusing circumstances of life, he understood the contingency of our choices and the necessity to make them. To assent to doubt would be to leave the world to those who do not doubt, those who do evil without reservation, those who perfect the world in their own image.

The ethos that developed from Levi's experience and guided his choices is one of defensive hedonism, where we do not know the good, but we are intimately acquainted with the bad. It is a sound basis of his flesh-and-blood liberalism, based on lived experience. It was forged in the Lager and developed over the rest of his life. He shows us how to regain our moral seriousness in times where weakness may provide an opening for those who lead others with moral certainty.

The views that the Holocaust proves that modernism provides the seeds of its own destruction, that modernism is a brief stopping point on the path to the Holocaust, or that modernism is no longer sustainable provide Levi with his intellectual adversaries. Levi's liberal hedonism is a hearty defense of modernism. If we fail, we fail as humans, not because of modernism and democracy, but because we are ill-constituted beings. If there is any provisional hope for us, we need to be better educated, more civilized.

Levi's thoughts and actions are in service of insuring that the chances are decreased for ghastly events recurring. He tells us how to respond to the contemporary public situation. In another of the many ironies that define man for him, intractable human nature and the structures of society that embody the contradictions of our nature seem so beyond our control. Yet there is the continual urge to be actively engaged.

The problem of education and action as it occurs in liberal democratic societies may be illustrated by again referring to M. in Levi's *"Force Majeure"* and stretching Levi's metaphorical situation. How can we keep up the fight to make sure that no more alleys are built? If they are, we must insist that they have niches and exits. All existing alleys must be widened and made visible to aggregates of people. We must fortify our education to make sure that our citizens do not act as the sailor did.[19] Bringing about these changes will meet resistance from the ignorant and the indifferent, but more important, these suggestions will be competing with the suggestions of others lobbying for other changes in the city. We will compete with

19. We are assuming for the sake of symmetry to the Holocaust that what happened to M. happened to a huge number in the city many years ago.

those trying to convince the public that there are more immanent dangers like flood, fire, pestilence, or environmental degradation. Opposition also will come from those who do not like "us" for who we are, and from those who have the effrontery to deny that the incident in the alley really happened. How can one with a serious concern be heard in the modern Tower of Babel?

Levi's experiences with survival force us to ask ourselves how we would act if we ever were under the same kind of imperatives and duress. He also prompts us to ask how we make life choices in the circumstances of ordinary life. He asks us to consider his rigorous defense of modernism and tells us why, considering that life is a losing proposition, we must leaven our pessimism with optimism. As part of his defense of modernism, he tries to convince us not to be carried away by leaders so certain of their ideas. He also argues that we should not abandon moral seriousness under the influence of another set of thinkers who tell us that knowledge lacks clarity and leave us with no defensible alternatives.

2

Hobbesian Hell

It was a Hobbesian life, a continuous war of everyone against everyone.

— *The Drowned and the Saved*

Imagine now a man who is deprived of everyone he loves, and at the same time of his house, his habits, his clothes, in short, of everything he possesses. . . . He will be a man whose life or death can be lightly decided with no sense of human affinity, in the most fortunate of cases, on the basis of a pure judgment of utility. It is in this way that one can understand the double sense of the term "extermination camp", and it is now clear what we seek to express with the phrase: "to lie on the bottom."

— *Survival in Auschwitz*

This chapter will examine the most consequential context for Primo Levi's ideas, the Monowitz Lager in the Auschwitz complex. Auschwitz itself was made up of forty separate units, enterprises sustained by slave labor, but these enterprises were but a temporary diversion in an overwhelming death machine that methodically killed Jews in great numbers.[1] In Monowitz Levi toiled, first in harsh physical labor, and later in a factory in the complex that was supposed to, but never did, produce synthetic rubber.

One of the keys to surveying our world and its circumstances is whether we decide there is any room for improvement in that world, or whether the human condition does not suggest possible better worlds. Usually the

---

1. The "politically correct" way to say this is that many groups had members killed, but the stark reality is that Auschwitz was overwhelmingly a death camp for Jews.

latter is expressed as a world with unrelieved misery. Irving Howe compared the world views of the novels *1984* and *Brave New World* to clarify this distinction.[2] He feels that George Orwell in *1984* sees no hope for redemption in a world suffused with the worst in human nature. On the other hand, Howe believes that Aldous Huxley's *Brave New World* shows the contrast between two worlds, the wilderness and the city, and offers hope for a better existence in the freedom of those lands beyond the city. Primo Levi falls into the latter camp, expecting and later finding a somewhat better world outside of the Lager. However, he does this with many qualifications: Nothing reaches the horror of the Holocaust, but the world after Auschwitz, although better, is a tragic one, always quivering at the brink of extinction. This, as we shall see, is an expression of his optimistic pessimism.

Auschwitz was a merciless world where if the prisoners were "lucky enough" to escape the initial selections, they were ground in the machine unto death. Levi observes what happens to a being under extreme circumstances, for "the Lager was a cruel laboratory in which one could witness situations and behaviors never seen before or after or anywhere else."[3] The learning that takes place under tragic circumstances is important to Levi both as a survival mechanism and a recurring source of ideas, but it does not provide sufficient compensation for what happened to him. The conditions of the Lager were unique and tended to nullify the life strategies the prisoners had become habituated to and brought with them—strategies carefully thought out in their lives prior to the Holocaust.

Levi encountered a number of political and metaphysical boundary conditions in the Lager: a Hobbesian scarcity, an irrational universe with no sign of God, and the dead heave of fate.

Relegation to the Lager was a descent into the hypothetical Hobbesian "state of nature," characterized by the individual's ceaseless exercise of power to satisfy a normal appetite in a situation of abnormal scarcity. In the end, there could be no appeal to a central authority to resolve disputes and restore order among the prisoners. This was a Hobbesian Hell calculated by the Germans to destroy the prisoners: "They [the Lager] were no longer designed to terrorize political opponents, but to destroy the Jews."[4]

When Levi arrived, conditions were only a little better: "At the end of

2. Howe, *A World More Attractive: A View of Modern Literature and Politics*, 216–26.
3. Levi, *Drowned*, 95. Future references will be cited parenthetically in the text.
4. Ferdinando Camon, *Conversations with Primo Levi*, 30.

'43—after Stalingrad—the shortage of manpower in Germany was so acute that it became indispensable to use everybody, even the Jews. It was at this time that Auschwitz emerged as a hybrid concentration-camp, or rather a hybrid concentration-camp 'empire': extermination plus exploitation, or rather extermination through exploitation" (*Drowned*, 30).

The prisoners were equal in their abject state, and their freedom to act was greatly circumscribed. In the Lager, prisoners resembled the individuals in Hobbes's state of nature, only they were worse off: The scarcity was real, not internally generated by their ceaseless appetites, but by the deliberate withholding of necessities for living.

Rousseau claimed that when Hobbes and Locke, both contract theorists, described man in the state of nature, "they spoke about savage man and they described civil man."[5] What Hobbes and Locke had understood about human nature was taken from observations of people in societies that already tyrannized over individuals. The Hobbesian Hell of the Lager might be aptly described as Rousseau's explanation of a Hobbesian universe. The society that tyrannizes over individuals forces its members into their "Hobbesian" behaviors. Also, Levi believes that the Hobbesian drives in man exacerbated the situation.

The Germans artificially manufactured scarcity in the Lager. It was not a relative scarcity that impelled the prisoners to action, but an absolute scarcity of the necessities of life: "A fortnight after my arrival I already had the prescribed hunger, that chronic hunger unknown to free men, which makes one dream at night and settles in all the limbs of one's body." The same went for water and clothing to keep oneself warm. Levi describes imposed scarcity when speaking of the lives of the slave laborers in the Lager: "Thousands of individuals, differing in age, condition, origin, language, culture and customs are enclosed within barbed wire: there they live a regular, controlled life which is identical for all and inadequate to all needs, and which is much more rigorous than any experimenter could have set up to establish what is essential and what adventitious to the conduct of the human animal in the struggle for life."[6]

Hobbesian scarcity was imposed from above and the behaviors that followed were a direct result of the mad logic of the Lager.[7] For those at the bottom, "All are enemies or rivals" (*Survival*, 42). If a prisoner chose to

---

5. Brian R. Nelson, *Western Political Thought,* 227.
6. Levi, *Survival in Auschwitz,* 87. Future references will be cited parenthetically in the text.
7. In the ensuing chapters we will describe these conditions in greater detail.

survive, he must supplement the given provisions by guile and theft, because nobody could survive on the food, water, and shelter they were allocated. A purpose of the Lager was "to have a pool of cheap, or rather no-cost labor. This fact had been calculated in a very rational way: they anticipated a survival period of three months."[8] This was no rationalized system of slavery where the idea was to maximize what labor one extracted from the slave. In the Lager, the prisoner was totally dispensable. The dead man would be replaced by another prisoner, one soon to be dead himself.

Rousseau saw us as fragile beings initially blessed with a modicum of pity so fragile that it could easily be destroyed by civilization. What Hobbes did not recognize is that "savage man . . . tempers the ardor he has for his own well-being by an innate repugnance Rousseau calls *pity,* the only natural virtue that human beings possess."[9] The conditions of scarcity in the Lager drove out not only the fragile pity, but the elements of learning that toughen these fragile sentiments. Levi does not believe that man, if left on his own and stripped of the reinforcements of civilization, can act as a Hobbesian free being. Physical limitations as well as the difficulty in overcoming learned inhibitions leave him in a very impaired state of readiness. It is difficult for us to understand this abject state, something we will later call the *musselmans* state of mind:

> We do not believe in the most obvious and facile deduction: that man is fundamentally brutal, egotistic and stupid in his conduct once every civilized institution is taken away, and that the Häftling [prisoner] is consequently nothing but a man without ambitions. We believe, rather, that the only conclusion to be drawn is that in the face of driving necessity and physical disabilities many social habits and instincts are reduced to silence. (*Survival,* 87)[10]

Many had already suffered deprivation and degradation in the ghettos before they were put on the trains bound for Auschwitz. Levi speaks of the additional horror of the transports: the deprivation of food and water, the extremes of temperature, the obscene crowded conditions, and the terrors caused by the lack of knowledge about where they were going and what their fate was to be. Whether they lost everything slowly or all at

8. Camon, *Conversations,* 30–31.
9. Nelson, *Western,* 227.
10. Later we will see that these instincts and habits in humans seem to be overwhelmed by a darker side of human nature.

once, the great leveler was the train, and if they survived the transport and the initial selection, it was clear that "[we] had reached the bottom. It is not possible to sink lower than this; no human condition is more miserable than this, nor could it conceivably be so. Nothing belongs to us anymore; they have taken away our clothes, our shoes, even our hair; if we speak, they will not listen to us, and if they listen, they will not understand. They will even take away our name" (*Survival,* 26–27).

In William James's terms, the "me" of the individual had been taken away: the material me, the social me, the spiritual me.[11] The Lager's enforced scarcity ravaged all of the material parts of the "me." We all begin with different ideas of what is our material me—our clothes, our houses, the luxuries we procure—but the Lager leveled the individual, for no longer did the individual have all he needed to survive.

A luxury in these conditions was an extra piece of bread, which did not remain in one's possession for long. The imperative of hunger and the rationalization, often true, that if you kept the bread it might be stolen, led more often than not to immediate consumption. Of course, surplus is a misnomer here, because even with an extra ration here and there, the individual did not have enough to eat to allow him to survive for an extended period of time.

The *häftlinge,* or prisoner, was deprived of the social me, the recognition that he gets from those around him. It became the Hobbesian war of all against all: "The Law of the Lager said: 'eat your own bread, and if you can, that of your neighbor,' and left no room for gratitude." There was very little place for collective efforts that might better the conditions of all (*Survival,* 160).[12]

Finally, "The spiritual 'me'" is "the entire collection of my states of consciousness, my psychic faculties and dispositions taken concretely."[13] This spiritual me virtually disappeared in the Lager because of the savage attacks on the material and social me. These assaults meant that the prisoners spent every waking moment of their day entirely on the minute-by-minute struggle for survival, negating the possibility of the sustained thought or reflection that constitutes the spiritual me. The Holocaust was a complete annihilation of its victims. In the Lager, the various aspects of the "me" would be destroyed, followed by the death of the shells of beings

---

11. James, *Psychology: The Briefer Course,* 44–46.
12. Exceptions to this will be noted later, because they form the core of a key debate on the degree of social cooperation in the Lager.
13. James, *Psychology,* 48.

that remained. Levi writes that "the entire history of the brief 'millennial Reich' can be reread as a war against memory, an Orwellian falsification of memory, falsification of reality, negation of reality" (*Drowned,* 17).

In sum, Auschwitz was a death camp in which the prisoners would not last more than three months. When all was done, none of the prisoners would be left alive, and nobody would know what had happened there. However, no system, even the Lager, is completely closed, and it is important to talk about some of its breaches. First we will explain why the annihilation of the existence of the camps utterly failed. Second, we will show how the prisoners were able to alleviate, if only slightly, the abject conditions of their Hobbesian scarcity.

Perhaps Hitler's biggest mistake was choosing to destroy a literate population that could tell its tale of horror. The Nazis' attempts to annihilate history by murdering everyone did not work. For example, in one death camp, Chelmno, where 400,000 were murdered and only two survived, the story was told. The Nazis were so smugly confident that they, the victors, would write history, that at first they did little to cover their tracks. When it was evident the war was lost, they began covering the evidence. Little did they suspect how much would become known from the traces they could not destroy—the diaries, notes, sketches, eyewitnesses, escapees, and partially destroyed physical facilities that would tell a part of the story. The Lager's secrets were not destroyed, despite the monumental efforts at eradication.

Also, in this Hobbesian Hell, control over the prisoners was not total; prisoners could supplement their absolute scarcity a bit and breach the isolation of the Lager. For instance, some civilians working in Germany when the war broke out, virtual prisoners themselves, worked in Auschwitz, but outside the Lager. One of them, Lorenzo, an Italian from Fossano, was instrumental in Levi's survival. Lorenzo had been a mason employed by an Italian firm working in France in 1939. They met in Auschwitz, and Lorenzo, at the risk of his life, supplied Levi with soup: "The Camp food supplied us with about sixteen hundred [calories], which was not enough to live on while working. Lorenzo's soup supplied another four or five hundred calories, still insufficient for a man of medium build, but Alberto [a *häftlinge* who shared everything with Levi] and I had already started out small and skinny, and our requirements were lower."[14]

14. Levi, *Moments of Reprieve,* 150, 154.

After the war, Levi discovered that Lorenzo had been giving an equal amount of aid to other Italian prisoners. Encounters with civilians in Monowitz were far from rare, but Lorenzo's courage and generosity were exceptional. Levi also suggests that Lorenzo offered more than material sustenance. The idea that someone could still do selfless acts kept him going amid the madness of the Lager. The social me may have evaporated, or been repressed, but Lorenzo reminded him of its existence.

None of these penetrations of the outside world made life in any sense bearable. There was always risk involved, and absolute scarcity that may be overcome for a time with clothing, food, or water was only a temporary victory on the way to the annihilation.

The market, not human generosity, usually provided the vehicle for interchange among the various levels of inhabitants of Monowitz. In total institutions like prisons, regardless of the surveillance or sanctions, markets form and precede any other form of social organization. This was true in Auschwitz, despite extraordinarily severe penalties for participation in trade between the *häftlinge* and the civilians: "[I]t is a crime explicitly foreseen by the camp regulations, and considered equivalent to 'political' crimes; so that it is punished with particular severity. The Häftling convicted of '*Handel mit Zivilisten,*' unless he can rely on powerful influences, ends up at Gleiwitz III, at Janina or at Heidebreck in the coal-mines; which means death from exhaustion in the course of a few weeks" (*Survival,* 82).

Civilians may suffer the same fate by being sent to the mines, but they were not in the same physical condition, had not been starved, tattooed, nor subjected to the selections. Theft was also punished, but the SS and the civilian administration had very different ideas about sanctioning it: "[T]heft in Buna, punished by the civil direction, is authorized and encouraged by the SS; theft in the camp, severely repressed by the SS, is considered by the civilians as a normal exchange operation; theft among the Häftlinge is generally punished, but the punishment strikes the thief and the victim with equal gravity" (*Survival,* 76).

Levi points out that anyone found taking something out of the camp was severely punished, for the SS assumed that everything of the prisoners would belong to them, even their gold teeth. Goods coming into the camp from the civilian-run Buna (the synthetic rubber factory in which Levi worked) were a different story. There "are the instances of brooms, paint, electric wire, grease for shoes" (*Survival,* 83). The Buna was under civilian control, and the SS were less concerned with theft from civilians:

> But against theft in itself, the direction of the camp has no prejudice. The attitude of open connivance by the SS as regards smuggling in the opposite direction [into the camp from the Buna] shows this clearly. . . . The exchanges occur in two places; in a "market" located at the point most distant from SS headquarters and in the infirmary, Ka-Be. The bargaining Market, run by the few Salonica Greeks left in the Lager, works efficiently. Their skills transform the bargaining Market into a monopoly on trade. The Salonica Jews and their aversion to gratuitous brutality, their amazing consciousness of the survival of at least a potential human dignity made of the Greeks the most coherent national nucleus in the Lager, and in this respect, the most civilized. (*Survival*, 79)

The Lager had no common currencies, like tobacco, that often appear in illegal markets. Low-grade tobacco entered the market, but not as the "official" currency: "Mahorca is a third-rate tobacco, crude and wooden, which is officially on sale at the canteen in one and a half ounce packets, in exchange for the prize-coupons that the Buna [s]ought to distribute to the best [civilian] workers." The coupons floated around the market and took their value in terms of supply and demand, the closest thing to money. For the most part, however, each item had a price that fluctuated with the supplies of the item. Only the price of very few items remained stable: "At the Market you can find specialists in kitchen thefts, their jackets swollen with strange bulges. While there is a virtually stable price for soup (half a ration of bread for two pints), the quotations for turnips, carrots, potatoes are extremely variable and depend greatly, among other factors, on the diligence and the corruptibility of the guards at the stores" (*Survival*, 79–80).

John Locke initially suggests that each individual should keep only the fruits of his labor that will not spoil in his possession. To justify existing conditions of inequality in England, he decides that money is not perishable and that individuals can keep as much of it as they can, thus justifying great inequality in an economy. In the Lager, limitations to wealth existed because there were no laws to insure that stealing in this Hobbesian universe did not take place or that contracts would be honored: "In trade with trustworthy civilians, a rare occurrence, it is possible to give them something and they will pay you in a few installments of bread. . . . [T]he maximum total of any transaction negotiated *within* the camp is four rations of bread, because it would be practically impossible either to make contracts on credit, or to preserve a larger quantity of bread from the greed of others or one's own hunger" (*Survival*, 82).

What prompts people to take such risks incurred by continuing to trade is the condition of absolute scarcity. The prisoner needs more than what is given of soup, bread, and clothing in order to survive for very long. The market benefits those who steal or find negotiable items in order to "buy" the essentials. The trade is constant, because in this universe, any kind of hoarding does not work.

The market could enhance the chances of the veterans of the Lager to survive, but it was devastating to the newcomers. The newcomers' meager belongings, from bowl and spoon to items of clothing, were often left unprotected in their first days in the Lager and ended up in the market. We will see how different strategies of survival emerged in the Lager, where the market provided a few opportunities for extending a doomed life.

The second set of boundary conditions that defined the miserable life in the Lager for Levi is the godless, irrational universe. From his earliest years to his death, Levi's views on the existence of God never changed: "Like [philosopher Jean] Améry, I too entered the Lager as a nonbeliever, and as a nonbeliever I was liberated and have lived to this day. Actually, the experience of the Lager with its frightful iniquity confirmed me in my nonbelief" (*Drowned*, 145). His atheism was sorely tested when he was about to file past the "commission" that would make the selection: Would he live or die?

> For one instant I felt the need to ask for help and asylum; then, despite my anguish, equanimity prevailed: one does not change the rules of the game at the end of the match, not when you are losing. A prayer under these conditions would have been not only absurd (what rights could I claim? And from whom?) but blasphemous, obscene, laden with the greatest impiety of which a nonbeliever is capable. I rejected that temptation: I knew that otherwise, were I to survive, I would have to be ashamed of it. (*Drowned*, 146)

Primo Levi discussed the existence or the nonexistence of God with another Auschwitz survivor, Elie Wiesel. Wiesel writes in reference to his own experiences in the Holocaust:

My doubts and my revolt gripped me only later. Why so much later? My comrade and future friend Primo Levi asked me that question. How did I surmount these doubts and this revolt? He refused to understand how I, his former companion of Auschwitz III, could still call himself a believer, for he, Primo, was not and didn't want to be. He had seen too much suffering not to rebel against any religion that sought to impose a meaning upon it. I understood him, and asked him to understand me, for I had seen too much suffering to break with the past and reject the heritage of those who had suffered. . . . He was a chemist; I was nothing at all. The system needed him, but not me. He had influential friends to help and protect him; I had only my father.[15]

Wiesel's arguments are pragmatic ones, suffused with integrity. He did not want to break the bonds of his heritage by breaking with the past, nor did he want to give up the solidarity with those he knew. By the way of a Jamesian pragmatic will, Wiesel says, "I needed God, Primo did not."[16]

Joseph Heller makes the point that even atheists have a conception of what the god they do not believe in is like. Levi's God is a god of paradox. Wiesel insightfully suggests that "for Primo Levi, the problem of faith after Auschwitz was posed in stark terms: Either God is God and therefore all-powerful and hence guilty of letting the murderers do as they pleased, or his power is limited, in which case he is not God. In other words, if God is God, then He is present everywhere. But if He refuses to show Himself, he becomes immoral and inhuman, the enemy's ally or accomplice."[17]

Levi, a nonbeliever from a secular background, often makes reference to incidents in the Bible and frequently quotes scripture. When he was asked in what sense he was a Jew, he answered: "A simple matter of culture. If it hadn't been for the racial laws and the concentration camp, I'd probably no longer be a Jew, except for my last name. . . . At this point I'm a Jew, they've sewn the Star of David on me and not only on my clothes."[18] He had no prior beliefs to be challenged, nor was there a community of believers to betray. What remained was a cultural solidarity.

Both Elie Wiesel and Primo Levi remained true to their prior principles and developed very different but equally interesting life philosophies spawned by the Holocaust and their return to "ordinary life." Levi strained to be a believer, but he never could bring himself to be one: "There

15. Wiesel, *All Rivers Run to the Sea: Memoirs,* 82–83.
16. Ibid.
17. Heller, *Catch-22,* 185; Wiesel, *All Rivers Run to the Sea,* 83.
18. Camon, *Conversations,* 68.

is Auschwitz and so there cannot be God. [*On the typescript, he added in pencil:* I don't find a solution to this dilemma. I keep looking, but I don't find it]."[19] Levi wanted to believe, but faith kept running up against his rationalism. He knew there are pragmatic reasons for belief, for he reported, as did other survivors, that those who had and maintained a religious faith were more likely to survive the Holocaust: "Sorrow, in them or around them, was decipherable and therefore did not overflow into despair" (*Drowned,* 146).[20] In the end, however, he could not breech his own reason.

Levi realizes that not believing in God has many consequences. For instance, he sacrifices the idea of a rational, intelligible universe by not believing in God or some other all-encompassing ideology. Whether survivors are Marxists or believers in God, overall, they have an easier time of it, for they can find some compensation for what is happening to them: "Not only during the crucial moments of the selection or the aerial bombings but also in the grid of everyday life, the believers lived better." The universe was more comprehensible to them, for they were sacrificing for tomorrow, "a place in heaven or on earth where justice and compassion had won, or would win in a perhaps remote but certain future: Moscow, or the celestial or terrestrial Jerusalem" (*Drowned,* 146).

For Levi, the Lager remains an irrational universe, for it cannot be reconciled with the existence of God. Levi, in several of his short stories, creates a god who is trying to devise man as an intelligent creature at home in his surroundings. This god, Levi's inventive surrogate, is always devising experiments with human nature. "God" continually fails before the material conditions of existence.

Although Levi tried to make his experience comprehensible, the Lager seemed impermeable to reason. First, it was difficult to make sense of his experience. Although he viewed his circumstances with his particular detachment, he saw it only from his restricted view from the depths of the Lager; he never got an overall view of the Lager in the year he spent there: "I had never had either the curiosity or the occasion to investigate the complex structure of the hierarchy of the camp."[21] After his return he read extensively about the Holocaust, but he relied primarily on firsthand experience. For instance, in *Survival in Auschwitz,* he stays close to what he

19. Ibid.
20. Levi uses the term *ordinary life* in *Survival,* 88. We will make liberal use of this term to describe Levi's life before and after the Holocaust.
21. Levi, *The Reawakening,* 4.

knows firsthand so that he is believed. Ever the careful scientist, he makes clear the sources of the data for his argument. From his detached scientific perspective, the evidence of the organization and structure of the Lager is all too unclear, and it would be speculation on his part to understand the whole concentrationary universe and its raison d'être.

Levi warns us of a second methodological caveat in the way of explaining what happened in the Lager. He tells us that even though we want to understand the mind of the Nazis, we cannot put ourselves in the place of the murderers as a methodological ploy. We cannot use some variant of Max Weber's *verstehen,* because to do that would be trying to imagine ourselves doing the unimaginable. *Verstehen* and the empathy that often accompanies it softens our thoughts about the perpetrators. This happens when we know more of the murderer or the rapist and begin excusing his behaviors as inevitable, the results of childhood trauma and other past occurrences. Lezak Kolakowski says it best when he asks what happened to evil in the modern world; his answer is that evil has been explained away by social science. Primo Levi wants to avoid excusing those who perpetrated the Holocaust.[22]

In addition to these two methodological limitations on the "damned observer," for Levi, there is the fundamental fact that that the *universe concentrationaire* violated every law and expectation a person from ordinary life carries with him. Auschwitz was a universe turned upside down and, in fact, it was counterproductive to survival there to think about why things happen. When he first came to the Lager, he asked questions and was told by other prisoners: "There is no 'why' here." This serves as a description of the circumstances, and it serves as a useful tactical maxim in terms of survival. In ordinary life, even if we can never be sure of the why, we do act on reasonable assumptions and order our life in terms of probabilities. In contrast, the Lager was a universe in which very little of one's past knowledge could be used, for it was simply irrelevant or even harmful. The prisoner was better off reacting alertly to circumstances than trying to fathom what was happening; the latter would lead to despair, futility, and further confusion.

This does not mean that Levi and others did not try to explain what was happening to them. Levi sees that it is a useful, and perhaps an inevitable, trait of man to try to explain the unexplainable, and one thing that sets us

---

22. For Weber's concept of *verstehen,* see his *Economy and Society,* 8–9. Kolakowski, *"The Key to Heaven" and "Conversations with the Devil,"* 117–25.

apart from other species is that we must learn how to live with this truth: We must admit when things are presently inexplicable.[23]

In the Lager, when the slaves tried to come to an understanding, they usually clutched on to extreme positions and vacillated between these extremes: "If we were logical, we would resign ourselves to the evidence that our fate is beyond human knowledge, that every conjecture is arbitrary and demonstrably devoid of foundation. But men are rarely logical when their own fate is at stake" (*Survival*, 35). Reason was irresistible but generally unhelpful. Levi gives several examples of seemingly parallel transactions in the Lager and ordinary life, but in the Lager, the transaction has the twisted logic of a nightmare. When Levi "interviews" for a job in the Buna factory, Dr. Panwitz interrogated him. Even though the job turned out to be completely menial, the interview was handled as if it were an ordinary interview for a job under ordinary circumstances. A surreal veneer of normalcy hung before the backdrop of an interview between master and slave; the polished versus the discomfited; the fastidious engaged with dirty prisoner in the *häftlinge* garb: "Panwitz is tall, thin, blond; he has eyes, hair and nose as all Germans ought to have them, and sits formidably behind a complicated writing-table. I, Häftling 174517 [Levi's tatoo number], stand in his office, which is a real office, shining, clean and ordered, and I feel that I would leave a dirty stain whatever I touched." Panwitz became emblematic of all Levi's oppressors, and Levi felt that if he understood Panwitz, perhaps everything would be comprehensible: "Because that look was not one between two men; and if I had known how completely to explain the nature of that look which came as if across the glass window of an aquarium between two beings who live in different worlds, I would also have explained the essence of the great insanity of the third Germany" (*Survival*, 105–6).[24]

From the beginning, when Levi was first caught in the snare of Hitler's Europe, he tried to use reason to understand what was happening. Yet, he

---

23. Yet in one of the literally hundreds of ironies in Levi's thoughts, he does try to understand the mentality of the Germans and their social organizations, just as he tried to understand the Lager while a prisoner. It apparently arises out of an irresistible, but dysfunctional, curiosity, or more likely, in his case, the need to witness the events.

24. We will see later in this work that reason actually did help Levi and others come to grips with their circumstances. This involved process will be described in detail and will be contrasted with his pessimism, which indicated that the prisoners were crushed in the Lager and never recovered. It is the internal conflict in the Italian in *"Force Majeure"* between the total destruction of the psyche that occurred in the alley and the continuing struggle to overcome it.

still had great difficulty making the events intelligible to himself. A crime is a breech of the public order, some act a person commits that can be viewed as a threat to the public weal. His "crime" was being Jewish, a cultural status for him. Even though he knew of the historical persecution of the Jews, Levi was still working from a civilized discourse that would suggest that his "real" crime against the state was treason: "During the interrogations that followed [my capture as a partisan], I preferred to admit my status of 'Italian citizen of Jewish race.' I felt that otherwise I would be unable to justify my presence in places too secluded even for an evacuee; while I believed (wrongly as was subsequently seen) that the admission of my political activity would have meant torture and certain death" (*Survival*, 13–14).

For Levi, not understanding the "new logic" meant being deported as a Jew to Auschwitz, a much more severe consequence than would have occurred if Levi had admitted to being a partisan, a declared enemy of the state. Levi and other Jews could not accept being tagged for extinction for just belonging to a category. The guilt for which Jews were charged was the same crime of which Kafka's K finally decides that he must be guilty, for he can find no other charge: Levi and K are guilty for having been born. It was extremely difficult ever coming to grips with the new "logic."

"Useless violence" was everywhere in the concentrationary universe. There was the degradation on the transports, the ridiculous rules and regulations of the Lager—a bizarre parody of German militarism—the meaningless work, and in these and in other circumstances, brutal acts of violence to no visible end. Occasionally, it was possible to make sense of the senseless violence from the point of view of the oppressors. Jewish deportees were given advice or orders to bring all their valuables on the journey: "In fact, this was self-plunder, a simple and ingenious ruse to bring valuables into the Reich, without publicity, bureaucratic complications, special transports, or fear of thefts en route—and sure enough, upon arrival, everything was seized" (*Drowned*, 109).

Much more often, the behaviors of the oppressors made no sense to Levi. None of the diabolical goals were at stake. Some of the transports took as long as two weeks to get to their final destination. The German authorities "literally did not provide anything, neither foodstuffs, nor water, nor mats, nor straw to cover the wooden floor, nor receptacles for bodily needs, nor did they bother to alert anyone to provide these. A notice would not have cost anything: rather, this systematic negligence became a useless cruelty, a deliberate creation of pain that was an end in itself"

(*Drowned,* 109). For example, the prisoners had to scramble, grovel, and steal for spoons, but when the camp was liberated they found tens of thousands of spoons of all varieties that had been taken from the deportees. Levi concludes from the point of view of the Nazis: "So it was not a matter of thrift but a precise intent to humiliate." Other rituals, like standing in ranks for hours to be counted, probably had some rationale for the Germans, but they were perceived by the prisoners as "an empty and ceremonial ritual" (*Drowned,* 114–15).

While in the Lager, figuring out the logic of the system was counterproductive: There was no "why" there. Forty years later in his retrospective book, *The Drowned and the Saved,* he begins to try to come to grips with the unfathomable, focusing his attention on the useless violence described above. He defines useless violence by contrasting it with violence, however awful, that at least aims at some purpose: "Wars are detestable, they are a very bad way to settle controversies between nations or factions, but they cannot be called useless: they aim at a goal, although it may be wicked or perverse. They are not gratuitous, their purpose is not to inflict suffering; suffering is there, it is collective, anguishing, unjust, but it is a byproduct, something extra" (105).

He accuses the whole regime of useless violence: "Now I believe that the twelve Hitlerian years shared their violence with many other historical space-times, but they were characterized by widespread useless violence, as an end in itself, with the sole purpose of inflicting pain, occasionally having a purpose, yet always redundant, always disproportionate to the purpose itself" (106).

Levi comes close here to St. Augustine's and Lezak Kolakowski's definition of evil as a deed done for no other motive than to inflict harm. Only when social scientists try to explain away the deed by the perpetrator's historical being, his early upbringing, does evil disappear. This is why Levi does not want to know the motives of his captors—knowing might diminish the bad feelings. He does not want to diminish the evil.

The cruelty is all the more inexplicable because it was done by formerly ordinary citizens and not by easily labeled monsters. From the point of view of the prisoners who know that they are destined to die in the camps, the extra cruelty is completely unexplainable. Still, Levi attempts to understand the basis for this violence. He struggles to find anything in Nietzsche that he agrees with, for while he finds his thoughts repugnant, for him, even Nietzsche does not go nearly as far as the Nazis on gratuitous violence: "His [Nietzsche's] oracular tone irritates me, yet it seems to me that a desire for the sufferings of others cannot be found in it. Indifference, yes, almost on every page, but never *schadenfreude,* the joy in deliberately inflicting suffering. Pain the elect inflict on others is necessary, a minor evil, but for Nietzsche it is in no way desirable" (107). Many of the needless cruelties Levi mentions are contrary to the purposes of the war machine because they take time, manpower, and money:

> Would it not have been simpler, more 'economical' to let them [two ninety year old women were put on his transport] die, or perhaps kill them in their beds, instead of adding their agony to the collective agony of the transport? One is truly led to think that, in the Third Reich, the best choice, the choice imposed from above, was the one that entailed the greatest affliction, the greatest waste, the greatest physical and moral suffering. (120)

Levi suggests two possible explanations for the war in general and specifically for the useless violence: "Were we witnessing the rational development of an inhuman plan or a manifestation (unique in history and still unsatisfactorily explained) of collective madness? Logic intent on evil or the absence of logic. As so often happens in human affairs, the two alternatives coexisted" (106). These alternatives appear at the beginning of his chapter on "Useless Violence" in *The Drowned and the Saved.* A quote from Stangl, the ex-commandant of Treblinka, caps off the chapter. A reporter asks Stangl, "Considering that you [Stangl] were going to kill them all . . . what was the point of the humiliations, the cruelties?" Stangl replies, "To condition those who were to be the material executors of the operations. To make it possible for them to do what they were doing" (125). This is a monstrous explanation, but it must be taken seriously: "In other words, before dying the victim must be degraded, so that the murderer will be less burdened by guilt. This is an explanation not devoid of logic but it shouts to heaven: it is the sole usefulness of useless violence" (126).[25] The explanation, one of cultural madness, a world turned upside down, was one that Levi held at the time of the Holocaust. In the boundary conditions for Levi at the time, the Lager was a form of madness, a universe where none of the usual rules applied. Only in retrospect did he

25. Many, including Lucy Dawidowicz in *The War against the Jews, 1933–1945,* Saul Friedlander in *Nazi Germany and the Jews,* vol. 1, *The Years of Persecution, 1933–1938,* and Raul Hilberg in *The Destruction of the European Jews,* have come up with information to buttress the Stangl explanation.

hear of Stangl's response, and only then was Levi able to put it in perspective. In addition, even if Levi and others guessed why there was useless violence, the Lager would not seem any more intelligible. No strategy could be derived from understanding the possibility that they are being degraded to make their murder easier. How can humans be so cruel and calculating? At the time, they were better off not asking these questions.

Fate is the third and final boundary condition of the Lager. In part, the two other boundary conditions explain why Levi believed in fate playing such a decisive role in the Holocaust. The scarcity was so severe that virtually no one in the early transports survived. The prisoners, the Special Squad, forced into building crematoria and removing clothes and bodies were systematically murdered so as to leave no witnesses. Part of Levi's luck was being one of the later arrivals.

Levi does not believe that God intervened on behalf of any of the survivors; that would have been perverse for him, because, as he says in *The Drowned and the Saved,* the best people were not the survivors. Nor is there any explanation of why so many died and for what reason. As an irrational universe, survival strategies played a small part, for the vast majority of the Jews were slaughtered without the chance to even think of strategy. Whether the prisoner was a man or woman, young or old played a key role in survival, but there was little individuals could do to control those circumstances.

In several places, Levi gives examples of how fate altered his circumstances in the Lager. Lorenzo's unsolicited kindness toward Levi led directly to his survival. In the Buna factory, he accidentally discovered bars of cerium, and with his friend Alberto, he fashioned the bars into flints for lighters, which bought them some extra rations of soup and bread. Of course, they helped fate along a bit, something Levi is too modest to take credit for. He knew what cerium can be used for, and they had the courage and ingenuity to carry the flints onto the illegal market.[26]

In his writings, Levi suggests that seemingly insignificant events may alter the whole course of history. For want of a nail in the horse's shoe, the battle is lost. In the example he uses, the history of the Mediterranean area would have been completely different had Cleopatra's nose been a little longer. In his life and that of Alberto, one such nail had deadly implications. When Alberto was a child, he contracted scarlet fever, giving him

---

26. Levi, *The Periodic Table,* 139–46.

adult immunity from the disease. Levi, who had no exposure to the disease, contracted it in his last month in Auschwitz. Because he came down with scarlet fever, Levi was left in the camp. All of the prisoners expected that the Nazis would murder those left behind in the infirmary, or if simply left unattended, that they would all die of disease. All the "fortunate," the able bodied, were to march toward the interior of Germany, and if there was any hope for living it was to go on that march. Alberto, along with the vast majority of those who marched, lost their lives, and Levi lived.

Much of our lives are spent trying to convince ourselves and others that we have some control over what happens to us, that luck is far around the corner. When the word came in October 1944 that there would be another "selection," the prisoners reassured each other, in an almost universal act of kindness, that he would not be "selected": "Nobody refuses this charity to another: nobody is so sure of his own lot to be able to condemn others. I brazenly lied to old Wertheimer." He told Wertheimer reasons, all lies, why he should be confident, and the latter relaxed. Levi's real feelings were that "it is absurd of Wertheimer to hope: he looks sixty, he has enormous varicose veins, he hardly even notices the hunger any more" (*Survival,* 125). Most knew that they were lying, but it was a lie to salve feelings. Even Levi grew more confident when someone bolstered his hypothetical chances for surviving the selection.

The selections did not follow any predictable path, even though the Germans put their pseudologic into action—the unhealthy were to be selected for the gas. It was done at such great speed: "In three or four minutes a hut of two hundred men is 'done,' as is the whole camp of twelve thousand men in the course of the afternoon." Sheer numbers to be murdered took priority over careful selection. During the selections, as they ran by their judge, Levi and most of the others looked back to see which way, left or right, their cards were delivered to the functionaries on the left or right of the SS Subaltern making the selections. After looking at whose card was delivered to the left and whose to the right, even accounting for the "mistakes"—healthy-looking people who were selected—they determined that if their cards went to the left they had been selected for extinction. Levi discussed with Alberto whether the chance, which let him live, occurred when someone before him, a healthy person, may have had his card taken instead of Levi's: "Rene passed the commission immediately in front of me and there could have been a mistake with our cards. I think about it, discuss it with Alberto, and we agree that the hypothesis is probable" (*Sur-*

vival, 128). These examples and many others like them convinced Levi that survival, in great part, is a matter of luck.

Every once in a while the prisoners played some role in the fate of their friends, but it was almost always a political prisoner who had this influence: "We, the almost total majority of common prisoners, did not know about them [influential political prisoners] and did not even suspect their existence." He witnessed one episode of their influence that he did not recognize at the time. A relatively benign Kapo—at this juncture, a fellow prisoner put in charge of his group—was replaced with a malicious one, who Levi surmised was probably mentally ill: "Now, the new *Kapo* gave his beatings in a different way, in a convulsive, malicious, perverse way: on the nose, the shin, the genitals. He beat to hurt, to cause suffering and humiliation." Levi spoke with a fellow prisoner, a Jewish Croatian Communist, and asked him what they should do about the Kapo. "He gave me a strange smile and simply said: 'You'll see, he won't last long.' In fact, the beater vanishes within a week." Many years later, Levi found out from survivors that there were political prisoners attached to the "Work Office" who had "the terrifying power of switching the registration numbers on the lists of prisoners destined to be gassed" (*Drowned*, 73, 74). For the vast majority of the prisoners, the power to effect someone's destiny, and to even know that someone has that power, is beyond comprehension.

One of the situations that quickly brought Levi to anger was when people in groups he addressed about the Holocaust would tell him that his fate was in his own hands, if only he had acted the hero. This "Hobbesian hero," the individual whose security is threatened by others or by the state, has the obligation to save himself through individual self-defense or escape. This striving to survive is for Hobbes a natural law, a behavior, not a moral law, where the individual will try to save himself. Levi patiently shows that this heroism is the stuff of modern mass culture, a fiction unknown to those who were forced into the camps, and inapplicable for the few who might have contemplated flight or rebellion. Escaping before the Holocaust swallowed up people, rebelling, and escape from the Lager once entrapped was, for the most part, romantic fiction. For some it actually happened, but for most it was beyond the reach of possibility. An ex post facto analysis of conditions before a comfortable fire in order to decide how one would act in unprecedented conditions while physically and mentally debilitated is not in the same universe with being there. The Hobbesian social contract, which is forged following dangerous conditions in the hypothetical state of nature, imply time and circumstances for deliberation, conditions absent in the Lager. The best the prisoners could do was try to survive for another day.

Thus for Levi, who lived and who died was a matter of fate—a childhood disease, a social category, a mistake, late capture when not everyone went to the gas chambers, or some other scrap of luck. Regardless of the strategies to survive, unconscious or deliberate, the vast majority, no matter their life philosophies, perished.

Scarcity, the godless, irrational universe, and fate were the boundary conditions for Levi in the Lager. The urge remains to try to understand, by a great leap of imagination, how we would have coped with such a loathsome, constricting universe. In our relatively comfortable existence, we too might hold that there are relative scarcities that cause greed and conflict; that we live in a godless, irrational universe; and that fate can take us in its clutches. Still, the difference is that we who have time for deliberation can do it in some comfort and believe that we might give fate a big shove. In order to understand Levi, we must put aside the fantasy of existential heroics.

Ill-Constituted Beings

3

Ill-Constituted Beings

"Gentlemen, it is my opinion which . . . can be amply documented, that in order to put together a Man answering to the prescribed characteristics, and at the same time vital, economical and reasonably durable, we should go back to the beginning and set up this animal along definitely new lines."

— "The Sixth Day"

Robert Nozick, in *The Examined Life,* recommends a thought experiment we might perform. It goes as follows: There is at least one planet in our universe for every person on earth, so that when we die, we might be given our own world to construct as we please. How would we go about doing it? In a short story, Primo Levi uses just such an experiment to explore human nature and see if humans could construct a better world than the present one.[1]

In "The Sixth Day," Levi has a committee of bureaucrats trying to decide what characteristics they should give "Man." The Committee includes specialists, such as the Psychological Advisor, the Minister of Waterways, the Comptroller, the Anatomy Advisor, the Chemical Advisor, the Mechanical Advisor, and two generalists who are chairing the meeting, Arimane and Ormuz. The latter two urge the Committee to decide on essential human characteristics. Far from remaining neutral, they insistently lobby for their favorite qualities.[2]

Early in the proceedings, Arimane suggests that there is not enough time to design an entirely new model, as the Psychological Advisor wants. Even-

1. Nozick, *The Examined Life,* 25–26, 47.
2. See Levi, "The Sixth Day," in *"The Sixth Day" and Other Tales,* 90–106. Future references will be cited parenthetically in the text.

tually, everyone, including the Psychological Advisor, agrees: Man should not be a unique being, but instead should be generated from the existing models of life forms on Earth. For example, one of the available models, a sea creature, is the preference of the Minister of Waterways. Others raise questions about the vulnerability of a sea creature and whether he can gain dominion over the whole planet. Still others try out the idea of a reptile, but since reptiles cannot adapt to cold climates, this alternative also drops out of the discussion.

More suggestions are brought forth, debated, and discarded. Arimane chides Ormuz for his hopeless utopian scheme:

> Let it be said among us—those attempts of yours to produce Super-beasts, all brain and balance, filled *ab ovum* with geometry, music and wisdom, would make a cat laugh. They smacked of antiseptic and in-organic chemistry. For anyone with a certain experience of the things of the world, or for that matter any other world, their incompatibili-ty with the environment surrounding them would have been easily in-tuited, an environment that is of necessity both florid and putrid, pul-lulating, confused, changeable. (93)

Calculated reason is insufficient for dealing with the confusing world; its practitioners would suffer endless frustration.

The drift of the debate is that regardless of whatever ideal Man is pro-posed, be he mammal, reptile, fish, or bird, he will be an ill-constituted be-ing. He will carry out some of his express purposes his makers designate for him, but he will fail at others.

The discussion shifts to the underlying theme that Man's purpose is sur-vival. The committee is ambitious for Man and wants him to survive, but they cannot agree on the answer to the question: For what? Built into each bureaucrat's individual discourse is a purpose or multiple purposes for his "Man" and an argument as to how Man will fulfill his purpose or pur-poses. Can and should Man dominate the planet? Balance the existing planet? Allow reason to reign? Have other, not yet mentioned purposes?

Others ask how, given a posited purpose, Man will fulfill other tasks. Ormuz, for instance, is concerned with "the dangers connected with the insertion of so-called Man into the present planetary balance" (92). Will he then be able to defend himself?

A bit later in the discussion, the Psychological Advisor suggests reason will be a feature of Man: "But there is much more: it seems clear to me, from at least three or four subsections of the motion, that Man is implicitly understood to be reasonable" (96). For him, it appears that reason can and will be used to dominate the planet. If Man is a bird, the Psychological Advisor points out, then his first advantage is that he can go anywhere and dominate the planet, because there will be no artificial territorial divisions between Man and Man. This ties into a second advantage, which is domination: "There is no need for me to insist on the other, more immediate advantages offered by rapid flight, as regards defense and offense against all earthbound and aquatic species, and as regards the prompt discovery of ever new territories suited for hunting, cultivation and exploitation: so that it seems legitimate to me to formulate the axiom: 'The animal that flies does not go hungry.'" (102)

What does this do to planetary balance?

The Committee has an edict from "above" to create a sustainable Man, but for what? They seem to agree that Man will have a large brain so that he may reason, have an articulated language, and maintain a social life (96). These characteristics will distinguish Man from other beasts, but we still have no answer as to his purpose. The functionaries and advisors are technicians, not metaphysicians: They invent tasks for the beast, but they have no agreement on any overall theory to justify their suggestions.

Arimane submits that the Committee needs compromise solutions to create Man; this is how committees resolve issues. However, they never get to compromise, because as the argument continues and the arguments become more complex, God goes ahead and places Man on the planet. All the functionaries can do is wish the new creature well. Man, as we know him, embodies all of the difficulties the functionaries had anticipated. It was as if God simply stopped the discussion because it was going nowhere; he created Man with all his contradictions because the functionaries would never be able to resolve their difficulties.

"The Sixth Day" leaves the reader with the impression that we are equipped with an incomplete and sometimes contradictory set of tools for survival and no agreed-upon reason for being. Simply put, we have no answer to these ultimate questions about meaning, and our fellow humans can come to no provisional agreement among themselves on the purpose of being. We have a variety of traits and no essential purpose; it is left for us to decide the essential questions, questions we are not ultimately equipped to answer. Other than try to survive, what are we to do? Every trait seems to work for some purpose and against others. Do we make decisions by reason or emotion? Are we to be at peace with our role in na-

ture and live in harmony with others, or are we to be dominant? Is the re-
productive process a calculation or an instinct?

We are ill-constituted beings, and it is clear to Levi that the best minds
could not do a better job of re-engineering us through technology. Our imperfection, as Levi sees it, does not lead to Descartes's conclusion that our
imperfection suggests a perfected being, a creator. We are left with our own
flesh and bone, and the possibilities and tragedies of existence are ours
alone.[3]

Levi does not hesitate, however, as many empiricists do, to express his
preferences. He finds that many of our behaviors in Hobbesian and even
normal circumstances are appalling, and actively argues on behalf of behaviors that appear to him our much weaker and more remote possibilities—for example, compassion for the less fortunate. Later chapters will
explore in detail his ethos, but it is important to acknowledge up front that
Levi believes we must take sides in the war of purposes and not remain by-
standers to action.

Levi's philosophy is in most essentials modern, but he disagrees in one
major way with the early modernists.[4] For Levi, there is no progress. In
many of his other short stories—in addition to "The Sixth Day"—the protagonists tinker with some individual trait of man. The motivation is not
evil, but scientific curiosity, and depending on the project, the hope is to
make a better man or a better life for man. In "The Sleeping Beauty in the
Fridge," for example, an experiment brings a woman back from a cryo-
genic state every few years to observe the changing world. In the next succession of stories, his protagonist uses a duplicating machine to clone people. In "The Angelic Butterfly," a Nazi attempt to create a creature with
wings fails. Needless to say, none of these stories has a happy ending. Finally, in the short story "Versamina," suffused with desperation, a scientist turns what people normally perceive as "pain" into "pleasure"; his
character ends up throwing himself in front of a car, the ultimate pleasure
in this fictional world.[5] All of his protagonists' experiments fail to make
man better or the world a better place. We are ill-constituted beings.

---

3. In his short stories and essays, Levi works out other broad theoretical concerns. His
acute observations of human behavior in normal and extreme circumstances supply him
with his evidence. Levi is a masterful empiricist. In addition, some of his generalizations
about the nature of man come from his observation of insects and mammals, which serve
as testable metaphors for human behavior.

4. The word *modern* is used here in the way contemporary philosophers use it, with no
relation to the way that Italian Fascists used the term.

5. These stories all appear in Levi's *"The Sixth Day" and Other Tales*. See: "The Sleeping Beauty in the Fridge," 55–70; "The Angelic Butterfly," 19–25; "Versamina," 45–54.

Given the presence of other people, a world not of our own making, and substandard equipment to deal with existence, there is struggle but no progress. We are tragic beings. In Shakespeare's classic tragedies *Hamlet* and *King Lear,* the heroes' tragic flaws are their undoing. Similarly, in Levi's stories and essays, each of our fundamental traits carries the potential for our undoing. Characteristics like aggression, which fuel our strength in one direction, may be necessary for our survival, but they also cause our unhappiness or death. Even more drastic, they may lead to our annihilation as a species. We always seem to be faced with tragic circumstances and no clear choice of how to act; agonic doubt sets in. Every trait for the good has a potential for thwarting other purposes—even our very existence.[6]

Levi's essays and personal accounts highlight specific tragic tendencies in human nature, like hierarchy, Manicheanism, violence, lack of social solidarity, and reason.[7] When these characteristics are carried to excess, as can happen with violence or hierarchy, the consequences are very negative. Thus, the tragic perspective on life, one where we understand our frailties and struggle against ourselves with the aid of education, is our only avenue of action against these traits of human nature, perfected and treated as absolutes. This tragic perspective promises no progress, but for Levi, it is the only assumption upon which he can proceed with his life. Reason will try to guide our atavistic tendencies, not by glorifying them or denying them, but by trying to put them at reason's service. As suggested, he differs from the early modernists because he throws himself into the struggle, even though he is doubtful of the outcome. Levi's perspective on civilization resembles that of Freud, who once commented in a letter to Albert Einstein that it is surprising civilization has prevailed as well as it has, given man's tragic and tenuous makeup.

As tenuous as existence is in terms of human happiness and our ultimate survival, Levi also recognizes that we have a cushion of surplus capabilities that may serve us well. These are not the result of a teleological nature, but simply luck. As Stephen J. Gould points out, one of the common mistakes Darwin's interpreters make is in believing that all of our being is to be understood as behavior that leads to survival: We are perfected survival machines. Through the luck of natural selection, as a species

6. Future chapters will spell out what Levi means by the good, but for now it is well to note that the achievable good for Levi, in most instances, is the absence of pain.

7. This chapter will touch on the vagaries of reason, and the topic will appear in other chapters as well, especially in the context of reason and technology.

we have a cushion for survival, unlike the badly adapted pandas, described by Gould, who have to eat bamboo all day just to survive. Unlike the panda, we do not live completely on the edge of extinction.[8]

Thus, though we are ill-constituted beings, we still have room to make mistakes and survive. World War II was a huge slaughter, but the larger part of mankind survived and is even more plentiful than before the war. In the essay "The Man Who Flies," Levi marvels at the fact that man can survive in space, something not tested until recent years: "The ease with which man adjusts to the absence of weight is a fascinating mystery," he writes, noting that there is little in our evolutionary history to prepare us for the experience of weightlessness. Although the body is defenseless toward many things, including viruses and weapons, we have comfort zones: "So we do have vast and unforeseen margins of safety."[9]

We are ill-constituted beings with margins for survival, but for two reasons, we cannot be smug. First, given our atavistic tendencies, we have ways—as with hydrogen bombs or chemical and biological warfare, for instance—to annihilate ourselves. In this sense, we may be as fragile as the panda dependent on bamboo for survival. We are captive to weapons of our own making and only protected by the thin veneer of intelligence that cautions restraint.

Second, even though we may survive many mistakes, and even survive a devastating war that only temporarily retards the growth of human populations, the acceptance of mass murder is unallowable for us. It is distasteful to Levi to hear arguments that killing is correct as long as our side comes out the victor. Levi is an individualist, and his life and the lives of others count above the power of overriding causes and ideologies. As we will see, Levi clearly is in the court of the civilized liberal modernist.

The remaining pages of this chapter will investigate Levi's specific observations on the darker uses of our tendencies, especially our Manicheanism, lack of social cohesion, and propensity for hierarchy. We will see how all of these come to the fore in the Lager, where the thin protective veneer of civilization so quickly vanished. The following chapter will examine the difficulties we have with our propensities toward violence and reason.

8. Gould, *The Panda's Thumb*, 19–34.
9. Levi, "The Man Who Flies," in *"The Mirror Maker": Stories and Essays by Primo Levi*, 143.

The observation of group cohesion in both animal societies and human societies led Aristotle to declare that man is a social animal. Political organizations have many virtues, prominent among them the fact that they allow us to defend ourselves against outside threats, whether from animals, other humans, or natural disasters. Polemarchus's argument in *The Republic of Plato* is that justice is the rewarding of one's friends and the punishing of one's enemies. As Socrates aptly points out, this definition unfortunately gives us no instruction on what qualities allow us to differentiate between friends and enemies. Polemarchus's definition of justice was most familiar to Athenian citizens, and today it still holds great currency with the public. We share a propensity to organize to defend friends and fend off enemies, but the basis for distinguishing between friends and enemies appears to be more rationalization than reason.[10]

Levi finds Polemarchus's definition of justice deeply rooted in the nature of humanity. Fundamental to us is our Manichean attachment to others: "Perhaps for reasons that go back to our origins as social animals, the need to divide the field into 'we' and 'they' is so strong that this pattern, this bipartition—friend/enemy—prevails over all others." History taught in schools reflects this Manichean tendency. Our sports and entertainments, with their clearly defined winners and losers, and our identification with the "good guys" is further evidence of this either/or tendency in man. This is a simplifying tendency we use to comprehend our environment. Of course, we must fight this Manichean tendency, which is not reflective of our complex reality where most people fall into "gray zones" rather than the easily conceptualized friend and enemy. In general, Levi notes that we have a strong aversion to outsiders and a weak attachment to insiders. Levi finds himself disposed to the same tendency in several situations in terms of finding difference, but very far short of acting on murderous impulses.[11] In his attitudes toward the newcomer to the Lager, "It is probable that the hostility toward the *Zugang* [newcomer] was in substance motivated like all other forms of intolerance, that is, it consisted in an unconscious attempt to consolidate the 'we' at the expense of the 'they,' to create, in short, that solidarity among the oppressed whose absence was the source of additional suffering, even though not perceived openly."[12]

10. See Allan Bloom's translation of *The Republic of Plato*, 7–8.
11. This is a huge qualitative difference. What he did is a far cry from Nazi brutality and much closer to the simple vigilance we use against strangers. There is no moral equivalence.
12. Levi, *The Drowned and the Saved*, 36–37, 39–40. Future references will be cited parenthetically in the text.

We tend to segregate outsiders on the basis of many perceived differences, including race, religion, ethnicity, infirmity, age, sex, country, or physical proximity. This propensity may be useful in self-defense with respect to recognizing potential danger and simplifying the multitudinous messages received from "outsiders."

The Nazis, of course, had a Manichean outlook on life, and brutally acted upon it; this tendency permeates much of reality. The Germans "perfected" these Manichean tendencies by going to great lengths to use their pseudoscience, myth, and outright lies to make two clear camps and then try to eliminate "the others" by murder.[13] Since unadulterated Manichean attitudes historically have had murderous consequences, Levi believes that we must be educated to accept difference and nuance when we think about and associate with others. He worries about man's inclination to simplify the relationship between groups by categorically deciding who are friends and who are enemies.

In addition the Lager, much to his horror, taught him that our attachments with friends, our solidarity with others, is tenuous. In the Hobbesian circumstances of the Lager, virtually everyone became an enemy, and it happened quickly. One of the serious debates in the literature of the Holocaust regards the extent of human solidarity among the prisoners of the Lagers. For instance, in showing the arguments for solidarity, Istvan Deak notes that Levi actually provides evidence for solidarity despite his overall picture of a bleak universe: "[Tzvetan] Todorov, however, finds many exceptions to the law of the jungle in concentration camp literature and points out that Primo Levi and other pessimists themselves performed quiet acts of compassion and heroism. Not everyone became demoralized, and survival was often a question of mutual assistance and sympathy."[14]

Lorenzo, a civilian Italian laborer, brought soup to Levi every day, and Todorov uses this human contact as evidence of social solidarity.[15] Levi brings much to this controversy by making critical distinctions. In general, the worse conditions were, the more solidarity disappeared. It was a Hobbesian universe, and if people in the state of nature had that small

13. Levi noted the strength of national habits in the Lager, which was overwhelmingly Jewish. The differences were between Polish Jews, Italian Jews, Hungarian Jews, etc. Although difference in the Lager was manifest on the basis of nationality, crimes and solidarity did not seem to be based on national differences.

14. Deak, "Memories of Hell," 39.

15. Ibid.

modicum of pity as Rousseau suggests, the Lager quickly dispatched it. Levi comments about the folly of a Hungarian Jew named Kraus, who believed in solidarity and the virtue of hard work: "He works too much and too vigorously: he has not yet learnt our underground art of economizing on everything, on breath, movements, even thoughts. . . . [H]e seems to think that his present situation is like outside, where it is honest and logical to work, as well as being of advantage, because according to what everyone says, the more one works the more one earns and eats."[16]

Levi and the others went along with Kraus's optimistic fantasy, but they had no respect for him, thought little about him, secretly resented when they had to work with him, and gave him little chance to survive. Levi concludes: "Poor silly Kraus. If he only knew that it is not true, that I have really dreamt nothing about him, that he is nothing to me except for a brief moment, nothing like everything is nothing down here, except the hunger inside and the cold and the rain around." Levi so grimly states: "The law of the lager said: 'eat your own bread, and if you can, that of your neighbor,' and left no room for gratitude" (*Survival*, 132, 160). This, not conviviality and concern, was the harsh reality of the Lager.

Deak and Todorov are correct in suggesting that Levi found solidarity; it is just that the few traces he found took on the narrowly circumscribed form of "us-ism." The fact is, there was no common law to deal with disputes among prisoners, a truly Hobbesian condition. Fragile bonds between individuals were aggravated by scarcity. If the prisoners shared everything, there would not be enough to go around.

Between pure selfishness and Kraus's dream of generosity and sharing, there was the occasional example of us-ism: "I chose the third path, that of selfishness extended to the person closest to you, which in distant times a friend of mine appropriately called us-ism" (*Drowned*, 80). One day, Levi found a pipe with a small amount of water in it. He could have shared it with everyone, which would have left mere drops for everyone, or he could have taken it all for himself. Instead, he shared it with Alberto. In another instance, when Levi and a few others had been accepted to work in the chemical factory, "[m]any comrades congratulate us; Alberto first of all, with genuine joy, without a shadow of envy. Alberto holds nothing against my fortune, he is really very pleased, both because of our friendship and because he will also gain from it. In fact, by now we two are

---

16. Levi, *Survival in Auschwitz,* 132. Future references will be cited parenthetically in the text.

bound by a tight bond of alliance, by which every 'organized' scrap is divided into two strictly equal parts" (*Survival*, 138).

In Aristotelian terms, Levi's friendship with Alberto was based on an induction of feelings, true friendship, and utility reinforced the ties.[17] The us-ism between Lorenzo and Levi and between Levi and Alberto helped keep the latter two alive, but according to Levi, it was exceptional in the Hobbesian Lager.[18] The only other example of us-ism is what we might call implied social contracts, "tacit pacts of non-aggression with neighbors" (*Survival*, 56).

Thus, despite the occasional us-isms, the seemingly natural ability for categorization and the inevitable aversion toward others, and the weak bonds between so-called friends, are clear propensities in humans. Auschwitz greatly accelerated these processes. The cultivation of an understanding of difference with others and cultivating the bonds of friendship prove very fragile under conditions of adversity, a situation that Levi very much lamented.

Levi's explanation of human behavior with respect to hierarchy follows the same pattern as his clarification of Manichean propensities and human solidarity. Intitially, there is a human tendency to hierarchy, which may be useful in human organization. As Levi suggests, "There is no proof that power is intrinsically harmful to the collectivity." Power that becomes organized in hierarchy is fundamental to our nature: "Power exists in all the varieties of the human social organization, more or less controlled, usurped, conferred from above or recognized from below, assigned by merit, corporate solidarity, blood, or position. Probably a certain degree of man's domination over man is inscribed in our genetic patrimony as gregarious animals" (*Drowned*, 46).

Levi recognized the same tendency in himself and in other prisoners when they were faced with the *Zugang*, the newcomers to the Lager. The "old-timers" tried to establish their superiority: "Vying for prestige also came into play, a seemingly irrepressible need in our civilization: the despised crowd of seniors was prone to recognize in the new arrival a target on which to vent its humiliation, to find compensation at his expense, to

17. Generally, Levi's idea of causality in social relations is that social causes are overdetermined. He is thereby in accord with Aristotle on this matter.

18. Interestingly, after the war, Levi discovered that Lorenzo was supplying many other Italian prisoners with extra rations at no benefit to himself. Levi tried to get to the bottom of this extraordinary behavior, but he ultimately could not.

build for itself and at his expense a figure of a lower rank on whom to discharge the burden of the offenses received from above" (*Drowned*, 39–40).

The seduction of these satraps is universal, and the social organization of the Lager brought out some of the very worst aspects of hierarchy. The Germans preyed on these tendencies, which made the Lager that much worse for the prisoners: "In history and in life one sometimes seems to glimpse a ferocious law which states: 'to he that has, will be given; to he that has not, will be taken away.' In the Lager, where man is alone and where the struggle for life is reduced to its primordial mechanism, this unjust law is openly in force, is recognized by all" (*Survival*, 88–89).

For instance, in the Lager, numerous satraps existed at the lower ends of power; the most well known of these was the position of Kapo. Their power was unlimited: "[O]r, more accurately put, a lower limit was imposed on their violence, in the sense that they were punished or deposed if they did not prove to be sufficiently harsh, but there was no upper limit. . . . Until the end of 1943, it was not unusual for a prisoner to be beaten to death by a *Kapo* without the latter having to fear any sanctions" (*Drowned*, 46).

Specific circumstances exacerbate the atavistic tendency in us to dominate. Where only a few are at the top of an organization, positions of power tend to proliferate. As Levi points out, the Nazi regime of the final years could not have done without auxiliaries like the Kapos and still have carried out the war. He also discusses the behavior of those prisoners who, as Anna Freud and Bruno Bettleheim describe, identify with the aggressors (*Drowned*, 48, 42). It grieves Levi greatly that man has a penchant to do to those below him what has been done to him from above, behavior that Elias Canetti refers to as "the sting."[19]

In *Democracy in America*, Alexis de Tocqueville reinforces the notion of a tendency toward hierarchy in man when he suggests that democracies can't quell the human desire for superiority. In democracies, individuals are unleashed to seek their fortunes under the guise that one is as good as the other. It can be argued that few in a democracy are striving to be equal, for they are really striving to be superior in some way. Democracy simply gives vent to that ambition. In the Hobbesian state of nature in the Lager, everyone at the bottom was equal, and it is possible that this condition gave an added push to the prisoners' hierarchical tendencies. Levi regret-

19. Freud, *The Ego and Mechanisms of Defense*, 109–21. For Bettleheim, see Carl Secord and Carl W. Backman, *Social Psychology*, 223. Canetti, *Crowds and Power*, 315–16.

fully recognizes that hierarchy is a ubiquitous phenomenon: "The ascent of the privileged, not only in the Lager but in all human coexistence, is an anguishing but unfailing phenomenon: only in utopias is it absent" (*Drowned,* 42).

Thomas Hobbes sees violence stemming from competition, diffidence and glory.[20] It is glory where the advantage is not material, but simply something one can laud over others. Levi and Alberto got themselves a *menaschka,* or zinc bucket, to carry the extra rations of soup Lorenzo provided: "In the whole camp, there are only a few Greeks who have a *menaschka* larger than ours. Besides the material advantages, it carries with it a perceptible improvement in our social standing" (*Survival,* 145).

Levi despised the pervasive and pernicious effects of hierarchy. These atavistic traits must be challenged, but the battle is endless, for as he explains above, only utopian fantasies are free of privilege. Levi concludes that man must continue the battle against privilege, but as suggested earlier, he is not a progressivist: "It is the duty of righteous men to make war on all undeserved privilege, but one must not forget that this is a war without end" (*Drowned,* 42).

In conclusion, we are ill-constituted beings in ordinary life, and we suffer from our deficiencies even more under the boundary conditions of the Lagers. Our Manichean tendencies come out in our relations with those we perceive as different from ourselves, but even our solidarity toward our friends is excessively fragile. In addition, we have a very strong inclination toward hierarchy regardless of whether or not it is useful.

20. Hobbes, *Leviathan,* 76.

4

Violence

We had worked together for a long time in the Polish mud. All of us had fallen in the deep slippery workyard mud but, thanks to that bit of animal nobility that survives even in a man reduced to despair, we struggled to avoid falling, and to minimize its effects; in fact, a man prostrate on the ground is endangered, for he stirs fierce instincts, and inspires derision rather than pity.

—*Moments of Reprieve*

The human ashes coming from the crematoria, tons daily, were easily recognized as such, because they often contained teeth or vertebrae. Nevertheless, they were employed for several purposes: . . . and especially notable, they were used instead of gravel to cover the paths of the SS village located near the camp, whether out of pure callousness or because, due to their origins, they were regarded as material to be trampled on, I couldn't say.

—*The Drowned and the Saved*

Primo Levi's work is replete with keen insights on violence, from the descriptions and analyses of the Holocaust in *Survival in Auschwitz* to his retrospective thoughts on the Lager forty years later as carefully rendered in *The Drowned and the Saved*. In his initial writings, Levi closely works with what he observed about violence firsthand. In his later works, he collects his observations on nature and, in addition, returns to the Holocaust to try and understand many of the incidents of violence that those at the bottom, including Levi himself, didn't know about. By engaging himself in the questions of why the Holocaust occurred, he avoids the problem that Omer Bartov speaks of when analysts choose to talk either of the perpetrators or the victims.[1] Levi takes a hard look at violence against victims, but he also tries to understand why this violence came about at the hands of perpetrators. In his writing he makes a sharp moral distinction between what violence was done to the victims and what, in turn, some of the victims did to one another.

Levi's thoughts on violence, as with his thoughts on social cohesion and hierarchy, are consistent with his insights on nature, nurture, and the tragedy of being human. First, we will discuss the "atavistic" aspects of violence in man and how they clash with "civilized man," who through learning tries to restrain himself from committing violent acts. Second, we will consider the problematic aspects of reason with respect to violence—for example, when reason embraces violent acts and destructive technology. Third, we will discuss Levi's arguments against the use of violence. In conclusion, we shall examine our infinite capacity for rationalization when it comes to sanctioning violence and destruction. This detailed discussion of our violent proclivities will also serve as an introduction to some of Levi's key concepts, such as civilized liberalism, moral education, the tragic sense, and man the toolmaker.

Levi frequently remarks about the ubiquity of violence in nature, whether in animal or human life. In his essay on carbon in *The Periodic Table,* he traces one of the building blocks of living matter, a single carbon atom. The play of life on this planet, illustrated by the journey of the single carbon atom, involves beauty and the prevalence of life and death struggles: "I could recount an endless number of stories about carbon atoms that become colors or perfumes in flowers; of others which, from tiny algae to small crustaceans to fish, gradually return as carbon dioxide to the waters of the sea, in a perpetual, frightening round-dance of life and death, in which every devourer is immediately devoured."[2]

This dance is built into the nature of being and gives Levi pause about how we are featured in it. His look at the murderous course of nature sets up a major agony in his thought with respect to violence. If he falls into the naturalistic fallacy that whatever is, is good, then he would have no basis for condemning the violence that was done to him and millions of others. Thus, his ethos against violence comes from other than the naturalistic source.

1. Omer Bartov, "The Penultimate Horror," 49.
2. Levi, *The Periodic Table,* 232.

In his science fiction story "His Own Blacksmith: To Italo Calvino," Levi speculates about human nature and its possible consequences. Again, he comes to the same conclusion: violence predominates on this planet. Levi has the main character speak historically about his own ancestry. Where the main character, the blacksmith, differs from the rest of us is that he can remember his adventures as he moves up the phyllogenetic scale. He is the architect of genetic changes from slime to man as he moves through generations.

In recounting his past adventures, the blacksmith cannot help but comment on violence. He describes the hazards to himself when he lived in the sea, and then of the dangers he faced when he moved onto land: "We have landed: there wasn't much choice, the sea is getting colder and saltier, and besides it is filling up with animals that I don't like too much, fishes with teeth, more than six meters long, and others that are smaller but poisonous and extremely voracious." When he becomes a land animal, life is no less dangerous, for there as well, all is kill or be killed: "Dear diary, today I had a close call: an enormous beast, I don't know what it's called, came out of the swamp and pursued me for almost an hour. As soon as I got my breath back, I made up my mind: in this world it is imprudent to go about unarmed."[3]

In this story, Levi describes in an anthropomorphic, personal way, the evolutionary process that randomly led from slime to man: "I thought about it, I made a few sketches, then I made my choice. I built myself a beautiful armor of bony shields, four horns on the forehead, a nail on every finger, and eight poisonous stings on the tip of my tail" (199). At least the early armor and the later toolmaking ability that allowed the development of offensive weapons gave the human species and the individual a chance for survival.

When the transformation is made into man, the blacksmith has the violent characteristics that were with us from the beginning, whether we need them today or not. Man is a thinking creature, but he seems to be thinking with his hands as much as with his brain. With the combination of both he builds weapons for defense and offense: "With your hands—not that it is easy—but with your hands you can also chip a flint and tie the chip to the end of a stick, in short make yourself an axe, and with that axe protect your territory or perhaps even enlarge it" (201). Man puts

3. Levi, "His Own Blacksmith: To Italo Calvino," in *"The Sixth Day" and Other Tales*, 97, 99. Future references will be cited parenthetically in the text.

the axe to a variety of violent uses; it is used to hurt, intimidate, or fend off those whose only "crime" is to be different. Levi's protagonist uses the weapon to "bash in the heads of certain other 'I's that are in my way, or court my wife, or are even only whiter or blacker or hairier or less hairy than me, or speak with a different accent" (202).

The protagonist ends the diary here because human nature is fixed. In the future, his progeny will confront a different set of adventures, but they will face them with the same set of attributes: "But here this diary might as well end. With these last transformations and inventions of mine, the major part of the job is now accomplished: since then, nothing essential has happened to me, nor do I think is going to happen to me in the future" (202). We are set with a propensity toward violence, and we are "creative" in the ways that we apply it to our lives.

As discussed in the last chapter, the tendency to differentiate between "us" and "them" seems to Levi to be built into our constitution. He can understand how people, especially the young, want simplification; Alexis de Tocqueville made the same point when he talked of our desire to generalize in order to simplify. For Tocqueville, only God can know everything in its particularity, and humans, to make sense of things, must use some method of simplification to organize what we know. Levi indicates that the complications of life limit our ability for concision: "This *desire* for simplification is justified, but the same does not always apply to simplification itself, which is a working hypothesis, useful as long as it is recognized as such and not mistaken for reality."[4] In making necessary judgments about human beings and their activities, Levi recognizes the tension between the need to simply make judgments and the possibility that simplification brings on a real distortion of a complex reality.

In specific situations, Levi takes into account our Manichean tendencies. For instance, he warns us against simplification when we discuss whether or not to hold people accountable for what happened among the prisoners in Auschwitz. The vast majority of behaviors lie within a "gray zone" that does not fit into the Manichean categories of good and evil. Atavistic Manichean simplification is at the heart of why groups are singled out by others for different treatment and placed into the categories of "us" and "them."

Levi sees nationalism as the important organizing focus for our

---

4. Levi, *The Drowned and the Saved*, 37. Future references will be cited parenthetically in the text.

Manichean tendencies. Even in the Lager, nationalism persisted: the constant was that virtually all the prisoners were Jewish, and the variable was that they were also Hungarians, Poles, Greeks, Czechs, French, etc. However, it is not necessarily a slippery slope from nationalism to violence. These differences, for instance, did not lead to violence in the Lager, but where leaders use difference to separate "us" and "them," nationalism rests at the base of competition and violence in society. Virulent nationalism flourishes when it is unrestrained by intelligent citizens' understanding of the relationship between simplifying concepts and the complexities of reality. For instance, the philosopher-sociologist Georg Simmel suggests that if we think about it carefully, we will realize that we can never be the same or identify completely with another human being. Such subtle thoughts in individuals, however, fall before the strong Manichean tendencies to fully identify with our friends and hate our enemies.[5]

During the Holocaust, the Germans, either wittingly or unwittingly, used manipulative tactics to accentuate differences between "us" and "them." As explained earlier, Levi endeavors to understand why there is so much gratuitous violence that is not connected to the manifest goals of the oppressors. The only explanation Levi can find is that the Germans wanted to degrade the Jews, to make them seem subhuman, unlike Germans, so that killing them would be easy. The trick is to accentuate the "us" and the "them." Levi sees us as ill-constituted human beings that evolved with the protective mechanisms that help us differentiate friend and foe, but in an untutored form, they can turn us into murderous beasts.

Levi believes it is our responsibility to overcome our atavistic tendencies where they would wreak havoc on other human beings. We can be educated to overcome these tendencies; if we are not, our atavistic tendencies, often magnified by a poor education, accentuate the worst in us. Levi rejects the idea that his oppressors were specially selected brutes, some subspecies of humans more prone to these atavistic tendencies than others. Nor does he accept the assumption that there is original sin we must overcome. At the conclusion of *The Drowned and the Saved* he indicates that he has been asked repeatedly what his "torturers" were like. He answers as follows: "The term *torturers* alludes to our ex-guardians, the SS, and is in my opinion inappropriate: it brings to mind twisted individuals, ill-born, sadists, afflicted by an original flaw. Instead, they were made of the same cloth as we, they were average human beings, averagely intelli-

5. Donald N. Levine, ed., *Georg Simmel: On Individuality and Social Forms*, 147–49.

gent, averagely wicked: save the exceptions, they were not monsters, they had our faces, but they had been reared badly" (202).

He refers here to the "terrifying miseducation" of the Germans under Hitler. The Nazis, instead of teaching the necessary virtues, simply accentuated the violent, atavistic tendencies. Often, social learning through propaganda is used to explain the exceptional violence, but Levi will not excuse any of those so blinded by the words of Hitler. Instead, Levi holds us to the civilized notion that we are all responsible.

The Enlightenment faith in education as inoculation against savagery was very strong prior to World War II. As a youth, Elie Wiesel shared a similar notion about the Germans' cultural tradition: "The truth is that, in spite of everything we knew about Nazi Germany, we had an inexplicable confidence in German culture and humanism. We kept telling ourselves that this was, after all, a civilized people, that we must not give credence to exaggerated rumors about its army's behavior."[6]

Obviously, these beliefs were dashed by the conflagration. The youthful Enlightenment optimism of both Primo Levi and Elie Wiesel was sorely tested by the brutality of the Nazis and the fact that such crimes came from the most civilized of nations, coupled with the postwar unveiling of the Western powers' colonial record. As we shall see, Levi's political philosophy is in large part an attempt to salvage Enlightenment assumptions by abandoning the myth of progress and embracing the tragic sense of life. For instance, later we will explore Levi's argument that the original modern education was not bad. The Enlightenment did not carry its own seeds of destruction; it was simply that the re-education of the Germans by the Nazis was so powerful and toxic.

Levi sees violence from two perspectives to try to understand why it reaches the levels it does among us. His first view is close to the Freudian-Rousseauian position; the second is elaborated by Friedrich Nietzsche. These views are set into tension with each other. For Levi, as it is for Freud, the veneer of civilization is very thin. When Levi looks at the behavior of animals and man, he comes to Freud's conclusion; it is surprising that we do not have more violence. Our primal powers and the fragility of social learning fuel violence. Initially, when the prisoners entered Auschwitz we have in them Rousseau's modicum of pity reinforced by early learning, but it quickly became erased as the pressures of survival imploded on them.

6. Wiesel, *All Rivers Run to the Sea: Memoirs,* 27.

We described in the last chapter the quick destruction of solidarity and the instant activation of survival instincts of violence and superiority among the prisoners. Circumstances overwhelmed social learning in the Lager.

Levi's chapter "The Gray Zone" in *The Drowned and the Saved* stakes out the most frequent rest stop for moral behavior in humans, the large expanse of gray zone between good and evil. Survivors of the Lager often fall in the gray zone because of the extreme Hobbesian pressures on an already vulnerable population: "But there are extenuating circumstances: an infernal order such as National Socialism exercises a frightful power of corruption, against which it is difficult to guard oneself. It degrades its victims and makes them similar to itself, because it needs both great and small complicities" (68). Extreme circumstances drive people inward in defense of themselves and the thin veneer of civilization is overwhelmed, and "the harsher the oppression, the more widespread among the oppressed is the willingness, with all its infinite nuances and motivations, to collaborate: terror, ideological seduction, servile imitation of the victor, myopic desire for any power whatsoever, even though ridiculously circumscribed in space and time, cowardice, and finally, lucid calculation aimed at eluding the imposed orders and order" (43).

For those who are brought under the death grip of the Nazi machine in the Lager, there are mitigating circumstances, but Levi does not extend them to the perpetrators. In the modern totalitarian state there are several reasons why citizens may fall into uncivilized patterns of behavior: "Its weapons are substantially three: direct propaganda or propaganda camouflaged as upbringing, instruction, and popular culture; the barrier erected against pluralism of information; and terror" (*Drowned*, 29). He is aware that propaganda should not have worked on that vast group that had come to consciousness before the twelve years of the Third Reich. As well, he is aware that terror was rarely needed and that it might have been only a nudge that the citizenry needed when it came to uncivilized behavior.[7] This is why Levi has no sympathy for the perpetrators. In addition, conditions were nowhere as severe for the Germans as for the prisoners; the former had choices.

Thus, Levi first tries to understand the levels of violence among humans by suggesting that we are ill-constituted beings and that violence is not far

---

7. Of course, if Daniel Goldhagen in *Hitler's Willing Executioners* is correct, a nudge may not have even been needed.

below the surface in individuals and civilizations.[8] His second perspective, set against the first, recognizes the power of culture, often ignored, which exerts considerable influence on the ways of man. From the perspective of culture, violent acts are the overcoming of socialization that takes place in society against violence. These habits can be very strong, and it is difficult to act against them, regardless of our original endowments. This second position is one that Nietzsche reluctantly comes to when he assays human motivations. It occurs to him that in all his writings he asserts a will to life, but most people do not part from their habits of culture. Perhaps there is a will to conform that is stronger than the will to life and individuality. Nietzsche preaches self-assertion against a backdrop of what he classifies as conformist behavior by all but the few. He describes a psyche socialized to make people timid creatures. For Nietzsche, there must be a will to this type of conservatism in human behavior, the acceptance of conventional learning, which must be overcome.

What is repugnant to Nietzsche is a glimmer of hope to Levi. It means, for Levi, that civilization and prior learning are not easy to give up. In Levi's own experience, it was difficult, having been brought up to cherish peace and civility, to assume a more violent mode of action toward the adversities of the Lager. We can make many responses to adversity, including withdrawal, acquiescence, physical illness, mental illness, negotiation, and finally violence. We may pick up these responses by accident of development, or deliberately through individual or collective learning. No two people will respond in the same way to similar circumstances. "Atavistic" capabilities reside within us, but there is no necessity to the use of any one of these, for there is no necessary quantum of instinctual energy that the individual has to discharge. From this Nietzschean perspective, education and civilization can be very powerful, and violence might need an effective boost to overcome them.

Levi issues personal testimony to the fact that reticence toward violence may be built in. He gives credit to Jewish and Italian culture. He was trained to use the mind, not physical force, to encounter adversity. He cannot find in his background instances where he was tempted toward or actively engaged in physical violence. If he engaged in such force, he would have to deal the rest of his life with the prohibitions, which would find ex-

---

8. Levi fully understands the special circumstances of the Holocaust and the Nazi's virulent hatred of the Jews, but when speaking of violence and the human condition he recognizes the ubiquity of violence in the human condition. He is taking a long view of history.

pression through guilt. This actually occurred to Levi when stealing became a necessity for him in the Lager. The prohibition against stealing and violence had to be overcome. Levi's reticence, gained through habit and self-control, differed from Jean Améry's ability to "return the blow" to the enemy. Levi simply did not have this ability in his repertoire. He speculates as to why: "I have never known how to 'return the blow,' not out of evangelic saintliness or intellectual aristocracy, but due to an intrinsic incapacity. Perhaps because of the lack of a serious political education: in fact, there does not exist a political program, even the most moderate, even the least violent that does not allow for some form of active defense" (*Drowned*, 136).

Levi uses his ideas to control his urges. He describes with extreme distaste his fight with Elias the Dwarf in the Lager, a fight not of Levi's own making. Primal urges were there, but social learning prevailed. When students asked him why there were no expressions of hate and revenge against the Germans, he gave this reply: "I must admit that if I had in front of me one of our persecutors of those days, certain known faces, certain old lies, I would be tempted to hate, and with violence too; but exactly because I am not a Fascist or a Nazi, I refuse to give way to this temptation."[9] Self-control, of course, is one of the virtues taught in a civilized society: "I believe in reason and in discussion as supreme instruments of progress, and therefore I repress hatred even within myself: I prefer justice." (*Reawakening*, 196). He goes on to say that his writings are his revenge, and to be believed they must be in a sober and not a vengeful tone. An education that bans violence from our central repertoire of potential alternatives works in tandem with a society that reinforces the suppression of violent proclivities.

In question and answer sessions, a member of Levi's audience inevitably would ask, in an accusatory fashion, why the prisoners did not escape or rebel. The moral force of this question comes from the current popular culture that espouses rebellion as a duty, but Levi was not schooled in such a culture.[10] More important, Levi feels the "brave" inquisitors are very naïve about the circumstances faced by those in the Lager. In *The Reawakening*, he persuasively insists that the physical and mental destruction of

9. Levi, *The Reawakening*, 196. Future references will be cited parenthetically in the text.

10. Levi answered such questions formally in both *The Reawakening* and in *The Drowned and the Saved*. Also included in the list of inevitable questions was: "Why didn't you flee before the Holocaust?"

the prisoners virtually precluded bravado: "Even outside the camps, struggles are rarely waged by *Lumpenproletariat*. People in rags do not revolt" (203). In his writings forty years after Auschwitz, his views did not change. Freedom is espoused by the comfortable when escape and capture do not mean death. The obligation to resist and rebel had, and still has, its strongest roots in military, not civilian culture. Western allied soldiers, who were subject to humane treatment, could escape again and again, while death was the only prescription for the Lager resident (*Drowned*, 151–52). Even the Russian soldiers who had been taught the obligation to escape and rebel rarely did so. Finally, there were escapes and rebellions in the Lager by the civilian prisoners under such extreme circumstances.

Levi's first reason for the lack of rebellion, the lack of a cultural tradition, suggests that the response of violence is simply not instinctual, but is learned. In many cultures, socialization has to be overcome before violence can take place. Levi's inclination to resist comes when he joins the partisans, knowing nothing about how to mount a refusal. He is arrested the day after joining the partisan group. He lacks the skills, guile, and experience: "They [his partisan group] did not get a chance to fight: the local units had been infiltrated by some former army officers, who worked for the Fascist militia and who led a raid on the partisan hideouts."[11]

His novel *If Not Now, When?*, a possible wish fulfillment, shows what happens to Jews who join a resistance movement and become successful partisans. Mendel the watchmaker, the main protagonist, and his friends use skills from their professions, book learning, guile, and instruction from partisans to teach themselves to make weapons, to organize, and to fight. In some ways it parallels the lessons that early Zionists in Israel had to learn after overcoming prior historical habits. Levi is chronicling a turning point in Jewish history where the Jews were not prepared for the violence done to them, and certainly not prepared to resist evil in a military way. For Levi, this reticence is a glaring indication that we cannot simply talk of instinct when we talk of violence. He makes the same point when he shows how defeat turned the Germans he encountered on his way home to Turin into broken men incapable of resistance. They were even fearful of the ragged, displaced Jews still wandering through Europe at the end of the war.

Levi points out that the Jews submerged and killed in the Holocaust could have done little to save themselves even if they had been militant at

11. Mirna Cicioni, *Primo Levi: Bridges of Knowledge*, 15–16.

the time. The more you can blame the victim, the less culpable the enemy. For his theory of violence, he wanted to show that through education, Jews as well as the Germans going in reverse could successively learn and un-learn violence, and that education through formal learning and circum-stances is as critical as our atavistic leanings toward violence. Learning can move a people from a nonviolent position to a role as active, effective fight-ers; it is not solely instinct that explains violence. Isaac Bashevis Singer's protagonist in *The Penitent*, Joseph Shapiro, suggests that Jewish behav-ior has ranged from the lusty days of King David to the peaceful Hassidic Jews of Eastern Europe to the warriors of modern Israel. For Shapiro and other modern Jews, they have a full range of actions to call upon: one can decide what type of Jew to be.

In sum, the veneer of civilization is very fragile and there is an atavistic tendency toward violence, but at the same time powerful influences can be built in by the strength of education and civilization. A fateful struggle is set up. Levi obviously believes that buttressing civilization and education against violence is crucial; the battle must be fought. This tension in Levi's thought resonates throughout his works: "It has been obscenely said that there is a need for conflict: that mankind cannot do without it. It has also been said that local conflicts, violence in the streets, factories, and stadi-ums, are an equivalent of generalized war and preserve us from it, as petit mal, the epileptic equivalent, preserves from grand mal." Levi goes on to say: "These are captious and suspect arguments. Satan is not necessary: there is no need for wars or violence, under any circumstances" (*Drowned*, 200).

His evidence is that in the forty years between the end of the war and the writing of *The Drowned and the Saved*, there had been no war in Eu-rope; however, most historians treat this as an historical anomaly. For Levi, this interlude from war appears to him proof that wars are not nec-essary. He sees no need to accept the idea of original sin, or the social sci-ence hypothesis of the constant valence of energy from the aggressive in-stinct. Hence, there is no credence to the hypothesis of catharsis, which makes functional small acts of violence in order to avoid larger confla-grations. Levi's critique of catharsis appears to be aimed at James's moral equivalent of war and the Freudian notion of catharsis, both of which as-sume a quantity of aggression that must be dispatched.

Carol Tavris, in her book *Anger*, supports Levi's contention that vio-lence is not necessary: Violence when it occurs between groups, or by in-dividuals against groups, does not necessarily bring cathartic relief to the perpetrators.[12] A violent response to persecution may bring no relief—for instance, when prescribed by Franz Fanon as a cleansing action of the soul—to those previously persecuted. What may be more important to the victims' state of mind is their initial disposition and whether or not they feel superior to the perpetrators. As Elie Wiesel points out, the Jews did not respond to the violence of the Poles, and this lack of response is made easy because they had no respect for their tormentors. Status superiority and other variables make the catharsis hypothesis irrelevant.[13]

We move now to Levi's discussion of our penchant for reason and the relationship it has with violence, concentrating on violence both as a means to an end and as an end in itself to see how violence is used and abused through the use of reason. In his carefully calculated way, Levi shows that reason in the service of violence is not always a bad idea. For instance, he does not counter our warlike tendencies with pacific suggestions under all circumstances, because he understands that sometimes violence is a useful means in our arsenal, a tool that may be necessary to ward off evil.[14] As Tavris puts it, we would not want to do away with the hiss of the snake, for example, that wards off attackers.

Scientists use instrumental reason to perfect the means of violence; Levi tries to discern the motives of those who tinker with these war toys, which end up as instruments of violence. It is by now a cliché that we have mad scientists who are bent on discovering something simply for the technological virtuosity involved, regardless of the consequences. Levi adds to the discussion because he is a scientist and knows how they think. In his youth, Levi tried to explain to his friend Sandro the ideal of being a chemist, an explorer of nature, a toolmaker: "That the nobility of Man, acquired in a hundred centuries of trial and error, lay in making himself the conqueror of matter, and that I had enrolled in chemistry because I wanted to remain faithful to this nobility."[15] Many of his great adventures as a chemist came when he uncovered the "secrets" of nature by manipulating different materials.

This "greatness of man" can also turn sour when his technology is used

---

12. Tavris, *Anger*, 45–47.

13. Later chapters will explore what Levi thinks about the idea of catharsis and our ability to do away with violence. He is revealed as far less optimistic than portrayed here.

14. As suggested earlier, Levi indicates that he is constitutionally incapable of using violence himself.

15. Levi, *Periodic*, 41.

for certain purposes. In a short story "Some Applications of the Mimer," he tells of Gilberto, a tinkerer who repairs refrigerators, electric razors, and watches. In addition, "he builds devices to turn on the radiators in the morning, photoelectric locks, flying models, acoustic probes to play with at the seaside. As for automobiles, they last him only a few months: he disassembles and assembles them continually; polishes, lubricates, modifies them." In an adventure that Levi carries through several short stories, Gilberto obtains a mimer, a device that makes perfect copies of paper, including the exact fiber content and arrangement of the molecules of the original. He breaks the mimer down and builds a much larger version, which he uses to duplicate his wife, Emma. Gilberto is "a dangerous man, a small noxious Prometheus: he is ingenious and irresponsible, arrogant and foolish. He is the child of the century, as I have said before. Indeed, he is a symbol of our century. I've always thought that, if the occasion arose, he would have been able to build an atom bomb and drop it on Milan 'to see the effect it would have.'"[16]

Again, we are ill-constituted beings because the toolmaker can do ill as well as good on a massive scale. In an essay called "Hatching the Cobra," Levi speaks of the 1974 Nobel Prize–winning scientist Martin Ryle, who suggests a drastic solution to the problem that toolmaking can be for good, but especially for ill. Ryle's work contributed to the development of measures to confuse the German radar. He was repelled by war and understood that discoveries that might have been conceived for good ended up supporting evil. Ryle knew that astronomers did not have clean hands: "For instance, to measure with precision the intensity of the gravitational field surrounding the Earth is doubtless of theoretical interest, but it also serves to improve the aim of intercontinental ballistic missiles. According to Ryle's data, 40 percent of all English engineers and physicists are involved in the study of instruments of destruction." Ryle's solution, one he made shortly before he died in 1948, was to "'Stop science now.'"[17]

Levi calls Ryle's proposal "extremist" and "utopian." The toolmaker is too central to our selves to be excluded by ukase: "We are what we are: each one of us, even the peasant, even the most modest artisan, is a researcher, has always been that."[18] The toolmaker, as Levi reiterates many times in his books, cannot be rooted out of us. Besides, would we want to root him

16. Levi, "Some Applications of the Mimer," in *"Sixth,"* 39.
17. Levi, "Hatching the Cobra," in *"The Mirror Maker": Stories and Essays by Primo Levi,* 175.
18. Ibid.

out? Man the maker is central to who we are, and what is more, is close to the center of our virtue. Once again, Levi's solution is moral education, for the toolmaker needs to be taught responsibility and humility. Whether he acts himself or passes the technology on to others for them to use, the tinkerer should be made aware and hence responsible for his actions.

The tinkerer is of great concern, but so are those in power who use the new technologies of violence to carry out their evil intentions. Levi recognizes that violence has defensive uses, but he is most concerned when violence is used to carry out the Holocaust. In the *Drowned and the Saved,* Levi raises the question of whether the Holocaust is part of a design or whether it is just some form of collective madness: "[O]ne feels torn between two opinions: Were we witnessing the rational development of an inhuman plan or a manifestation (unique in history and still unsatisfactorily explained) of collective madness? Was it logic intent on evil or the absence of logic? As so often happens in human affairs, the two alternatives coexisted" (106). In accord with the writings of Lucy Dawidowicz, he takes the position that the intentions are there and the design for evil is in place: "Hateful but not insane were also the means foreseen to achieve these ends: to unleash military aggressions or ruthless wars, to support internal fifth columns, to transfer or remove entire populations, to subjugate, sterilize, or exterminate them." The ends violence served drew theoreticians, leaders, and followers further and further from the human community. They "became progressively removed from reality as little by little their morality came unglued from the morality common to all times and to all civilizations, an integral part of our human heritage which in the end must be acknowledged" (107).[19]

The fundamental problem with the ideas of the leaders is not that they were rational or brilliant, but that they were believed by the masses: "The ideas they [Hitler and Mussolini] proclaimed were not always the same and were, in general, aberrant or silly or cruel." Such ideas will always be in the air. The problem is with the followers, "ordinary men," who carry the ideas out and take dangerous initiatives on their own: "More dangerous are the common men, the functionaries ready to believe and to act without asking questions, like Hoss, the commandant of Auschwitz; like Stangl, commandant of Treblinka; like the French military of twenty years later, slaughterers in Algeria; like the Khmer Rouge of the late seventies, slaughterers in Cambodia" (*Reawakening*, 214).

19. Note Levi's understanding of the values of civilization as universal.

Public willingness in no way excuses the leaders; they are the triggers and must be punished. However, the real danger, for Levi, is not madmen in our midst: "Monsters exist, but they are too few in number to be truly dangerous" (*Reawakening,* 214). They may be biological mistakes, or socialized in a diabolical way; they cannot be educated. They are difficult to identify early, and in later life it is too late to re-educate them. Therefore, the focus of prevention must be on the followers. Leaders first propose the ends of terror and the means to carry out a plan, but without followers, it will never happen. In almost a parody of what Nietzsche said about Socrates—that he was a buffoon who was believed—Levi believes there are always buffoons around, and the key is whether they are believed: "In the Third World [violence useless or useful] is endemic or epidemic. It only awaits its new buffoon" (*Drowned,* 199). The cultures of these and other countries are truly frightening when they invite such violence to occur.

Niccolo Machiavelli most clearly lays out a blueprint for the rational capture and consolidation of power. Calculating man is at the center of control. Machiavelli is considered a realist because power appears to be more realizable than negotiation or some form of community. Human affairs inevitably degenerate into violence, the common denominator of societies. Empirically, as we look back in history, the "bad" seems more "real" than the "good." Realism is the hard-boiled view of humans when you strip them of sentimentality or ideals. Machiavelli believes that through violence in the service of reason, the consolidation of the five Italian states could occur. As commentators suggest, his preference was for the type of democracy propounded in the *Discourses,* but the Italy of his time was in no position to accept democracy; it was "unrealistic." Machiavelli himself gives credence to this view when, in an implicit criticism of Plato's *Republic* in *The Prince,* he tells us that the ideal is far from the actual:

> But my intention being to write something of use to those who understand, it appears to me more proper to go to the real truth of the matter than to its imagination; and many have imagined republics and principalities which have never been seen or known to exist in reality; for how we live is so far removed from how we ought to live, that he who abandons what is done for what ought to be done, will rather learn to bring about his own ruin than his preservation.[20]

20. Machiavelli, *"The Prince" and "The Discourses,"* 56.

If realism is the assessment of a society and a prescription of the possible, then Machiavelli was not a realist. Italy surprisingly did not bend to the will of Machiavelli's generation or those few in future generations who carefully read *The Prince*. Even if violence used in the service of reason is evil, or we consider it amoral, it is no less of an ideal than some utopian ideal proposed for the "good." The "real" was supposed to dominate as the prince tries to stay alive and in power by a series of shrewd and ruthless moves. The leader who took power in Machiavelli's time might rule for a short time, by his means or otherwise, but consolidating power or just keeping it might cost him his life and certainly win him little respect. Holding power was not "realistic." In addition, where could this disciplined prince be found, who was so willing to use force and yet so under control that he could consolidate power?

It is too easy to read Machiavelli, ignore his comments about *fortuna,* and assume that by strength of will and calculating reason, a leader can dominate regardless of the circumstances. While leaders, often madmen with schemes, are plentiful, there are seldom enough of them to constitute whole governments. Today, without the participation of the culture, the most evil of schemes is as idealistic as the utopias of Plato, Bellamy, or More. In Machiavelli's times, the feuding aristocrats prevented the princes from ascending to and keeping power. In modern times, Levi puts the burden for prevention of the ruthless prince on the intelligence of the people, who must be educated to stave off the occasional buffoon.

Although Levi felt that an informed public was the antidote to the prince, he never lost his fear of the prince himself. Levi explores Machiavellian themes in *The Reawakening,* where cultural differences are played out in the character of two individuals, Mordo and Cesare, Auschwitz survivors who accompanied Levi at different times on his journey home. Mordo was a calculating, single-minded individual. Levi admired these qualities in the Lager:

> That this wisdom [about commerce] was transformed in the camp into the systematic and scientific practice of theft and seizure of positions and the monopoly of the bargaining Market, should not let one forget that their aversion to gratuitous brutality, their amazing consciousness of the survival of at least a potential human dignity made of the Greeks the most coherent national nucleus in the Lager, and in this respect, the most civilized. (*Survival,* 72)

The Salonica Greeks, by relentlessly pursuing their mercantile ends, staved off personal and collective destruction as long as possible. Mordo's skills and his ruthless pursuit were also helpful to Levi on his journey home, but personally he found Mordo cold and a bit scary. What frightened Levi and put him off about the Salonica Greeks is the possibility in us of such single-mindedness. Levi had begun to relax while on the way home and assumed the war was over: "'There is always war,' replied Mordo Nahum memorably." Certainly, that perspective was strengthened by the Lager experience that both Mordo and Levi shared in common, but to Mordo, the Lager was simply a confirmation of what he had already known. Mordo treated those he traded with as enemies in the war he was determined to win. He also was affected by aesthetic and humanitarian concerns. He simply compartmentalized the latter by only thinking about them when the day was over:

> The biography of my Greek was linear; it was that of a strong and cold man, solitary and logical, who had acted from his infancy within the rigid framework of a mercantile society. He was also (or had been) open to other claims; he was not indifferent to the sky and the sea of his own country, to the pleasures of the home and of the family, to dialectical encounters; but he had been conditioned to drive all this back to the margins of his day and life. (*Reawakening,* 38)

If the ends pursued are good, as they were with the Salonica Greeks, a group can give good service to civilization. There is no fear that they will pursue other, more diabolical ends, because they are so fixed in their beliefs reinforced by habit. What scares Levi about the Mordos in this world is that if people pursue evil ends with such single-mindedness, unspeakable crimes may occur. The trait of single-mindedness makes Mordo an unattractive character personally, as well as a constant reminder of the potential dangers of man. The dogmatic, instrumental use of reason may have tragic consequences.

Levi is more congenial with Italian mercantile culture, personified by Cesare, whom he met shortly after Mordo's exit on the journey home. The chapters on Mordo and Cesare in *The Reawakening* follow one another, and Levi draws many comparisons. For instance, Cesare was temperamentally incapable of seeing projects to their ultimate conclusion. The means to an end were ends in themselves; a form of joy and play rather

than some necessary imperative for war: "Not that Cesare is much concerned about acting legally; but he likes a sense of style, gamesmanship,
putting one over on the next man without making him suffer" (*Reawakening,* 64). Levi clearly preferred Cesare to Mordo: "One of them was free,
the other was a slave to himself; one was miserly and reasonable, the other prodigal and fantastic" (*Reawakening,* 66). In Levi's account, Cesare
develops a scheme for injecting water into fish with a hypodermic needle
to make them look like part of a fresh catch. At another juncture, he sells
a ring to a group of peasants waiting at a train station, hoping the train
will pull out before the peasants realize the ring was worthless. Cesare sus-
tains himself by his endeavors, but the aesthetic value of his capers seem
to matter more to him. No matter that the two adventures spoken of above
and many others end in near disaster for Cesare: "The Greek was a lone
wolf, in an eternal war against all, old before his time, closed in the circle
of his own joyless pride; Cesare was a child of the sun, everybody's friend;
he knew no hatred or contempt, was as changeable as the sky, joyous, cunning and ingenuous, bold and cautious, very ignorant, very innocent and
very civilized" (*Reawakening,* 66).

Of course, Mordo and the Germans can never be compared, for as Levi
stated, the Salonica Greeks' behavior in the Lager was exemplary; they had
been well educated. However, the perspective of life as a joyless, endless war
to be pursued single-mindedly could do harm in the hands of a determined
people like the Germans, who were badly educated. Cesare, in contrast with
Mordo, could not get morbid and fixated on a purpose. For Cesare, means
are ends in themselves; life is a sense of play, a playful anarchism with a
sense of tragic limitation. Levi loved Italy and his fellow Italians. Italians
were not a population that could be easily mobilized for either good or evil.

In short, malignant individuals will exist, but Levi hopes the masses can
be educated against violence. This education, of course, is made difficult
if a people are so focused on means in their struggle for existence and es-
chew thoughtful, imaginative contemplation of means and ends. It is especially dangerous where moral education is lacking, because we have an
instinct for violence. Through our curiosity as toolmakers, we can esca-
late the damage we can do to one another.

Finally, as suggested in the discussion of Hobbesian Hell, Levi is most
distressed when violence is used as an end in itself, a horror he explores in
depth in the chapter "Useless Violence" in *The Drowned and the Saved.*
The Hitlerian years "were characterized by widespread useless violence,
as an end in itself, with the sole purpose of inflicting pain, occasionally

having a purpose, yet always redundant, always disproportionate to the purpose itself." From the transports to the Lager, "To humiliate, to make the 'enemy' suffer, was their everyday task; they did not reason about it, they had no ulterior ends: their end was simply that" (106, 121).

Levi believes we are ill-constituted because we are equipped to commit violence. Although violence may be necessary in response to the violence of others, it is a very destructive force. In addition, our facility of reason does not necessarily lessen the propensity to violence. The tinkerer can invent violent means in the name of progress that, in the wrong hands, can cause great destruction. Machiavelli shows us that violence, devoid of distracting passion, can be used in a chilling way to achieve a clear set of objectives. Levi believes people with destructive designs will always exist, but their numbers are not great enough to carry the horror by themselves. Even his tormentors in the Lager were not examples of evil seed: "[T]he Lager SS were obtuse brutes, not subtle demons. They had been raised to violence; violence ran in their veins" (*Drowned,* 121). Also, the cultures where people are habituated to means and efficient at reaching their ends make him nervous. People in these cultures are especially dangerous if they view mankind as participants in a war to be fought to the end.

Levi's solution is to make sure that there is a public educated to understand propensities towards violence, a public that can resist the ideas of the madmen and buffoons of the world. However, his optimism about education is clearly tempered by his belief that reason is an untrustworthy ally in resisting man's violent propensities. His optimism is further clouded by some disturbing tendencies in the human condition, elaborated upon earlier, which his experience in the Holocaust brutally engraved in his consciousness. Society is very fragile, and under conditions of scarcity it tends to fall into a war of all against all. There is a Manichean tendency to differentiate between friends and enemies. Among "friends" and against enemies, there is the propensity to find some means of superiority over others regardless of utility. The willingness to follow cultural norms or charismatic leaders without question, especially if they exaggerate the Manichean message, is also a dangerous tendency.

Given all of these problems of ill-constituted human beings, coupled with his conclusion that "kill or be killed" is the law in all of the nonhuman world, Levi is brought to the brink of the abyss.[21] Even the Holo-

---

21. Levi, *Other People's Trades,* 96. For example, "in nature's games there must after all be a winner and loser."

caust continues to have its ripple effects: "In actuality, many signs lead us to think of a genealogy of today's violence that branches out precisely from the violence that was dominant in Hitler's Germany." Ever the scientist, he finally gives the empirical assessment that war and violence among humans is not necessary or inevitable and resolves again that education must solve the problem: "Satan is not necessary: there is no need for wars or violence, under any circumstances" (*Drowned*, 200). Ortega y Gasset argues that reasoning is not constitutive of man; it must be earned through work.[22] In the same sense, Levi argues that nonviolence is not constitutive of man, but it can be earned through education.

Up to this point, we have simply assumed that the less violence there is, the better the world would be. Here we begin to piece together Levi's moral argument against violence, and the ensuing chapters will develop his moral theory more fully. The first argument against violence is the utilitarian argument of the flesh: We are beings who seek pleasure and suffer pain. We may not know how to achieve the former, but we must reduce pain. The Holocaust caused unspeakable pain and loss for those caught up in it. A crucial thrust of Levi's writings is that such pain should never have to be endured again.

Sometimes analysts carelessly assume that Nietzsche has said it all when he states that if an experience does not kill you, it will make you stronger. The implication is that pleasure and pain balance out in life if you come through a terrible experience with more strength and guile for the future. This form of argument would take the purveyors of misery off the hook; they could claim their brutality led to better people. Levi will not tolerate this line of reasoning. For instance, because of his experiences in Auschwitz, he becomes a writer, but his life as a writer does not come close to compensating him for the pains of his slavery. In the short story *"Force Majeure,"* Levi makes it clear that nothing can erase the pain and humiliation of the citizen who is crushed in the alley by the sailor. In his interview with Camon, Levi says that he wouldn't do it over again, but he "couldn't deny that it also had positive results. It seems to me that that was where I learned to know the facts about people." Camon asks Levi if sometimes a dreadful experience can have redemptive value if the trials make us a good person—in other words, suffering has meaning and use. Levi rejects the compensatory universe implicit in this type of thinking and

22. Ortega y Gasset, *"The Dehumanization of Art"* and *"Notes on the Novel,"* 183.

replies to Camon's question as follows: "I don't think I became a better person. I understood a few things, but that didn't make me good."[23]

We are people of flesh and bone and we should not suffer. There is no excuse for making another suffer, nor is redemption to be found in suffering. We do not have the right to make people "good" against their will, nor can the consequences of *force majeure* be overcome. Levi is a utilitarian when it comes to making sure that we do nothing to increase the sum of human misery; it is civilization's role to ensure that those already unfortunate are not made to suffer more.

Levi feels strongly about lessening human misery. He argues that pain is useful to our existence, but that it causes overwhelming misery. Pain is another part of the human condition that makes us ill-constituted beings. For example, in "Time Checkmated," he notes that our perception of time even works to increase the stock of human misery. The "observation that subjective time lengthens in the course of disagreeable experiences or conditions, such as toothache or seasickness, migraine, long waits, and such. However, because of the viciousness intrinsic to the human condition and nature, it becomes short, even evanescent, in the course of the opposite conditions."[24]

Pain is predominant in the human condition and must be alleviated. Yet, this appears to be impossible, because like all other features of our ill-constituted being, pain does serve some functions. Levi uses the story "Versamina" to show the results of an experiment to reduce suffering by making the sensation of pain its opposite, pleasure, and the sensation of pleasure its opposite, pain. Jacob Dessauer, the observer in "Versamina," comes back to his old laboratory after twelve years to see what progress his former colleagues have made. Jacob captures the dilemma perfectly: "He thought about one thing that he hadn't thought of for a long time, because he had suffered much: that pain cannot be taken away, must not, because it is our guardian. Often it is a foolish guardian, because it is inflexible, it is faithful to its orders with maniacal obstinacy, and never grows tired, whereas all other sensations grow tired, wear out, especially the pleasant ones."[25] Had they made any progress with respect to the alleviation of pain since he had left the Institute?

A former colleague of Dasseur's, Kleber, had previously stumbled upon

23. Ferdinando Camon, *Conversations with Primo Levi*, 60, 61.
24. Levi, "Time Checkmated," in *"Mirror,"* 72.
25. Levi, "Versamina," in *"Mirror,"* 53.

a drug that reversed pleasure and pain in a rabbit: "It refused food, and instead it chewed the wood, bit the wires of the cage, until it bled at the mouth." Another scientist who kept track of Kleber's experiments remembers "a German shepherd, for instance, that we wanted to keep alive at all costs, despite himself, because it seemed he had no other desire than to destroy himself. He sank his fangs into his paws and tail with wild ferocity, and when I put a muzzle on him he bit his tongue."[26] When Kleber experimented on himself, the results were just as self-destructive. He stopped eating, because eating is pleasurable. He died when he ran a red light and had a fatal traffic accident, a new ultimate in "pleasure." Pain, like violence, is built into human nature, but it causes grief as well. For Levi, pain predominates over pleasure in this world, a grim fact. "Versamina" demonstrates that a reversal of the feelings would be even more of a disaster.

Levi knew that the argument of the flesh would not satisfy all those he came in contact with, especially students and "intellectuals." A second argument against violence, which also builds on the suffering man of flesh and bone, is a pragmatic one. He lays out the facts of the Holocaust dispassionately so that he will be believed: "I have deliberately assumed the calm, sober language of the witness, neither the lamenting tones of the victim nor the irate voice of someone who seeks revenge" (*Reawakening,* 196).[27] If someone counters his argument and says that violence is a good, and suffering and death are good, the argument is at an end; the pragmatist can go no further than to argue that there can be no ultimate agreement on ends. Except in the all-too-clever dialectic of some philosophers—and we will get to that further on in the text—the argument that pain is an evil and not a good is very persuasive. Even those who try to minimize the extent of the Holocaust, or even deny it occurred, rarely attack the normative argument of evil. Instead, they try to minimize the impact of the events by making bogus empirical statements.

The third argument Levi raises against violence contains a political variant of the second. Levi marshals positive normative statements about civilization, self-imposed control, and the rule of law, all of which are features of civilized modernism. These features, which are found scattered throughout his writings, can reduce the sum of human misery. For in-

26. Ibid., 46, 49.
27. See also Anthony Rudolph, *At an Uncertain Hour: Primo Levi's War against Oblivion,* 34.

stance, in *Survival in Auschwitz*, Levi speaks of the horrors of the Hobbesian universe of the Lager and then goes on to say that in contrast with this hell, "one must take into account a definite cushioning effect exercised both by the law, and by the moral sense which constitutes a self-imposed law; for a country is considered the more civilized the more the wisdom and efficiency of its laws hinder a weak man from becoming too weak or a powerful one too powerful" (88).

Near the end of his life, in an interview with Camon, Levi's views remained unchanged: "Particularly where law turns out to be lacking, the law of the jungle is established, Darwinian law, by which the fittest, who are mostly the worst, prevail and survive by eating the living flesh of others."[28] Levi argues that because of our propensity to privilege, the struggle for justice in the interest of the weaker is never ending: "The ascent of the privileged, not only in the Lager, but in all human coexistence, is an anguishing but unfailing phenomenon: only in utopias is it absent. It is the duty of righteous men to make war on all undeserved privilege, but one must not forget that it is a war without end" (*Drowned*, 42).

Levi believes in liberal democracy and social justice and feels these ideas express "the morality common to all times and all civilizations, an integral art of our human heritage which in the end must be acknowledged" (*Drowned*, 107). These civilized norms are not forever established, but at least they are part of the dialogue in civilized societies, where, for instance, equality may be posed against economic freedom as a legitimate part of debate.

Clearly, Levi sets up a tragic tension between the atavistic tendency to dominance and the learned response of social justice. He feels it necessary to bolster the position of the weak, even though it tends to be a losing effort. Levi's argument for siding with the weak comes from compassion with those in pain. Also, for him there is the empirical possibility of a slippery slope, which begins with the toleration of excesses of power to the end of murder on a mass scale: "Where power is exercised by few or only one against the many, privilege is born and proliferates, even against the will of the power itself. On the other hand, it is normal for power to tolerate and encourage privilege" (*Drowned*, 42). In other words, power usually tolerates privilege, but privilege is so tenacious it can spread even against the will of the most powerful. Power, whether of the leader or his satraps, must be challenged. For Primo Levi, there is no doubt as to this

28. Camon, *Conversations*, 20.

slippery slope: In "every part of the world, wherever you begin by deny-ing the fundamental liberties of mankind, and equality among people, you move toward the concentration camp system, and it is a road on which it is difficult to halt" (*Reawakening*, 207).

We turn now to Levi's spirited arguments against those who rationalize their violent actions. What sets us apart from other species is that we sys-tematically experiment with violence and are adept at justifying the results. Scattered through Levi's texts are attacks on rationalizations, historical and contemporary, that have been used to justify such experiments with violence. His refutations heavily depend upon his utilitarian argument that the abatement of violence alleviates pain. First, we will talk about the re-lationship between the leader and the follower and speak of the leader's arguments for justifying violence. In this same section we consider the rea-sons followers give for following the words of their leader. Second, we will look at five rationalizations of violent behavior found in the ideas of philosophers, which Levi tries to counter in his works.

The tough chore discussing the rationalization of violence is that it is difficult to understand the motives of individuals, a task Levi suggests is a part of understanding human behavior. Individuals often switch from their initial rationalizations of violent acts, which they hold at the beginning of a conflict, to the fantastic rationalization of their behavior after defeat. These rationalizations may contain an unconscious component, because individuals may not be aware of how they are "weighing anchor" on the truth (*Drowned*, 26–27).[29]

Why would people alter their views to follow a cruel leader? One of the most important features of such a leader is his ability to use man's Manichean tendencies to persuade the masses to attack another group. The leader blames his group's actual deprivation or relative deprivation on an out-group, convincing his followers that life is a war of us against them, and that war is endemic to life. If human nature were different, we would not need to do ill by our neighbors. However, since it is a war of all against all, we must use all the means at our disposal before our enemy uses them against us. By inference, the leader argues that there is good in the world, whether it be self-preservation, ideology, or group solidarity. Violence is needed to protect our virtue. Joseph De Maistre, a precursor of fascism,

29. Like Gresham Sykes and David Matza in the criminology literature, "Techniques of Neutralization: A Theory of Delinquency," Levi assumes that for most in society, before committing violence, a rationalization must be found.

used the rationale described above to convince people that the course of violence is a sound one.[30]

When followers rationalize violence, they may take their cues from the leader or create their own from the violent context. As we have seen, not all of the individuals who participate in a leader's mad dreams are equal in culpability. Levi recognizes a gray zone of behaviors where judgment is much more difficult; in Auschwitz this zone is occupied by the prisoners, not the perpetrators. Among the prisoners, "the harsher the oppression, the more widespread among the oppressed is the willingness, with all its infinite nuances and motivations, to collaborate: terror, ideological seduction, servile imitation of the victor, myopic desire for any power whatsoever, even though ridiculously circumscribed in space and time, cowardice, and, finally, lucid calculation aimed at eluding the imposed orders and order" (*Drowned*, 43).

Levi recognized from his own slavery how quickly people can give in to the pressure of scarcity and abandon those close to them.

Culpability is different for those from the oppressor nation or nations. Levi knows that during the Nazi regime, many Germans could have refused to participate in the regime's crimes and received minimal sanctions, yet they chose to go along or even eagerly participate. It was not an either/or situation—obey or die—for the dilemma of participation could have been resolved by "(actually often was resolved) by some maneuver, some slowdown in career, moderate punishment, or, in the worst of cases, the objector's transfer to the front" (*Drowned*, 60).[31] All of the post hoc rationalizations sit badly with Levi:

> Expressed in different formulations and with greater or lesser arrogance, depending on the speaker's mental and cultural level, in the end they substantially all say the same things: I did it because I was ordered to; others (my superiors) have committed acts worse than mine; in view of the upbringing I received, and the environment in which I lived, I could not have acted differently; had I not done it, another would have done even more harshly in my place. For anyone who reads these justifications the first reaction is revulsion. (*Drowned*, 26)

30. Isaiah Berlin in *The Crooked Timber of Humanity*, 91–174, points out that Joseph De Maistre's views presaged the Nazis, but his thoughts were not used by them to originate or justify their beliefs.

31. See also, for example, Saul Friedlander, *Nazi Germany*, and Jonathan Goldhagen's introductory example of the SS colonel who objected to command orders in *Hitler's Willing Executioners*, 3–24.

What is important for Levi is that we not succumb to the initial all-too-human tendency to believe in a Manichean world and to feel that it is our role to gain any privilege in that world over others. As he suggests, there will always be leaders, comic and diabolical, with their slick rationalizations, but the trick is to see that there are no followers. In addition, we must account for those victims who fall into the gray zone of responsibility.

The remaining rationalizations come from intellectuals who occupy an ambiguous place in Levi's thought. One of their arguments, a postmodern argument, suggests no sanctions for what is most painful to Levi, violence done to those in the Lager. In the chapter "Useless Violence" in *The Drowned and the Saved,* he documents the numerous cruelties brought upon the prisoners for no apparent reason, for reasons of pure malice, and recognizes them as evil. A radical postmodern position is that evil is merely one more story or narrative among others. The concluding chapters will develop in detail Levi's response to this postmodern position.

A second rationalization of intellectuals is described in Lezak Kolakowski's explanation of the disappearance of evil in modern society. The enormity of crimes is softened when the discourse of social science replaces the language of evil. Modern man is embarrassed to speak of the devil because it comes from the language of religion, but more importantly evil has disappeared from the modern vocabulary because all evil can be explained away by science. In one of Kolakowski's essays, a demon explains this to his audience: "You have got your Freud to talk about aggression and the death wish, you have Jaspers who tells you about the night passions when Man seems to try to violate the secrets of the deity, you have your Nietzsche, you have your psychologists specializing in the 'will to power.' You know with which words to obscure something under the guise of revealing it."[32]

According to Kolakowski, evil is a "power which cannot be reduced to anything, explained by anything, justified in any way." It is "[a] destructive force which wishes for nothing else but sheer destruction."[33]

In the Afterword of *The Reawakening,* Levi answers the question about how the Nazi hatred of Jews can be explained. Unlike Kolakowski, Levi certainly would not want to bring back the context and language of good and evil, nor would he stand in the way of the social sciences, but he is al-

---

32. Kolakowski, *"The Key to Heaven" and "Conversations with the Devil,"* 121.
33. Ibid., 122.

most happy that social science does not succeed in explaining away the evil in Nazi Germany. He reviews the various explanations of Nazi hatred, but the explanations seem inadequate to him. He writes: "Perhaps one cannot, what is more one must not, understand what happened, because to understand is almost to justify. Let me explain: 'understanding' a proposal or human behavior means to 'contain' it, contain its author, put oneself in his place, identify with him. Now, no normal human being will ever be able to identify with Hitler, Himmler, Goebbels, Eichmann, and endless others" (*Reawakening*, 213).

The use of *verstehen* to identify with another human being and understand his thoughts luckily does not work with monsters: "This dismays us, and at the same time gives us a sense of relief, because perhaps it is desirable that their words (and also, unfortunately their deeds) cannot be comprehensible to us." It leaves us with Nazi hatred as the very definition of evil: "But there is no rationality in the Nazi hatred: it is a hate that is not in us; it is outside man, it is a poison fruit sprung from the deadly trunk of Fascism, but it is outside and beyond Fascism itself" (*Reawakening*, 214).

Not understanding does not mean that we give up our vigilance. On the contrary, as with Kolakowski, we are more alert to the hatred that cannot be explained than we are to the hatred that social science tamed and gave a human face: "We cannot understand it, but we can and must understand from where it springs and we must be on our guard" (*Reawakening*, 214).

As a toolmaker, Levi is never willing to give up the scientific quest for understanding either in the social or physical sciences. He is never willing to relinquish our basic curiosity, the quest for understanding, but he knows well that judging motives is a necessary, problematic, and yet, an interesting dilemma for the practicing social scientist. As Levi was afraid of the scientist-tinkerer, so is he afraid of the social scientist and his or her tendency to explain away the behavior of the monsters of society by lending them some human sympathy. So, when those who sought to understand the mind of the murderers failed, Levi is not disappointed.[34]

A third rationalization of intellectuals, that we are all capable of murder, works as well to blunt the force of the argument against the Nazis. It is a reworking of Dostoyevsky's idea that if God is dead, everything is

34. John Lukacs's recent book about Hitler, *The Hitler of History,* re-explores the issues of explaining the behaviors of a monster. The author reviews many of the attempts to decipher Hitler's behavior.

possible. Levi does not refer directly to Dostoyevsky, but he comments on the words of a film director who crudely expresses these sentiments:

> The film director Liliana Cavani, who was asked to express briefly the meaning of a beautiful and false film of hers, declared: "We are all victims or murderers and we accept these roles voluntarily. Only Sade and Dostoevsky [*sic*] have really understood this." She also said she believed "that in every environment, in every relationship, there is a victim-executioner dynamism more or less clearly expressed and generally lived on an unconscious level." (*Drowned*, 48)

For Levi, facile explanation makes it too easy for us all to be complicit in each crime, thus making those who committed them simply expressing our nature. Propensity is simply not the same as the deed itself: "I do not know, and it does not much interest me to know, whether in my depths there lurks a murderer, but I do know that I was a guiltless victim and I was not a murderer." To "confuse them [the murderers] with their victims is a moral disease or an aesthetic affectation or a sinister sign of complicity; above all, it is a precious service rendered (intentionally or not) to the negators of truth" (*Drowned*, 48–49). Dostoyevsky warns humanity that if God is dead, then anything is possible, but the key is that he understands the checks we might have against acting capriciously, such as moral strictures from prior education. His idea is a long way from the idea that with a wink from Cavani, we would all agree to secret collusion with murderers. To understand violence is neither to forgive nor to identify.

Fourth is an argument touched upon earlier in discussing violence as an end in itself. At the conclusion of the nineteenth century and the beginning of the twentieth century, some argued that war and aggressive behavior were constitutive of our nature, and that masculine virtues were lost when we found ourselves in a peaceful, nonheroic society. Nostalgia was for "heroes" like Napoleon. Just as Levi posits liberal values for us, others espouse the martial virtues to strengthen our "natural" inclinations. James called the part of the population that held this view the "war-regime." Nietzsche felt that the will to power was natural and if blocked would come out as ressentiment.

Levi is very much against those who preach violence as an end in itself. He talks about the dangers in the Germans' belief in the myth of the "Superman to whom everything is permitted in recognition of his dogmatic and congenital superiority." Levi, in contrast, recognizes a universal morality that we ignored at our own peril: "The fact that all of them, teachers and pupils, became progressively removed from reality as little by little their morality came unglued from the morality common to all times and all civilizations, an integral part of our human heritage which in the end must be acknowledged" (*Drowned*, 107).[35]

Unlike some of the other intellectual rationalizations, the fifth does not neutralize the explanation of evil as just another story, explain it away, weaken it by finding it everywhere, or justify it as an end in itself. Instead, it recognizes evil when done, but excuses the evil of the perpetrators. Nazi hunter Simon Wiesenthal, in *The Murderers among Us,* suggests, in line with Jewish tradition, that only those who are aggrieved can forgive those who committed the crimes.[36] It pains Levi greatly, as it did Wiesenthal, to see absolution given freely to murderers. He illustrates his distaste for easy absolution when he recalls a fable in *The Brothers Karamazov* about a terrible old woman who has gone to hell. Her guardian angel "recalls that she once, only once gave a beggar the gift of a little onion she had dug up from her garden. He holds the little onion out to her, and the old woman grasps it and is lifted out of the flames of hell." After living a terrible life, she is redeemed by a trifling: "This fable has always struck me as revolting: what human monster did not throughout his life make the gift of a little onion, if not to others, to his children, his wife, his dog?" (*Drowned,* 57–58).

In "Letters from Germans" in *The Drowned and the Saved,* Levi recounts letters he received after the war from Germans who had read *Survival in Auschwitz.* The letter writers often make excuses for their individual role and Germany's role in the war and subtly ask him for absolution. A typical letter from a Doctor T. H. of Hamburg came with a few lines at the end written by his wife:

> I often thought about this strange couple. He seems to me a typical specimen of the large mass of the German upper middle class: a not fanatical but opportunistic Nazi who repented when it was opportune to repent, stupid enough to believe that he can make me believe his

---

35. Nietzsche was a lot more careful than those who simply followed what they thought were his bloodthirsty conclusions, instead of paying attention to his call for the spiritualization of instincts—for instance, turning violence into competition and lust into love. Nietzsche called for creativity and necessary violence to achieve ends, but never useless violence. That did not deter his successors who misread him, or did not read him in any detail, but used him to their own purposes.

36. Wiesenthal, *The Sunflower: On the Possibilities and Limits of Forgiveness,* 99.

simplified version of recent history, and dares to have recourse to
Narses's and Goths' retroactive reprisals. She seems to me a little less
hypocritical than her husband but more bigoted. (178)

He wrote a long letter in response, summarizing some of the points he
made early in the letter. One of them pertains to the problem of absolution: "That no church offers indulgences to those who follow the Devil or
accepts as justification the attribution of one's sins to the Devil. That one
must answer personally for sins and errors, otherwise all trace of civilization would vanish from the face of the earth, as in fact it had vanished
from the Third Reich" (*Drowned,* 178).

In his usual agonic and measured way, Levi indicates that absolution is
not bad in all instances. Still, he will not refrain from his own judgment
or give in to easy absolution:

> All the same I would not want my abstaining from explicit judgment
> to be confused with an indiscriminate pardon. No, I have not forgiv-
> en any of the culprits, nor am I willing to forgive a single one of them,
> unless he has shown (with deeds, not words, and not long afterward)
> that he has become conscious of the crimes and errors of Italian and
> foreign Fascism and is determined to condemn them, uproot them,
> from his conscience and that of others. (*Reawakening,* 197)

To sum up, in the first intellectual rationalization of violence, the postmodern thinker gives parity to the myriad of "stories" and thereby weakens the argument against evil. In the second, the force of evil is blunted
again by using social science explanations of origins to downgrade the perpetrators' responsibility by providing "reasons" for their behavior. The
third intellectual rationalization, which declares that everyone is capable
of violence, also blunts the force of the argument against those who "just
happened" to do something we are all capable of doing. The fourth is the
argument with a naturalistic base: Violence is prevalent and is therefore a
good. Sometimes this is argued as a useful evolutionary outcome that is
"good" for the species, and at other times it is argued from the perspective
of creativity or catharsis as beneficial to humans. Finally, a fifth rationalization acknowledges that evil has been committed, but that we have the
right to absolve the perpetrators of their guilt. In order to make his case
for civilization and the reduction of pain, Levi, at different times in his
writings, counters each of the arguments.

Levi's views on violence expose the core of his approach to public morality. Scarcity and hierarchy are absorbed into his thoughts on violence. We are ill-constituted beings who have tendencies like violence, rapid disintegration under conditions of scarcity, and the need to display superiority over others under virtually all circumstances. Monsters will exist in every society; they are a given for Levi. The rest of the population must be educated to prevent the monsters from putting their ideas into action.

Levi's liberalism is urgent and strident because as a man of flesh and bone he has seen and experienced the worst. Most liberal ideas begin with the assumption that contemporary society is inadequate and could be improved in accordance with liberal values. Levi's picture of us as ill-constituted and his experience in Auschwitz draws his energies to participation in the continuance of a liberal society based on the deep shadows of murderous regimes lurking just off stage. He is less apt to criticize present day liberal democratic regimes, especially when that criticism could undermine the liberal foundations of society that remain the fundamental bulwark against pain and horror. The concluding chapter will examine these notions within the spectrum of his political ideas.

Levi's discourses about the nature of violence are aggregated above: first, the arguments of pragmatism, flesh, and utility, which justify civilization; second, the arguments against the rationalizations of violence the leaders, masses, intellectuals, and religious figures put forth to lessen their feelings of responsibility. For now, it is enough to say that the danger to the people on one side is absolutism. On the other extreme, the affectation put forth by those who profess to not being able to make judgments about right and wrong leaves a void that absolutists would be glad to fill. Levi believes that learning must take place to counter the atavistic tendencies of man, and he is careful to indicate how precarious the battle is.

Levi feels passion for liberal values, but most courageous on his part is that he never denies or sweeps under the table those forces that mitigate against his views, creating agonic tension. On the individual level, Levi feels hatred, yet he recognizes the necessity to keep it under the control of reason: "I believe in reason and in discussion as supreme instruments of progress, and therefore I repress hatred even within myself: I prefer justice" (*Reawakening*, 196). He is dead set against the idea of catharsis when considering its use to prevent sporadic outbreaks; when he looks at the evidence from the Cold War, he almost tries to will the idea of catharsis away. However, his honesty keeps him from doing it. The Cold War proved we can be peaceful for a long time, yet it fostered a variety of surrogate wars:

> There are no problems that cannot be solved around a table, provided there is good will and reciprocal trust—or even reciprocal fear, as the present interminable stalled situation [cold war] seems to demonstrate, a situation in which the greatest powers confront each other with cordial or threatening faces but have no restraint when it comes to unleashing (or allowing the unleashing) of bloody wars among those "protected" by them, supplying sophisticated weapons, spies, mercenaries, and military advisers instead of arbiters of peace. (*Drowned*, 200)

This ambivalence is one more agony in trying to understand human beings.

The key to Levi's philosophy is that he never forgets our tragic sense, that we are ill-constituted beings, even when it would be convenient to ignore the evidence and try to live blissfully. He speaks of Chiam Rumkowski, a leader of the Lodz ghetto, who falls into the gray zone of people involved in the Holocaust. Rumkowski was certainly not the worst, but he was useful to the monsters who perpetrated the Holocaust: "At the foot of every absolute throne, men such as Rumkowski crowd in order to grab their small portion of power." Education begins, as it should have for Rumkowski, with an understanding of our essential tragic existence. To forget it assists monsters: "Like Rumkowski, we too are so dazzled by power and prestige as to forget our essential fragility." This fragility is a fundamental factor of life and "[w]illingly or not we come to terms with power" because we are finite beings (*Drowned*, 67, 69). At bottom, then, it is the intoxication with power made possible by the denial of the tragic sense that leads to destruction from atavistic tendencies.

Optimistic Pessimism

5

The Tragic Sense of Life

[O]ne perceived the heavy breath of a collective dream, of the dream emanating from exile and idleness, when work and troubles have ceased, and nothing acts as a screen between a man and himself; perhaps because we saw the impotence and nullity of our life and of life itself, and the hunch-backed crooked profiles of the monsters generated by the sleep of reason.

— *The Reawakening*

Willingly or not we come to terms with power, forgetting that we are all in the ghetto, that the ghetto is walled in, that outside the ghetto reign the lords of death, and that close by the train is waiting.

— *The Drowned and the Saved*

This chapter will explore how Primo Levi contemplates his own life from within and devises his personal morality of action against the background of lived existence. It relays Levi's reflections on his terrible experience— his personal response to the abyss, a lived doubt made manifest by the horror. Personal morality involves the difficulties and possibilities of overcoming oneself and the challenges put forth by others. His experiences in the Lager caused him to discover many interesting ideas about himself and other people; he has unique insights into the luck, natural faculties, and will that contributed to the survival of a few prisoners.

Despite the boundaries of scarcity, irrationality, and fate imposed on the prisoners in the Lager, Levi recounts ideas and actions that suggest how individuals used little-known abilities and some ingenuity to their advantage: "It [*Survival in Auschwitz*] has not been written in order to formulate new accusations; it should be able, rather, to furnish documentation for a quiet study of certain aspects of the human mind." He approaches his analysis of Auschwitz in the same way that he looks at his practice of chemistry and his naturalistic observations of animals—as the consummate scientist. Levi carefully documents regularities that he observed among all of the prisoners as well as differentiating individual responses to the same adversity; he is both sociologist and psychologist. Below, he sets up his sociological observations:

> [T]he Lager was pre-eminently a gigantic biological and social experiment. Thousands of individuals, differing in age, condition, origin, language, culture and customs, are enclosed within barbed wire: there they live a regular, controlled life which is identical for all and inadequate to all needs, and which is more rigorous than any experimenter could have set up to establish what is essential and what adventitious to the conduct of the human animal in the struggle for life.[1]

Levi's writings on his experience are a testament to his ruthless honesty, for he could have dwelled on the terrors and pains of the Lager, trying to draw more attention and sympathy to his personal misfortune. If Levi wanted to start a personal campaign for martyrdom, he could have emphasized will and courage in survival over chance and craven opportunism. Instead, he emphasizes the latter and concludes that those who survived were not the best. He prefers to be the scientific observer, not the hero or martyr.

Levi's personal meditations on survival are thus based on his careful, ruthless empiricism. His unique experiences in the Holocaust give him a very different base than most philosophers when it comes to formulating his basic presuppositions. His concept of "forced doubt," for example, differs from the more methodical doubt of many of his predecessors. For many modern philosophers, the self-conscious meditation on philosophy begins when they suffer radical doubts about existence. The methodical doubter begins a process of methodical doubt so that he can find some basis for certainty, a foundation for knowing upon which he can re-orient himself to the world. William James suffers from "panic fear"; he uses

1. Levi, *Survival in Auschwitz*, 9, 87. Future references will be cited parenthetically in the text.

sheer tenacity to pull himself out of this condition and to avoid sliding further into the abyss. He keeps himself afloat by continually repeating certain prayers as if they were mantras. Some philosophers, like James, are overcome by sudden anxiety about their existence, and others, like Descartes, face it less as a spiritual crisis and more as an intellectual challenge. Descartes can face these doubts without the same pressing sense of urgency. Most philosophers have the leisure to think about their engagements with the world before they decide upon a way back. The "fear and trembling" makes this condition extremely uncomfortable, and their mood may demand a quick resolution, but their current circumstances are not changed, only the perception of reality has been altered. As they cope with themselves they can keep their actions toward the world a constant. Descartes even used this constancy as a principle to insure himself the luxury of deliberation without anyone questioning his politics. Sometimes, as with the philosopher Amiel, the anguishing mood and the constancy of the world provides the time for him to find his way back, but as with Amiel, it does not guarantee resolution. The Swiss humanist recorded his agonies in his diaries published after his death. Amiel reviewed all his options for making it back from the abyss, but he couldn't commit himself to a single one. Thus, he never made it back.

Levi's experience is completely different. The horrible circumstances that forced him to face the abyss did not allow him ample time and space to turn his back on the world to think his way through his anguish. He was left to face a return to a life of deranged circumstances not of his choosing, in which almost none of his prior beliefs was of any use. Levi's experience was harsh and the conditions that caused it were relentless. The Lager provided him neither with the opportunity to meditate on his circumstances nor the latitude to experiment with his thoughts and actions. That means that he did not have the luxury of a stable set of outside circumstances within which he might find his way back from the abyss.

Whether the crisis is caused by internal or external circumstances, the anxiety provoked is acute in either case, but for Levi, the possibilities of gathering one's reason were much more limited. Many of his choices were the result of a reflex during confinement, a few were reasoned and rationalized, and as they developed, they tended to be consistent with one another.[2] His philosophy did not come from some epiphany: some ideas

2. I have tried in the pages below to put together his argument, but it would be hubris to criticize Levi for what he might not have intended in the first place: a systematic body of thought on doubt.

came to him when he was able to withdraw ever so briefly in the Lager to use his powers of observation and reason. He began a more formal synthesis in some of his earliest post-Holocaust writings, which were a meditation on his slavery, and some mature reflection appears retrospectively in Levi's later writings and personal interviews.

Doubt about the grounds of existence comes to many philosophers as a betrayal, because existence did not deliver what was promised. In most cases, it is not the world that has precipitously changed, but only the philosopher's view of it. What compounds this estrangement is that others around them go on much the same as always because their view of the world has not changed.

After considerable thought, the person who feels betrayed by existence may emerge to try and convince others of the radical contingencies of existence and how his new insight should change practical existence, or he may keep practical existence a constant, free of necessary modifications suggested by his views. In the former category we have William James, who feels the radical contingency of existence and then returns to the world on the tenuous grounds of practical reason. Although he leaves the abyss behind, he never forgets his insight that the epileptic he saw in the hospital could have been himself. This translates into his inward tolerance for all of his ideas as well as those of others. His leap into practice in life is done with a backward glance at his radical uncertainty. In this latter category where the philosopher keeps practical life as a comforting constant, we have Descartes, who traverses the wilderness and then returns to the world secure in his own existence. He holds as a constant his political ideas while he explores other areas where his new insights may have an impact on thought.

In Levi's case, we have an instance of forced doubt. With death's knell as the incentive, he made the necessary jump back into practicality. Even in "ordinary life" he vowed never to forget certain elements of the abyss, while simultaneously trying to minimize the pain that accompanied his basic insight into it.

The experience of loneliness and abandonment in the universe usually has three stages: the development of an initial set of assumptions about the world, a betrayal of these assumptions, and a recovery that includes the attempt to live in the world with a new provisional strategy. Betrayal frequently means that someone is seen as having deceived the individual about the nature of the world. That one may be God, our parents, or our formal or informal teachers: those who teach that being is good. If we do not assume that life is a communication to others, but an internal dialogue, then we may conceptualize the betrayal in the following way: The betrayal is brutal destruction of the naïve self's early domination over the knowing skeptical self. Betrayal means that the assumed experts in life are no longer trustworthy, whether the expert is God, the self, or others.

In doubt, there is no unseen hand of good guiding the universe. The links to practicality that were previously forged no longer pertain to the changed circumstances of life, regardless of whether the derangement was caused by a shift of perspective brought about by the systematic doubt of a Descartes, or by the circumstances that forced doubt upon Primo Levi. What has been lost is the trust in practicality. There is no longer a basis in wisdom, nor is there the sheer will to return to society.

Like Levi, those who eventually return often exemplify the courage to continually acknowledge the great leap they take out of nothingness in order to grasp onto practicality, to understand the weakness of the threads they spin over the abyss, and the fragility of being as they gingerly tiptoe on these threads. Betrayal presupposes the first stage in the process of abandonment, a secure universe where there has not been a betrayal of ordinary existence. For betrayal to take place, we must assume or consciously work out a prior set of beliefs about existence. In this prior universe of nature, God, and others, being is good.

The above picture has an exception, however. We might be comfortable with a universe where we know from the beginning that we have no home. Betrayal then comes when we find good in God, nature, or others and do not quite trust our new judgment or our old one. We don't usually think of such a condition as "betrayal," except in the sense that through actions or words, significant others first teach us the bitter ironies of existence. Then the possibility of good shows itself. For example, in Stanton Samenow's study of hardened criminals, his subjects determined at an early age that those who believed in goodness were fools and dupes. The criminals never believed that being is good. Treatment to make them conform to a set of moral strictures seems like a betrayal of what they knew from an early age.[3] In general, however, we will be speaking of betrayal as the destruction of the stable, dependable, even helpful universe.

For most, after their initial assumptions that being is good, followed by betrayal, there is a return to the world with a new synthesis, one that em-

3. Samenow, *Inside the Criminal Mind*, 211–43.

bodies the tension of tentative resolve. There are again exceptions. A few, like Amiel, do not choose to return to the world with some form of practical synthesis. As suggested, he had no clear avenue for return. In addition are the countless others who return but leave no written record of their return. Those who return and leave a written record usually do so by coming to terms with their prior ideas about the universe; they recover them, reconstitute them, reshape them, or reject them for a new set of assumptions. Every return from betrayal is unique: for some it is a complete reaffirmation of their prior universe; for others, a creative synthesis of old and new; and for others, a complete rejection of the old universe.

We will study the cycle of Primo Levi's ideas starting with his initial assumption that being is good, proceeding to the betrayal of this assumption he encounters in the Lager, and ending with his return to the world with the aid of practical reason.

Before his deportation, Primo Levi was a young nonbelieving cynic, so in that sense his betrayal was only partial—he had no expectation that God was the prime mover. Still, he believed that the universe was benign and that things would continue to go well for him: All things worked for the best. For Levi, some unseen and rarely thought about mechanism made this a compensatory universe. He held to these optimistic assumptions even as the politics of his Italy fell increasingly under the shadows of Nazi Germany.

In his youth he simultaneously held views to the contrary, thoughts at the fringes of his mind that contrasted with his idea of being as good. For example, in his youthful naturalistic observations he had glimpses into the brutality of the world. However, in his youthful exuberance about the fullness of life and feelings of youthful immortality, the fringe feelings about the finite aspects of life and the anomalous experiences that contradicted the good were mere annoyances for his happy soul. They were not fully conscious grounds for doubting that life was good.

On the heels of his early life came the forced doubt, which came upon him when he was on the eve of deportation to Auschwitz. He survived the initial selection and did not make a martyr of himself. He faced a world in which all that belonged to the self was taken from him and a world in which all that he acquired by learning, all his adaptive mechanisms, no longer worked. In William James's terms, every material, spiritual, and social aspect of the self had been stripped away.

Levi gives a vivid description of his existential meltdown. The terror of the prisoners' position and the realization of what was happening to them came crushing down all at once as he and the other prisoners waited for the train. Their whole world and the assumptions that went with it had disappeared: "Dawn came on us like a betrayer. . . . The different emotions that overcame us, of resignation, of futile rebellion, of religious abandon, of fear, of despair, now joined together after a sleepless night in a collective, uncontrolled panic." Conduct was so bad that for the first and last time, Levi finds it better not to tell the story: "Many things were then said and done among us; but of these it is better that there remain no memory" (*Survival*, 16).[4]

Levi describes this existential meltdown, this reaching of the bottom, in a variety of ways:

> Then for the first time we became aware that our language lacks words to express this offence, the demolition of a man. In a moment, with almost prophetic intuition, the reality was revealed to us: we had reached the bottom. It is not possible to sink lower than this; no human condition is more miserable than this, nor could it conceivably be so. Nothing belongs to us any more; they have taken away our clothes, our shoes, even our hair; if we speak, they will not listen to us, and if they listen, they will not understand. (*Survival*, 26–27)

Levi does an excellent job of describing the circumstances that lead to the demolition of man and the mental turmoil it causes: "Imagine now a man who is deprived of everyone he loves, and at the same time of his house, his habits, his clothes, in short, of everything he possesses: he will be a hollow man, reduced to suffering and needs, forgetful of dignity and restraint, for he who loses all often easily loses himself" (*Survival*, 27). Levi and the others found themselves helpless before their new circumstances. What they knew about the world no longer worked. They couldn't reason with the guards for mercy. They couldn't ask questions and get answers. Brutality was the gratuitous norm. As Levi suggests, this is the "bottom." Most of us have no way of understanding what this forced doubt is like, and even common words like *cold, hunger,* and *pain* need new words to describe what the prisoners went through. We only can imperfectly try to understand.

---

4. Levi suggests that what we call "existential meltdown" should be privileged and not told to others, much in the same way and for the same reasons that Elie Wiesel suggests that a person's last struggle with death be kept private. He does, without individual attribution, describe meltdown as a process.

From the bottom, Levi began to work his way back from this "New World" of crushing practicality without the benefit of meditation on his circumstances. First, however, it is necessary to describe the elements of doubt built into experience and try to understand the different levels on which doubt occurs. To do this, we may contrast the existential crisis of William James with the contingent perspective of John Dewey. For James, the crisis is at the existential level and throws into question everything about existence. It brings a mind shift that suggests our insufficiency toward the world, others, and ourselves. Not only are we inadequate when struggling with existence, but we have only ourselves to rely upon. John Dewey, in contrast, acknowledges the temporary derangement of material existence and believes in a subsequent readjustment, which optimistically will make the world a better place. It is not as deep a crisis as felt by James and involves a pragmatic response to external difficulties. In terms of Irving Howe's distinction, given the internal mind shift for James, the world will never be whole again, but for Dewey there can be progress. James sees the abyss, but we can never be the same in working our way back. When he comes back with tenacity he can see, as Dewey does, the possibilities of a better world, but we can never get all the way back. For Dewey, we can ultimately have more control over this varied, contingent experience, though it is fraught with dangers.

Return for Dewey is accomplished by a "selective emphasis" on the experience of betrayal. Each unique perspective has many avenues back to practical existence.[5] With the exception of Amiel, most make it back to practical existence. Those like James are driven by sorrow, while those like Dewey are driven by nostalgia.

Although the distinction is arbitrary, we can attempt in a summary way to indicate how Levi is affected on both levels. On the existential level, he never believed in the benign hand of God, but gone is any inchoate sense that being is good and that some vague sense of providence sets things right. What he brought back from his experience of betrayal was stitched into his soul, and he could not get rid of the ideas even if he so desired. Perhaps some can repress the experience of the Holocaust, but it always will be with him and he intends to keep it that way. He cannot turn back to a benign universe either emotionally or as a rational strategy of return. We alone are responsible for our existence, and with our limited abilities

---

5. I am fully cognizant here of the differences in mindset between those who have been in the Lagers and those who have not.

we must recognize the conflict within ourselves and the conflicts we have with others. In order to fight the losing battle against these conflicts, our only alternative is to use our natural proclivity for will and guile.

Before Auschwitz, Levi believed that we could muddle through events and that, in the end, everything works out for the good. His experiences in the Lager and afterward led him to conclude that, as a species, we are inadequate to existence. He works to comprehend hierarchy, selfishness, and violence and understands them to be part of the human condition. We have tendencies that may have been consequential to survival at one time in our evolutionary history, but they are no longer so useful. Only our reason can be used against these atavistic tendencies, and educated reason is our only path to a quick exit from the abyss, a flimsy one at that. In addition, flight from the abyss is only a temporary respite, for death borders our existence. Levi can never forget that we are finite beings within a frame where we have the possibilities of limited autonomy. Our human frailties make our lives a losing battle.

On the level of deranged experience, Levi believes that humans can make it back to a point where self and societal restraint, instead of atavistic behaviors, can prevail. He comes to believe this in the Lager because of the kindness of his fellow countryman, Lorenzo. In the Deweyian sense, he recovers the possibility of a fragile world with some modicum of enlightenment. His encounter with Lorenzo allows him to hold on to a vision of the possibility of finite good in experience and, as he suggests, this belief plays no small part in his ability to survive:

> I believe that it was really due to Lorenzo that I am alive today; and not so much for his material aid, as for his having constantly reminded me by his presence, by his natural and plain manner of being good, that there still existed a just world outside our own, something and someone still pure and whole, not corrupt, not savage, extraneous to hatred and terror; something difficult to define, a remote possibility of good, but for which it was worth surviving. (*Survival*, 121)

It is at this Deweyian level that Levi's optimism exists, the possibilities of the restoration of life and finite good.

Generalizing from his pre-betrayal beliefs, Levi rejects the idea that we are Hobbesian individuals from the beginning, creatures ceaselessly tied up in a struggle for power. He finally accepts, although never explicitly states, the historical sequence described by Rousseau that we begin with a modicum of pity, which is so easily lost in times of adversity. What shocks Levi is the complete fragility of the synthesis for good, which he saw crumble so quickly and completely and with so little resistance in the Lager itself. Feelings for other men deserted the prisoners so easily: "We do not believe in the most obvious and facile deduction: that man is fundamentally brutal, egoistic and stupid in his conduct is taken away, and that the Häftling is consequently nothing but a man without inhibitions. We believe, rather, that the only conclusion to be drawn is that in the face of driving necessity and physical disabilities many social habits and instincts are reduced to silence" (*Survival*, 87).

Levi cannot fathom what had happened to his captors to cause their brutality, but he is more perplexed with his fellow prisoners. He is not surprised that they finally gave in to the overwhelming force, but he is shocked by how easily the demolition of man was accomplished.

The remainder of this chapter will report how Levi responds to the abyss and the derangement of experience to return to the world, as much as possible, on his own terms. Return, for Levi, was made at two different times in his life, meaning that he had to make two separate adjustments. First was the return made in Auschwitz, a return necessitated by his slavery, which forced him to react immediately to pain and immanent death. Second, a return occurred when he found his way home to postwar Italy and civilian life.

In Auschwitz, Levi made the leap back to the world helped by a combination of fortuitous circumstances and modestly unacknowledged personal strengths. He had the innate strengths we possess that surface only in terrible circumstances, and he had no time to contemplate killing himself. In addition, he had a "useful metaphysic," sheer tenacity, a little guile, and a lot of luck.[6] He made it through, carrying with him some new principles, and some recovered from his past.

In ordinary life upon his return from Auschwitz, Levi dropped some skills, repellent to him, that had been expedient for survival in the camp. Levi never forgot the abyss and the derangement of experience. In his return, there was a reaffirmation of much in his pre-Auschwitz days, especially in his views on civilization and equality. However, his views are

---

6. I speak of a "useful metaphysic" in the same sense that Lawrence Durrell uses the term: the whole set of assumptions that orient a person to life. See Durrell, *Reflections on a Marine Venus*, 35.

much more complex than simple nostalgia for the past. Gone are his youthful assumptions that guaranteed a safe and just world.

The first steps back from existential meltdown are made with desperate determination, and it is difficult for Levi to fathom the psychological mechanisms. The whole world was turned upside down, and nothing that he knew about responding to adversity now worked. Honesty, hard work, solidarity, and helpfulness to those in need were all counterproductive to survival.

Perhaps his successful return is best explained by his sheer tenacity and his "metaphysic" of scientific curiosity. His tenacity is partially a product of useful prior experiences. In *The Periodic Table,* he describes the mental toughness he developed toward adversity when he went on physical adventures with his friend Sandro: "He dragged me along on exhausting treks through the fresh snow, far from any sign of human life, following routes that he seemed to intuit like a savage." Accomplishments did not count for Sandro: "What mattered was to know his limitations, to test and improve himself; more obscurely, he felt the need to prepare himself (and to prepare me) for an iron future, drawing closer month by month."[7]

A scientific metaphysic helped Levi fathom new rules of survival and gave him the ability to drop long-held hypotheses that proved unworkable in the Lager. As well, his observational skills, honed in the practice of chemistry and in the observation of the human species, allowed him, whenever possible, to distance himself from the immediacy of action. These skills provided him with purpose, some emotional distance from the plight of others, and a limited mental space to devise useful strategies for his own survival. His tenacity and his scientific metaphysic thus made up part of what led him out of the existential meltdown, and they served him well throughout his life.

In *Survival in Auschwitz,* Levi periodically lists new maxims that one has to understand and use to allow for survival in the Lager. These often reverse long-held rules for living. For example, prisoners were not to ask the question "Why?" in this universe. There was no "why" in the Lager, and to try and answer such questions led to total frustration. Stealing was the rule for survival, as was the necessity of sheer selfishness and callousness toward those less fortunate. Understanding German was the prerequisite for quickly learning the endless formal and informal rules. It quickly became clear to Levi that those who failed to learn the language of the

7. Levi, *The Periodic Table,* 45.

Lager could not survive: "Knowing German meant life: I only had to look around me. My Italian companions did not understand it, that is, almost all with the exception of a few from Trieste were drowning one by one in the stormy sea of not-understanding."[8]

If the prisoner survived existential meltdown, the initial mindset, three states of mind typified those few who remained. They were martyrs and saints, *musselmans* or "Hobbesian men." Few were in the first category, because those who were martyrs and saints initially confronted their captors without giving in to the new morality of the Lager. The few who stood up to the Germans in these circumstances did not last long: "Survival without renunciation of any part of one's own moral world—apart from powerful and direct interventions by fortune—was conceded only to very few superior individuals, made of the stuff of martyrs and saints" (*Survival,* 92). Even fewer saints and martyrs went along with their captors in the early going, only to rebel when they decided they had received one last indignity; they would not walk that last mile.

Levi gives a vivid description of the *musselmans,* the second category of those left after the initial selections: "They crowd my memory with their faceless presences, and if I could enclose all the evil of our time in one image, I would choose this image which is familiar to me: an emaciated man, with head dropped and shoulders curved, on whose face and in whose eyes not a trace of a thought is to be seen" (*Survival,* 90).

In ordinary life, we are not aware as much about those who are at the bottom, the *musselmans,* because there are, in Levi's terms, fewer of them. Where they exist, for instance, in our mental institutions or on the streets of our cities, we do a "good" job of keeping them from public view. Levi believes there are far fewer *musselmans* in normal society, for in civilization, man is more caring:

> This division is much less evident in ordinary life; for there it rarely happens that a man loses himself. A man is normally not alone, and in his rise or fall is tied to the destinies of his neighbours; so that it is exceptional for anyone to acquire unlimited power, or to fall by a succession of defeats into utter ruin. Moreover, everyone is normally in possession of such spiritual, physical and even financial resources that the probabilities of a shipwreck, of total inadequacy in the face of life, are relatively small. And one must take into account a definite cush-

8. Levi, *The Drowned and the Saved,* 95–96.

ioning effect exercised both by law, and by the moral sense which constitutes a self-imposed law. (*Survival*, 88)

In the Lager, *musselmans* were socially isolated because the other prisoners were bereft of pity; pity is an expenditure of precious energy, and they saw no material advantage to dealing with *musselmans*, for the latter would be dead shortly: "But with the *musselmans*, the men in decay, it is not even worth speaking because one knows already that they will complain and will speak about what they used to eat at home. Even less worthwhile is it to make friends with them, because they do not gain any extra rations, they do not work in profitable Kommandos and they know no secret method of organizing" (*Survival*, 89).

He gives a powerful description of the *musselmans'* terrible end: "Although engulfed and swept along without rest by the innumerable crowd of those similar to them, they suffer and drag themselves along in an opaque intimate solitude, and in solitude they die or disappear, without leaving a trace in anyone's memory." All of the prisoners were degraded in the eyes of their captors. The *musselmans* underwent a double degradation as their fellow prisoners began to distance themselves: "One hesitates to call them living: one hesitates to call their death death, in the face of which they have no fear, as they are too tired to understand" (*Survival*, 89–90).

By his own account, Levi fell into the third category of those who survived the initial selections, the Hobbesian men.[9] The prisoner was Hobbesian in two senses. First, he adopted the view that the universe was one of scarcity and that he must selfishly do anything he could to survive. If the prisoner did not understand this, inevitably he would sink to the level of the *musselman*: "To sink is the easiest of matters; it is enough to carry out all the orders one receives, to eat only the ration, to observe the discipline of the work and the camp. Experience showed that only exceptionally could one survive more than three months in this way" (*Survival*, 90). Slaves had to forget their prior moral universe, because in this state of nature, if they were to survive, former moral strictures got in the way. It was counterproductive to think of the morally correct actions. Power ruled completely.

The prisoners were not only Hobbesians in the sense of understanding

9. Levi understands that part of his luck came with his late deportation to Auschwitz, where in contrast to the early days of camp, the Germans spared a few for a time for slave labor.

that the Lager was a Hobbesian universe and acting on that principle; they also understood that they entered into the Hobbesian social contract of "your obedience or your life." They gave up any other social obligations when they made the continuing agreement with their captors to stay alive for at least another moment. A Hobbesian contract is based on power, not obligation. The wily prisoners understood this. Practically, this Hobbesian bargain meant that the prisoners would conform, whenever they had to, to the rules the SS set down, and go through the prescribed motions of discipline and work. They differed from the *musselmans,* who were indifferent in their mental state to the rules, sleepwalked through the day, and abandoned any effort at all to secure survival through their own guile. They were the walking dead.

Hobbesians were found in two moral camps. First were those who did everything to survive regardless of the damage they do to others. They observed Machiavellian reason not to weaken in the quest to enhance personal power. Second were those like Levi's inseparable partner Alberto, who understood the necessity of acting on the assumptions of a Hobbesian universe that necessitates moral backsliding, but in doing so tried to compromise as few of their former ideals as necessary: "Without hesitating, Alberto prefers the uncertainties and battles of the 'free profession' to a good employment" (*Survival,* 139). That "free profession" meant preferring to work in a backbreaking gang doing menial work rather than looking for some sinecure like the position of Kapo, where one's well being was greatly enhanced at the expense of others.

Levi goes to great lengths to describe the users of the two strategies. The first conformed to the wishes of their captors, sometimes even exceeding them in their enthusiasm on their way to some small advantage. The others, like Alberto, tried to minimize their complicity. Levi pointedly describes the two tendencies:

> One has to fight against the current; to battle every day and every hour against exhaustion, hunger, cold and the resulting inertia; to resist enemies and have no pity for rivals; to sharpen one's wits, build up one's patience, strengthen one's will-power. Or else, to throttle all dignity and kill all conscience, to climb down into the arena as a beast against other beasts, to let oneself be guided by those unsuspected subterranean forces." (*Survival,* 92)

If one was to live, he had to ruthlessly look after his interests. The choice came when there was any inclination to try to minimize harm to others.

Psychologically, one of Levi's greatest fears was that he would sink to the state of the *musselmans*. He saw individuals all around him slipping into the *musselmans* state. Some went into this state when they were first on the transports or initially arrived at the Lagers. Some never pulled out of the existential meltdown and lasted only a few days or weeks. Others survived that early crisis only to sink later to the level of the *musselmans*. The latter group terrified Levi, because he knew that he could become one of them, and they were never coming back.

The Hobbesians' state of mind is but a short distance from that of the *musselmans*. It is not often talked about, and it can be described best by metaphor. At times we are a furnace on low heat, functioning on automatic pilot, or a light fixture with the dimmer switch on. Our critical facilities are on hold, and we simply go along with the situation imposed from above. In obeisance to a Hobbesian atmosphere of compliance, nonconformity would lead to dire consequences, and there appears to be no way out. Protesting the circumstances is no use, so the pilot light or dimmer switch turns low to dull the pain. In this somnambulant state, Levi must have wondered how far it is to the point where the dimmer switch cannot be turned up again. Hobbesians could behave like *musselmans,* but Hobbesians could turn the switch on and off. For the *musselmans,* the switch no longer functioned.

As we shall point out in great detail later, the Hobbesian men, who were forced to shed the vestiges of prewar morality to survive, paid a terrible price. This became obvious to Levi when he and fellow prisoners were forced to witness the hanging of a prisoner who was rumored to have taken part in the destruction of one of the crematoriums in Birkenau. Just before he was hanged, the prisoner shouted: *"Kamaraden, ich bin der Letz!"* (Comrades, I am the last one!). When the prisoner shouted, Levi was ashamed to say, the prisoners who were lined up to witness the execution showed not even a nod of solidarity: "We remained bent and grey, our heads dropped, and we did not uncover our heads until the German ordered us to do so." Levi and Alberto couldn't even look at each other afterward: "To destroy a man is difficult, almost as difficult as to create one: it has not been easy, nor quick, but you Germans have succeeded. Here we are, docile under your gaze; from our side you have nothing more to fear; no acts of violence, no words of defiance, not even a look of judgement." This was the moment when he felt that even if they survived by a stroke of luck, they would never be the same: "Because we are broken, conquered: even if we know how to adapt ourselves, even if we have finally learnt how to find our food and to resist the fatigue and cold, even if we return home" (*Survival,* 149, 150). For him, this was the permanent destruction that he so effectively writes about in "*Force Majeure.*"

As with Levi's youthful thoughts about a benign universe, his idea of morality was not systematically developed in the prewar years. He endeavored to be good in a loosely utilitarian way, but the Lager forced him to act in ways contrary to what he was taught in his family, religion, and school, forcing him to think about what he believed. That development continued throughout his life.

Primo Levi roughly followed a utilitarian standard of ethics in his life, from the relatively inchoate views of his student days to his formative time in the Lager to the years he managed the paint factory and then finally turned to writing full time. The Holocaust sharpened his utilitarian views. He enriched his position over time with important additions and exceptions, but utility remained the important standard.

In his student days, Levi's basis for the good came from several sources, one of which was a rudimentary utilitarianism. He was aware of the value of civilization in that it protected the less fortunate, those presumably in pain in modern society. Levi also touted the rough virtues of work in bringing pleasure. Love was problematical for him, as for most his age.[10] Although he was not religious, he was aware of the prescriptions handed down to him through generations. For example, minimizing harm and being kind to others seemed givens to him and in no need of additional justification, standing independent of utility. After his return to Turin, Levi developed justifications for these givens through a utilitarian calculus. He knew that maxims or commandments for what most people understand as good were not enough to convince everyone to act on them, and he needed further justification for himself.

It is not difficult to see how Levi, especially after Auschwitz, came to the same conclusions as Thomas Hobbes in looking at motives: We are self-regarding hedonists. For Hobbes, we are driven by utter necessity, caused by the constant striving of individuals. This is manifest in competition, diffidence, and glory, the sources of ceaseless conflict. For Levi, these are part of the makeup of our ill-constituted beings. In the Lager, these human propensities were intensified, because scarcity was absolute

10. Coincidentally, after he married, he said little about his married life and kept his views on love private.

and people, of necessity, fought over the spoils. As Hobbes suggests, many are the means that man devises to achieve his ends. For Levi in Auschwitz, "Many were the ways devised and put into effect by us in order not to die: as many as there are different human characters" (*Survival,* 92).

Hobbes sees this struggle for power over power as a manifestation of human nature, and in the Lager, Levi believes that man's hedonism was exacerbated under the strain of vital necessity. The Lager was a pure Hobbesian world. In the Lager there was no possibility of a nonutilitarian standard, no possibility of the self-control prescribed in the *Gita* or the self-control spoken of in the *Republic,* where the unhappy tyrant needs to develop the control of his or her appetites. The leisure needed to cultivate the higher good was virtually absent, and selfish hedonism reigned. In ordinary life, humans can act differently if they were only under the stress of their subjective needs and free of absolute deprivation, but Levi feels that they remain fundamentally hedonists.

For the prisoners, it was purely a life of defense, a life of minimizing the pain that they suffered. Most of the time, life in the Lagers resulted less from choices than from the frightful circumstances that forced the prisoners to concentrate on the relief of pain whenever they could. In Machiavelli's sense, to speak of the good in the Lager was a fantasy that had nothing to do with reality. The Lager was so far away from anything resembling the good that all one could do was run from pain, and the only good was the cessation of pain. Later in this section we will see whether Levi believes that pleasure in ordinary life can ever be more than the sudden disappearance of pain, but in the Lager, the cessation of pain was the only pleasure.

Also in the Lager, the flesh was the judge of the good and the bad. We may not know what the good is, but we indelibly know what the bad is, and utility is the cessation of pain. In the Lager, the focus of the person was almost always on the person himself and his pain. In the Lager, "When we reach the cylinder we unload the sleeper on the ground and I remain stiff, with empty eyes, open mouth and hanging arms, sunk in the ephemeral and negative ecstasy of the cessation of pain." The identical idea, happiness as the cessation of pain, appears again when he describes the Lager under bombing attack: "[T]here we lay inert, piled up on the top of each other like dead men, but still aware of the momentary pleasure of our bodies resting" (*Survival,* 67, 119).

In the concentration camp, there was no good standing by itself—only good as the absence of pain. With few exceptions, like his recitation of the

Cantos of Ulysses to a worker on the way back from work in the Lager, pleasure consisted simply of putting down a heavy object, getting off work to go to the latrine, a watery soup to slake hunger a bit, or the pleasure of ceasing work for the moment and huddling together while the Lager was bombed.

The Holocaust is a formidable obstacle for those who would like to argue that there are myriad ways in which we may talk about the good and the bad. When confronted with the Holocaust, they are forced to theorize about circumstances where pain is absolute sovereign and cessation of pain is the highest good. How can you face a survivor with the idea that the flesh and pain are not absolutes and need not be addressed immediately? There is no armchair luxury in these circumstances, and if one identifies with the victims in even the slightest way, it is identification with the destruction of the flesh in the most painful of ways, pain moving a person inexorably toward death. On the grounds of the Holocaust, philosophical abstraction withers under the immediate demands of the flesh.

Other than denying the empirical fact of the Holocaust, there is one more argument used to minimize the destruction of the flesh found in the Holocaust. It is one we have come across before, and it is similar to the one used in everyday life when looking at the victims of violent crimes. Somehow, they must take part of the blame because they put themselves in the wrong places and may have even gone so far as asking for it. If the victims contributed in any way to their own pain, then the perpetrators are partially forgiven. This is why it was so important for Levi to face his youthful accusers when they would ask him whether the victims contributed to their own demise: "Among the questions that are put to us, one is never absent; indeed, as the years go by, it is formulated with ever increasing persistence, and with an ever less hidden accent of accusation. More than a single question, it is a family of questions. Why did you not escape? Why did you not rebel? Why did you not avoid capture 'beforehand'?"[11] These accusations are personal for Levi, and guilt gnaws on that part of the psyche that knows that in almost any circumstance, one could have done more. His interrogators look at Auschwitz in hindsight and see the will to resist as "natural." Levi forcefully answers his questioners and their stereotyped views that victims should have put up a better fight and could easily have accomplished heroic actions. He ends his discussion by putting a daunting challenge to them: "So then? Are today's fears more or

11. *Drowned,* 150–51.

less founded than the fears of that time? When it comes to the future, we are just as blind as our fathers." He refers to the fact that we live in a dangerous nuclear world, which could envelop and destroy the Western world. There are sanctuaries, but we are not fleeing for them. "There are Polynesia, New Zealand, Tierra del Fuego, the Antarctic: perhaps they will remain unharmed. Obtaining a passport and entry visa is much easier than it was then, so why aren't we going? Why aren't we leaving our country? Why aren't we fleeing 'before'?"[12]

What Levi understands is that if perpetrators or generations of judges of a crime can show that someone is culpable in their own demise, then they can convince others that the consequences of the crime deserve mitigation. "He deserved it" may mean that you didn't like the victim, or he was out in the street at night in a dangerous neighborhood, or he did not imitate fiction and resemble one of the comic strip heroes of popular literature or films. This is the major defense against the idea of the unmitigated evil of crimes of the flesh, one used either out of naïveté or cunning subtlety. Instinctively, Levi did not let those with whom he engaged in dialogue implicate the victim. Even if the victim did not properly use will or discretion, the perpetrator is not excused. For instance, nobody has the right to attack a woman against her will even if she walks through a dangerous neighborhood naked.

The social extension of the criteria of utility and maximizing one's own pain and pleasure involves accepting the idea of the greatest good for the greatest number. In the Lager, this principle of majoritarianism was not operative. The prisoner was left by himself—for himself. Levi laments this lack of solidarity under pressure. *Musselmans,* for example, became nonpersons to the Hobbesian who was barely trying to hang on. After the Holocaust, survivors again had time to think of the unfortunate through the lens of their pre-Holocaust morality, adding greatly to the survivor's lifetime of suffering to know that he did nothing to help his fellow man. It was a disaster for those with a conscience in pre-Holocaust days to ignore people less fortunate than oneself, or to deliberately bring harm upon them. Conscience reemerged.

There were some acts of kindness, whether the small societies of "usism" or random acts of kindness, yet the disintegration of solidarity was swift and almost complete. All varieties of behavior existed in the Lager, but most of them involved saving oneself first. As suggested above, some

---

12. Ibid., 166.

Hobbesians took on their roles with glee and purposely forgot others, while some struggled to live and at the same time invested at least a little something in minimizing suffering. Unfortunately, under duress, we can quickly ignore other people's suffering.

The fact that the behavior of the prisoners deteriorated quickly into a selfish hedonism did not excuse them from the responsibility to minimize pain in others. Yet, Levi makes clear, the culpability of the victim does not come close to the responsibility of those who could have walked away with little consequence or of those who believed in their cruelty. The blame cannot be shifted to the victim. Nothing done by the Lager slaves was worse than what the Nazis did, for the latter put everyone in compromising positions, purposely degraded the victims and made collective solidarity virtually impossible. If one allows others to shift blame to the victim, then he enables them to downplay or ignore the crime. Anyone in terrible circumstances asks himself if he could have done more, but to accuse the survivors is to fall in with the purposes of Nazi propaganda, to further degrade the victim. In Levi's ruthlessly honest writings, he takes himself and others to task for doing less than they could have done. It is incorrect to treat the survivors as saints or heroes, but abominable to use their own honest self doubts against them.

Heroes and saints, Hobbesians and *musselmans* were all victims. Levi feels that the laws of a country and its inhabitants' self-restraint defined civilization, "for a country is considered the more civilized the more the wisdom and efficiency of its laws hinder a weak man from becoming too weak or a powerful one too powerful" (*Survival*, 88).

Civilization is defined as our concern for those who suffer the pain and indignity of being weak. Those in power must be restrained in order to protect the weak. In ordinary discourse, we hear often that the victim deserved it because the category they belong to is inferior to the rest of humanity, whether the category be race, religion, or sexual preference. They brought on the trouble by their nature, or they caused it by not pulling themselves up by their own bootstraps. In the concentration camps, the rationalization might be heard as the fact that the Hobbesians made it, so why couldn't the *musselmans?* In Levi's terms, however, our pain is identical to the pain of others. Ethics for Levi involves violations of the flesh, something shared equally among all humans, and we should care for others as well as ourselves when we are in pain. Trying to implicate the victim in the crime simply means that one can excuse oneself from the whole incident. Levi will not let that happen.

Others obviously have posed other ideas that are contrary to Levi's idea of civilization and happiness and his insistence that the relief of pain is a first key to happiness. His ethics are pragmatic: When we get to the point where one person talks about happiness as the relief of pain and suffering, and another person poses massive self-assertion leaving many "necessary victims" as the key virtue on the way to happiness, there is no way to resolve the disagreement. Levi might argue back that massive self-assertion, especially in the hands of rulers, leads to terrible pain for the rest of us, but this will probably have little impact on those who champion it.

The tragedy of being becomes evident through Levi's understanding of utilitarianism. He realizes that because of the nature of being and the nature of experience, no one can achieve perfect happiness, or perfect unhappiness. Even if war could be avoided, it would not change this tragic element of existence, which puts limits on the flights of fancy one might take to try and make a perfect world, including the perfect world that does not include the happiness of anyone but oneself. Levi describes the limits of happiness and unhappiness beautifully:

> Sooner or later in life everyone discovers that perfect happiness is unrealizable, but there are few who pause to consider the antithesis: that perfect unhappiness is equally unattainable. The obstacles preventing the realization of both these extreme states are of the same nature: they derive from our human condition, which is opposed to everything infinite. Our ever-insufficient knowledge of the future opposes it: and this is called, in the one instance, hope, and in the other, uncertainty of the following day. The certainty of death opposes it: for it places a limit on every joy, but also on every grief. The inevitable material cares oppose it: for as they poison every lasting happiness, they equally assiduously distract us from our misfortunes and make our consciousness of them intermittent and hence supportable. (*Survival,* 17)

First, perfect happiness is unattainable. We will die, and just that brutal fact will cloud any unbridled happiness we might have. Life is finite. It can be, using James's terms, that some happy souls never contemplate the abyss. Others can run away from their finitude to thoughts of an afterlife that includes them. For Levi—again using James's terms, a "sick soul"—there is neither a return to consolations nor a willed ignorance. On the existential level, there is no complete happiness for Levi.

Finite life keeps us from complete happiness, but in a strange way it protects us from complete unhappiness. Death is not an absolute evil for the psyche when pain is so overwhelming. The hope then comes from our finitude. In this way Levi answers the question of what happiness a person could have if he were in terrible pain. In such conditions, we hope that we will die; death becomes an awaited pleasure. Elie Wiesel describes this mental state so well in *Night,* where he depicts the horrible death march from Auschwitz to Buchenwald. If the prisoners didn't keep moving, they would be trampled to death or shot by the SS. A companion of Wiesel's had just disappeared:

> I quickly forgot him. I began to think of myself again. Because of my painful foot, a shudder went through me at each step. "A few more yards," I thought. "A few more yards and that will be the end. I shall fall. A spurt of red flame. A shot." Death wrapped itself around me till I was stifled. It stuck to me. I felt that I could touch it. The idea of dying, of no longer being, began to fascinate me. Not to exist any longer. Not to exist any longer. Not to feel the horrible pains in my foot. Not to feel anything, neither weariness, nor cold, nor anything. To break the ranks, to let oneself slide to the edge of the road . . . [13]

Thoughts of death provided relief at the time for Elie Wiesel, but he continued on in pain because he did not want to leave his father, who accompanied him.

Material circumstances also protect us from complete unhappiness by serving as distractions; they can keep us from a close look at the abyss or from seeing the derangement of experience. They serve as an anesthetic, keeping us from full unhappiness. In the following example Levi gives the material conditions that shield us from the horrors of existence by intervening between the self and the abyss. Heroic existential actions did not save him in the Lager, simply the immediacy of experience and the necessity of dealing with it: "It was the very discomfort, the blows, the cold, the thirst that kept us aloft in the void of bottomless despair, both during the journey and after. It was not the will to live, nor a conscious resignation: for few are the men capable of such resolution, and we were but a common sample of humanity" (*Survival,* 17).[14]

The problematic aspects of material experience prevent complete happiness as well. On his way home from the Lager at a very carefree inter-

---

13. Wiesel, *Night,* 98–99.
14. See the parallels to John Dewey in *Experience and Nature.*

val, Levi became immersed in the joys of watching a play, and afterward engaged in revelry with other refugees. Like Georg Groddeck's and Rollo May's insight into the intermixing of feelings of love and death, the feelings of happiness reminded Levi and his companions of less fortunate times and unhappy victims, contaminating his mood of joy: "We lit fires in the woods, and no one slept; we spent the rest of the night singing and dancing, recalling past adventures and remembering our lost companions—for it is not given to man to enjoy uncontaminated happiness."[15] As Levi suggests, material cares "poison every lasting happiness." Unhappiness is impatient; it does not wait for our enjoyments to end before it intrudes on our happiness.

Work is one of the material cares that seal us from the absolute best and worst of life. Work is Levi's joy, but it is also his anesthetic, something that allows him to block out the pain of his Auschwitz existence. It temporarily shields us from the abyss, and it is necessary in that way, much in the way that an obsessive-compulsive disorder might keep us from thinking about certain ideas we don't want to think about. He comes by this painful forgetting when he thinks about the destruction done to him in the Lager and whether he can possibly overcome the pain. Forgetting is only a temporary anesthetic to keep him from pain. His only consolation for the return of painful memories is that he does not want to forget altogether.

Levi's thinking may be divided into two different stages of his life, the Lager and "ordinary life." In his writings undertaken in ordinary life, he adds several layers of complexity to his utilitarianism beyond the experience of pain and its temporary cessation, for he now has the time and space to generate his own pleasures. However, in the Lager, there was the absence of freedom, and for the most part happiness was relegated to the relatively rare times where there was an absence of pain. Dealing with vital material concerns provided some distraction from pain, and on the existential level, these material concerns shielded him somewhat from thoughts of death. For example, when Levi and the other prisoners found out that there was to be a *"Selekcja,"* a selection, "the result is hardly a wave of despondency: our collective morale is too inarticulate and flat to be unstable. The fight against hunger, cold and work leaves little margin for thought, even for this thought" (*Survival,* 124–25).

For Levi, "ordinary life" began gradually on his journey home from

---

15. Levi, *Reawakening,* 163.

Auschwitz to Turin, where he settled into his old home and a job in a paint factory. In Anthony Rudolph's *At an Uncertain Hour: Primo Levi's War against Oblivion*, the author asks Levi if his paradise is the personal and professional world he depicts in *The Periodic Table*. Levi answers: "I don't think *The Periodic Table* describes a paradise unless you call normal life a paradise, which could be the case. If you are happy with daily life, living the life of a *mensch* freely, then yes you can describe it as my Paradiso."[16]

Although he experienced "higher pleasures," for the most part Levi saw day-to-day life as a striking contrast with his time in the Lager; a life relatively free of pain was of sufficient pleasure.

Levi's quotation about the paradise of ordinary life introduces the idea of freedom into the calculation of pain and pleasure. Levi puts the idea in sharper relief in *Survival in Auschwitz* when he describes a day when "the sun rose bright and clear for the first time from the horizon of mud. . . . and when even I felt its lukewarmth through my clothes I understood how men can worship the sun." The work was light that day and there were extra rations of food. At the end of this "good day," Levi says, "we feel good, the Kapo feels no urge to hit us, and we are able to think of our mothers and wives, which usually does not happen. For a few hours we can be unhappy in the manner of free men" (71, 76). Happiness or unhappiness is only decisive when freedom is first taken into account. Freedom certainly does not guarantee happiness, but it should be a prerequisite to our ordinary tragic lives. It is vital that we have some say in our own unhappiness or happiness.

Levi expresses these sentiments of freedom in his short story "The Hard Sellers." In this story, Levi's mouthpiece, identified only as "S.," turns down utopian happiness for the ordinary life of pleasure and pain. S. is receiving the hard sell from others who argue that he should be reborn on the distant planet Earth. Earth, he is told, is a paradise, but S. sees through the verbal descriptions and snapshots. He cuts through the sales pitch to discern the monumental social conflicts on the planet. Since S. sees the problems of the disadvantaged, the hard sellers offer him a good place in the social system, guaranteed by the right parentage. S. declines, for he wants to take his chances in the lottery of birth and forge his own destiny. "I accept, [being born on Earth] but I would like to be born at random, like everyone: among billions of beings to be born without a fate, among

16. Rudolph, *At an Uncertain Hour*, 25.

the predestined to servitude or contention from the cradle on, if in fact they have a cradle. I prefer to be born black, Indian, poor, without indulgences and without pardons."[17] Paradise is when you freely live your tragic existence.

S. anticipates the criticism of the bureaucrats who will make the birth arrangements: "You yourself said that each man is his own maker: well, it is best to be so fully, build oneself from the roots. I prefer to be the only one to fabricate myself, and I prefer the anger that I will need if I will be capable of it; if not, I will accept everyone else's destiny. The path of defenseless and blind humanity will be mine."[18] In other words, it is best to face life and its inherent miseries in one's own free way.[19]

Others arbitrarily imposed pain and insurmountable obstacles in the Lager. In ordinary life, however, surmountable obstacles are often freely chosen, a requisite for happiness. Levi begins his essay "The Struggle for Life" by quoting Bertrand Russell on the importance of struggle:

> On an unforgettable page of *The Conquest of Happiness*, Bertrand Russell reminds us that the animal man, like the other animals, has in his biological makeup a certain instinct to compete, that is, to engage in the struggle for life; that therefore anyone rich or powerful enough to satisfy all of his desires without effort is deprived of a fundamental ingredient of happiness; that therefore you cannot be happy if you are not deprived of at least some of the things that you desire![20]

When needs are not vital needs, happiness is achieved through self-control: "If the desires whose satisfaction we must renounce become too many, or if they are numbered among the vital needs, then it is no longer a matter of happiness." According to Russell, and apparently Levi agrees, excessive satisfaction of a need or the lack of struggle for life bring not happiness, but "Byronic Happiness." Most of what we call happiness comes from struggle, but not that of the continuous life and death struggle. As Levi suggests, "you cannot be happy if you are not deprived of at

17. Levi, "The Hard Sellers," in *"The Sixth Day" and Other Tales*, 160.

18. Ibid. Because Levi's penchant is for clarity, even in his fiction, his own point of view is rarely disguised.

19. Levi shares the importance of freedom with many of the existentialists who began to conceptualize about freedom during and after the war, but he also finds his difference with them.

20. Levi, "The Struggle for Life," in *"The Mirror Maker": Stories and Essays*, 98.

least some of the things that you desire!" Troubles overcome are not only good to tell, but lead to happiness. In the Lager, there was not happiness, but only the occasional freedom from pain.[21]

Levi also tells of times where the good may not be described in purely utilitarian terms, and it is here where he talks about higher happiness. In the years succeeding his time in Auschwitz, Levi can think about forms of Platonic happiness or John Stuart Mill's qualitative pleasures. Levi asserts that utility begins to appear inadequate when one contemplates the good as opposed to the earlier exclusive focus on the cessation of pain.

In his essay "The Moon and Man," he writes in celebration of the flight of American astronauts Borman, Lovell, and Anders on Apollo 8:

> We can see today, and yesterday we could see it less well: the enterprise was not to be judged on a utilitarian scale, or not chiefly in those terms. In the same way, an inquiry into the costs encountered in building the Parthenon would seem jarringly out of place; it is typical of man to act in an inspired and complex manner, perhaps adding up the costs beforehand, but not confining himself to the pure, imminent, or distant advantage, to take off for remote goals, with aims that are justification in themselves; to act in order to challenge a secret, enlarge his frontiers, express himself, test himself.[22]

With the possibility of the good, he rejects the calculation of utility to measure happiness and certainly does not think that happiness can be operationalized in terms of dollars and cents. As with Mill, the adoption of the idea of higher pleasures cause him to realize that utility is not sufficient with respect to talking about pleasure; the utilities would remain incalculable. Yet most of his writing is spent discussing defensive life, the running away from pain.

In summary, we should be free beings who can try to maximize pleasure and minimize pain in our existence. Since life is bordered with conditions that do not allow maximum pleasure and minimum pain, as well as material experience that inevitably leads to both pain and the absence of pain, existence is essentially tragic. Our finite lives and material cares intervene to prevent either pure happiness or unhappiness. Even to the extent we have pleasures, pleasurable experiences seem to be gone in a flash, whereas painful experiences seem to last forever.

21. Ibid. "Troubles overcome are good to tell" is an old Jewish proverb.
22. Levi, "The Moon and Man," in *"Mirror,"* 89–90.

6

Useful Qualities of Human Nature

So we do have vast and unforeseen margins of safety: . . . our poor
body, so defenseless when confronted by swords, guns, and viruses, is spaceproof.

—"The Man Who Flies"

In the preceding chapter, we have discussed that given the nature of the
psyche, perhaps "pure hell" is neither to be found in Auschwitz nor anywhere on this earth, for that matter. This chapter will illustrate how the
psyche functions under extreme duress to mitigate some of the pains of being and experience. What is it about our nature that allows us to minimize
pain in desperate situations? Before these mitigating circumstances are
outlined, two issues must be dispensed with. First, the fact that we cannot
experience pure hell in no way mitigates the crimes of the perpetrators. No
one can wish Levi's experience in Auschwitz on themselves or others. Terrible suffering and death were endured under conditions of slavery. The
psyche only provided a minor benefit against pure hell.

Second, the forgetting of the abyss and the terrors of existence has its
salutary aspects, but we may want to remind ourselves of life's tragic aspects. Some forgetting is necessary to blunt the pain, yet there is the obligation to bear witness. That is an agony Levi knows well.

This chapter will show that Levi finds a reservoir of qualities in humans
that allows us to survive extreme situations. Survival in the Lager was due
mostly to luck, but there were some fortuitous attributes in the prisoners
that worked to mitigate some of the worst of situations. The next chapter
will ask if personal choices could help a prisoner extend his life and achieve
some relief from the pain. Can the individual, of his own volition, blunt
the existential terrors and the terrors of existence faced in the Lager? Once

117

liberated, can he exert a modicum of will and guile to achieve some happiness in ordinary life? This chapter shows that some instinctive responses, ones that the prisoners did not know they possessed, may have worked for their own good. The next chapter illustrates our ingenuity under crushing pressure.

The earlier chapter "Ill-Constituted Beings" discussed Levi's idea that although we are insufficient beings, we manifest surprising strength in the face of adversity. As a species, we do not live on the edge of extinction like the panda, a creature that must spend almost all waking hours eating bamboo in order to live. In the essay "The Man who Flies," Levi marvels over the fact that man survives conditions of weightlessness in space with relatively little discomfort. Human flesh is often fragile, but we have surprising strengths: "[O]ur poor body, so defenseless when confronted by swords, guns, and viruses, is spaceproof." We manage to survive as we do in many unusual conditions: "So we do have vast and unforeseen margins of safety."[1] Here we will examine some of these surprising attributes of man.

The individual in the Lager first faced existential meltdown. Instinctively, the prisoner hunkered down, dug in and built a secure space for himself:

> Man's capacity to dig himself in, to secrete a shell, to build around himself a tenuous barrier of defence, even in apparently desperate circumstances, is astonishing and merits a serious study. It is based on an invaluable activity of adaptation, partly passive and unconscious, partly active: of hammering in a nail above his bunk from which to hang up his shoes; of concluding tacit pacts of non-aggression with neighbors; of understanding and accepting the customs and laws of a single Kommando, a single Block. By virtue of this work, one manages to gain a certain equilibrium after a few weeks, a certain degree of security in the face of the unforeseen; one has made oneself a nest, the trauma of the transplantation is over.[2]

If the prisoners managed to survive the transport and the initial existential meltdown, other useful qualities of human beings began to kick in.

---

1. Levi, "The Man Who Flies," in *"The Mirror Maker": Stories and Essays by Primo Levi*, 144, 143.
2. Levi, *Survival in Auschwitz*, 56. Future references will be cited parenthetically in the text.

During this time and afterward, several features of man went to work to allow for the possibilities of survival under the utmost physical and psychological pressure. As suggested in the last chapter, the material conditions of the Lager crowded out fears of death: "I almost never had the time to devote to death. I had many other things to keep me busy—finding a bit of bread, avoiding exhausting work, patching my shoes, stealing a broom, or interpreting the signs and faces around me."[3]

The prisoners, by virtue of their slavery, were in a "compulsory zen mode," focusing on the cold, their hunger, or the exhausting task in front of them. Material concerns forced them into the immediate present: "We had not only forgotten our country and our culture, but also our family, our past, the future we had imagined for ourselves, because, like animals, we were confined to the present moment" (*Drowned*, 75). In terms of compulsory zen, the prisoners lived like dogs with no chance of the reflexivity of thought.[4] Ironically, harsh slavery achieved what self-discipline most often cannot—the staving off of thoughts of death.

The focus of the prisoner's being on the immediacy of material circumstances in the Lager was accompanied by an anesthesia of the mind, the dulling of the senses. This stupefaction is experienced in normal life where a task is obligatory and extremely unpleasant. We can best describe it as a dulling of the senses while minimally focusing on the necessary circumstances of the task. The previous chapter described an involuntary servitude to circumstances, which causes the mind to go on automatic pilot. A mood of torpor envelops the human beast of burden.

Levi describes the *musselmans* as those who feared death the least. Their pilot light had gone out. He can visualize their torpor as they attended to present material concerns with almost complete indifference. They were in this state protected from pain and thoughts of death, but they had lost the ability to cling to the present. Other prisoners shunned them; they did not have long to live. We may describe them as being beneath life.

In the Lager, the dulling of pain occurred on a continuum. The most pain and thoughts of death remained with the alert Hobbesians in the Lager, and at the other end of the continuum we find the *musselmans*, who were almost completely anesthetized. Levi describes his state of mind, in

3. Levi, *The Drowned and the Saved*, 148. Future references will be cited parenthetically in the text.
4. The expression, "living like dogs," is used in the traditional way in Zen, indicating a good state of man with no reflexivity. Whether animals can "think" is in hot debate currently.

his later days in the Lager, as moving toward the *musselmans* end of the continuum: "As for us, we were too destroyed to be really afraid. The few who could still judge and feel rightly, drew new strength and hope from the bombardments. . . . But the greater number bore the new danger and the new discomforts with unchanged indifference: it was not a conscious resignation, but the opaque torpor of beasts broken in by blows, whom the blows no longer hurt" (*Survival*, 118).

This dulling of the senses, living like a dog in the present moment, was providential for Levi, for it precluded the possibility of any kind of speculative thought or the sapping of vital strength through emotion. Mercifully, there seems to be a threshold of pain that when passed leads to a shutdown of cares and sensitivity: "It [thinking] is harmful, because it keeps alive a sensitivity which is a source of pain, and which some providential natural law dulls when suffering passes a certain limit" (*Survival*, 171). In voluntary Zen, a spontaneity of action occurs in the person, and there is a oneness with the universe. In compulsory Zen, no such feelings arise. For the prisoner, there is a weariness with life, there is no will or zest that emanates from within.

This condition has very powerful effects. When Levi first became aware that the Lager was about to be liberated, his protective torpor had not worn off, and his former sensibilities had not yet returned: "I had no longer felt any pain, joy or fear, except in that detached and distant manner characteristic of the Lager, which might be described as conditional: if I still had my former sensitivity, I thought, this would be an extremely moving moment" (*Survival*, 152–53).

In addition to the general dulling of the individual, prisoners drew on other resources they unknowingly had in reserve. They led a defensive life against the threats of death, the humiliation of the whip, and the pains of exhaustion, disease, body traumas, cold, hunger, and thirst. Yet, according to Levi, the prisoners did not suffer them all at once. His psyche was organized in what can be called a "hierarchy of troubles," whereby the prisoners were confronted by the most serious threat, and the less serious threats were dully felt on the fringes of the mind, if at all. If the most prominent trouble was alleviated, then the next one became manifest. Levi rarely repeats himself, but as an exception he often brings up the importance of the hierarchy of troubles, which plays a protective function for the threatened human being. This hierarchy of troubles becomes operative after the existential meltdown, after he has survived all the concerns impinging on his psyche at once, and man has crept into his manmade security shell. It guards him from being engulfed once again by those conditions threatening him; it allows him to focus on the most insistent pain while ignoring the rest.[5]

We can be neither completely happy nor unhappy, and the hierarchy of troubles works to insure that this is the case. We cannot be completely happy because as soon as one care is put to bed, another care quickly arises to take its place. We will never be completely unhappy because all secondary troubles are masked by the predominant trouble. In one of his most comprehensive statements on the hierarchy of troubles, Levi says:

> For human nature is such that grief and pain—even simultaneously suffered—do not add up as a whole in our consciousness, but hide, the lesser behind the greater, according to a definite law of perspective. It is providential and is our means of surviving the camp. And this is the reason why so often in free life one hears it said that man is never content. . . . And if the most immediate cause of stress comes to an end, you are grievously amazed to see that another one lies behind; and in reality a whole series of others. (*Survival,* 73–74)

Levi goes on to give a concrete example of the hierarchy of troubles: "So that as soon as the cold, which throughout the winter had seemed our only enemy, had ceased, we became aware of our hunger; and repeating the same error, we now say: 'if it was not for the hunger!'" (*Survival,* 73).

There is a great psychic distance between the dominant concern and the rest that await their turn. In *The Periodic Table,* he describes that distance: "To eat, to get something to eat, was our prime stimulus, behind which, at a great distance, followed all the other problems of survival, and even still farther away the memories of home and the very fear of death."[6] In the last part of this statement we can see how the hierarchy of troubles is also part of the reason why death is kept from the door of concern. The process abets the dulling of the senses.

After the existential crisis is surpassed, this is the psyche's way of dealing with the horrors of the abyss and deranged experience—to focus on pains one at a time. The prisoners who had survived the longest were characterized by this short-term mindset: "For months and years, the problem

---

5. As we suggested, what is frightening to Levi is that we don't know the exact point at which the hierarchy of troubles dissolves and the individual is engulfed all at once by his troubles.

6. Levi, *The Periodic Table,* 140.

of the remote future has grown pale to them and has lost all intensity in face of the far more urgent and concrete problems of the near future: how much one will eat today, if it will snow, if there will be coal to unload."[7]

However merciful the hierarchy of troubles may be, the pains suffered in the Lager were unlike any the prisoners had ever known: "We were not normal because we were hungry. Our hunger at that time had nothing in common with the well-known (and not completely disagreeable) sensation of someone who has missed a meal and is certain that the next meal will not be missed: it was a need, a lack, a yearning that had accompanied us now for a year, had struck deep, permanent roots in us, lived in our cells and conditioned our behavior."[8]

Every other concern defers to the dominant pain, whether it is cold in winter, hunger in summer, or thirst, pains that cannot be measured by anything we experience in normal life. Other pains return when there is some period of respite, for example, in Ka-Be, the infirmary, where the prisoners were temporarily free of work and crushing routine: "When one works, one suffers and there is no time to think: our homes are less than a memory. But here [in Ka-Be] the time is ours." In Ka-Be, "we become aware, with amazement, that we have forgotten nothing, every memory evoked rises in front of us painfully clear." Sometimes, in the brief interludes, the prisoners deliberately willed concerns out of existence, helping reinforce the hierarchy of troubles. Levi says: "Here I am, then, at the bottom. One learns quickly enough to wipe out the past and the future when one is forced to."[9]

The concept of a hierarchy of troubles is also relevant when talking about the post-Holocaust, "ordinary life."[10] Rarely in the Lager, but often in normal life, where the future is somewhat within his grasp, Levi and others could try to manipulate the hierarchy of troubles, which dominated their defensive life.[11]

---

7. Ibid., 36.

8. Ibid., 140.

9. Ibid., 55, 33. It does no good to remember those in trouble left behind. When a prisoner in an Argentine jail, Jacobo Timerman expressed the same need to willfully repress thoughts of home. See Timerman, *Prisoner without a Name, Cell without a Number,* 88.

10. Levi faced the ontological problem that life after the Holocaust was never as real for him as it was during the awful tragedy. Levi means "real" in the sense that Robert Nozick means "real": that event or events that present themselves in such searing clarity, intensity, and immediacy. See Nozick, *The Examined Life,* 128–40.

11. In the Lager, the past and the future came back in Ka-Be and some small moments of respite, and a bit of planning did take place. We will document this shortly.

As suggested, most of the refugees relaxed their armor of defense on the journey home. Mordo, the Salonica Greek, pressed Levi to think systematically about the hierarchy of troubles when the former prisoners had temporarily relaxed their vigilance. Mordo believed that life is war, and he was still prepared to fulfill vital needs first. He believed that shoes, for example, were prior to food, because without shoes, one could not forage for food. Mordo scolded Levi who, after liberation, did not take care to find a good pair of shoes. In walking from Cracow, Levi underestimated the distance, and his shoes were virtually useless: "After about twenty minutes, my shoes were finished; the sole of one of them had come off, and the other began to unstitch itself." He sat down with Mordo, who did not take any of Levi's excuses for not having gotten a good pair of shoes after the liberation. Mordo was willing to risk everything for a pair of shoes: "I wanted the shoes, and so I walked to the back, I broke open a small window and I entered. So I got my shoe, and everything that is inside the sack, which will prove useful later on. That is foresight; yours is stupidity. It's a failure to understand the reality of things."[12]

Many Holocaust survivors, even months or years later, never took for granted their vital needs. Levi and Vladek Spiegelman, the Holocaust survivor described by his son Art in *Maus,* looked to the ground for months after being freed, habitually searching for scraps that might help with survival. Jerzy Kosinski, author and survivor, kept a survival kit in his car. In ordinary life, we rarely have to think in the terms of stark utility with respect to our vital needs; vital concerns may seem to recede and are taken care of as a matter of routine. The pressures were less for Mordo on the way home than they were in the Lager, but he reminded Levi of the importance of the "rational" calculation of vital concerns.

The hierarchy of troubles also comes into play in another way when we are living a normal life. As Levi suggests, even when we achieve the lessening of the burden of something weighing on our mind, we can never be completely happy. A lesser care rises insistently into consciousness and the felt need to do something about it begins all over again. The hierarchy is still there, but the strategies of self-defense become more confused. How do we order our existence, for when we are at leisure our pressing concerns are fed from below and they don't seem to be in any conscious order of priority? No longer do the vital needs demand immediate satisfaction, and the outer world competes with our historical inner beings, which

12. Levi, *Reawakening,* 28, 29.

throw up, one by one, concerns for the individual. As William James suggests, open spaces are threatening to man, and he begins to imagine all sorts of dangers. This is spelled out beautifully by Adam Phillips, who sees the need to quell the uncertainties of life. Normal life is filled with unseen dangers for us, and we use our imagination to conjure up the possibilities of danger. We seem to unconsciously set these priorities, and one by one they come back to us in the form of the hierarchy of troubles.[13]

There was little chance for imagination and imagining of troubles in the Lager because the most pressing material concerns were external and obvious. The creativity and madness of ordinary life were luxuries. In Auschwitz, if the prisoner did not attack the pressing vital need, he died. At times, the prisoners tried to resist the insistence of hunger, for example, to alleviate some other need. They might trade in rations for a spoon, thread, or some other vital object. Most of the time, the hunger was so insistent that they could not even save a scrap of bread for later in the day.

The calculations are much different in ordinary life. Here, we have to recapture existence from ourselves as often as from immediate circumstances. Our leisure, coupled with the fact that most vital needs have been taken care of, allows us to grasp our troubles and attempt to set priorities. Take, for instance, this trivial example: Top on a person's list of concerns may be the way he is dressed for an interview, the unhealthy lunch he ate, the slight he thinks he gave to his boss, or the party he must attend against his will. They all appear to arise from current circumstances, but none affects vital needs. Their order comes from within. To try and reorder them on some cognitive basis or on the basis of intuition may cause great anxiety, which becomes part of the cost of rearranging the hierarchy. It becomes even more complicated when one, consciously or unconsciously, tries to switch from a defensive mode of life based on handling successive evils, to a life based on calculating the good and moving to achieve it. Can we achieve the good, or is all life defensive life?

The fundamental deception for Rousseau is that society convinces those who live in it what their needs are and draws us further and further away from expressing our weak instinctual feelings of pity for others. He suggests that his pupil, Émile, read *Robinson Crusoe* in order to discover in himself what he truly needs and what is unnecessary luxury. Levi suggests that the hierarchy will decide for us if we do not find a way to order our own priorities in ordinary life.

13. Phillips, *On Kissing, Tickling and Being Bored,* 6, 7.

The hierarchy of troubles is a productive idea and its implications can be fruitfully explored. For instance, during an existential crisis, the whole hierarchy may suffer meltdown. Is it possible that with the *musselmans,* the hierarchy implodes and the person shuts down to lock out the cacophony of voices? The enemy seems to be coming from all corners. This may also happen to a person in ordinary life who is not overwhelmed by external circumstances like the *musselmans,* but is overwhelmed by an internal mind shift in combination with external situations.

Other paths can be explored. In psychoanalytic terms, it is possible that one worry simply is a stand-in for another one. For example, a compulsion that we act out may mask worry about a deeper underlying problem. Levi does not deal with these questions, but his hierarchy is an interesting concept and begs for more investigation.

For our interests, the hierarchy functions as part of that surplus of being that allows us to survive extraordinary circumstances. First, it directs us to deal with the problem utmost on the table before us. Second, by focusing on one problem at a time, it allows for the possibility that we will not suffer all of the lesser cares at the same time. Levi believes that dealing with the greater to the exclusion of the lesser is deeply rooted in humans. It helped him to survive in Auschwitz, and it becomes an interesting way to view ordinary life, where we find the continued insistence of the hierarchy of troubles.

In addition to the diminishment of the terrors of death and the hierarchy of troubles, which blunt all but the most pressing of concerns, there is the relative absence of guilt among the prisoners in the Lager. For the prisoners, this was merciful, because they were forced into many behaviors that went counter to what they had been taught before the war by their families and civil society. Behaviors that under ordinary conditions might have caused them a great deal of guilt brought no corresponding guilt in the Lager. Guilt or shame, concepts used synonymously by Levi, disappeared, because the prisoners were constantly being punished. Continual punishment made it easier to commit crimes against their own ideas and against other prisoners. He describes this mechanism in *The Drowned and the Saved* in a discussion of suicide, where he notes that it was more frequent after liberation than it was in the Lager. In "the majority of cases, suicide is born from a feeling of guilt that no punishment has attenuated; now, the harshness of imprisonment was perceived as punishment, and the feeling of guilt (if there is punishment, there must have been guilt) was relegated to the background, only to re-emerge after the Liberation. In other words, there was no need to punish oneself by suicide because of a (true or presumed) guilt: one was already expiating it by one's daily suffering" (76).

When there is some respite from the worst punishment, for example, in Ka-Be, conscience may return for the interlude:

> So that, whoever still has some seeds of conscience, feels his conscience re-awaken; and in the long empty days, one speaks of other things than hunger and work and one begins to consider what they have made us become, how much they have taken away from us, what this life is. In this Ka-Be, an enclosure of relative peace, we have learnt that our personality is fragile, that it is much more in danger than our life; and the old wise ones, instead of warning us 'remember that you must die', would have done much better to remind us of this great danger than threatens us. (*Survival*, 55)

Once again, in the chemical laboratory, these pangs of conscience return and remind him of "all my peaceful moments, of Ka-Be, of the rest-Sundays—the pain of remembering, the old ferocious suffering of feeling myself a man again, which attacks me like a dog the moment my conscience comes out of the gloom" (*Survival*, 142).

When the Lager was liberated, Levi did not feel lighthearted, for the sorrows way down on the hierarchy returned along with the attendant guilt: "the sorrows of men returned: the sorrow of the dispersed or lost family; the universal suffering all around; their own exhaustion, which seemed definitive, past cure; the problem of a life to begin over again amid the rubble, often alone." The emerging consciousness of these sorrows made liberation much less than a celebration. Liberation "coincided with a phase of anguish" (*Drowned*, 70). Anguish, Freud's anxiety, conveys those familiar feelings that indicate some underlying problems, perhaps a past or a future that are problematic for the person, but are not readily identifiable by consciousness: "Anguish is known to everyone, even children, and everyone knows that it is often blank, undifferentiated" (*Drowned*, 71). Guilt about the past and the future returned as soon as the pressures of the present relented and gave formerly dormant concerns a prominence in the psyche.

Levi asks himself rhetorically what guilt the prisoners might have and suggests that "on a rational plane, there should not have been much to be ashamed of, but shame persisted nevertheless, especially for the few bright

examples of those who had the strength and possibility to resist"
(*Drowned,* 77). For the rest of the prisoners, "When it was all over, the
awareness emerged that we had not done anything, or not enough against
the system into which we had been absorbed" (*Drowned,* 76). Levi also
says that he felt most humiliated when there was nothing he could do to
retaliate. Specifically, among other humiliations, Levi singles out his humiliation in front of the German girls when he sensed their condescension
as he worked among them, filthy and smelly. Humiliation also occurred
when he faced the German officer to take his chemical examination to try
and procure work inside in the chemical plant. He also speaks of an incident in Ka-Be where he was totally humiliated by a male nurse: "I wish I
had never spoken to the Pole: I feel as if I had never in all my life under-
gone an affront worse than this. . . . The nurse points to my ribs to show
the other, as if I was a corpse in an anatomy class: he alludes to my eye-
lids and my swollen cheeks and my thin neck, he stoops to press on my
tibia with his thumb, and shows the other the deep impression that his finger leaves in the pale flesh, as if it was wax" (*Survival,* 49).

Levi takes great care to indicate what generalizations can be made
about these circumstances, but not before warning us that each individual responded differently: "In my opinion, the feeling of shame or guilt
that coincided with reacquired freedom was extremely composite: it contained diverse elements, and in diverse proportions for each individual"
(*Drowned,* 75). He gives us the following generalizations: First, those who
returned from the Holocaust felt accused and judged by those who listened
to their stories. Second, in the Lager, "[t]he demand for solidarity, for a
human word, advice, even just a listening ear was permanent and universal but rarely satisfied." Survival necessitates that the survivor must come
first. In moments of reprieve, or upon "liberation," guilt inevitably surged
in. Third, there was the shame of being alive in the place of another, one
who may have been more worthy of life than you: "It is no more than a
supposition, indeed the shadow of a suspicion: that each man is his broth-
er's Cain, that each one of us (but this time I say 'us' in a much vaster, indeed, universal sense) has usurped his neighbor's place and lived in his
stead" (*Drowned,* 78, 81–82). Fourth, "there is another, vaster shame, the
shame of the world. . . . [E]very bell tolls for everyone. And yet there are
those who, faced by the crime of others or their own, turn their backs so
as not to see it and not feel touched by it. This is what the majority of Germans did during the twelve Hitlerian years, deluding themselves that not
seeing was a way of not knowing, and that not knowing relieved them of

their share of complicity of connivance." Ironically, the Germans could avoid the shame in this way, "But we [the prisoners] were denied the screen of willed ignorance, T. S. Eliot's "partial shelter": we were not able not to see" (*Drowned*, 85–86).

These hurtful self-accusations arose only after liberation or briefly during the fleeting moments of reprieve in the Lager. The survivors faced the guilt and loss of self-respect, feelings that were mercifully blunted during their captivity. In the Lager they were continually undergoing hardships that served as punishment for whatever self-accusations they might have had. Liberation left them with humiliation and guilt, feelings they could never cast away. In his description of the alley in "*Force Majeure*," this is the part of the soul that is crushed by the sailor, never to be repaired.

Levi gives us a prototype of his guilt and its dynamics in the following example. He found a pipe with water dripping from it and shared it with Alberto. If he shared it with others, everyone in the barracks would have gotten merely a drop. An acquaintance, Daniele, spotted them in the rubble and guessed what they were up to: "He curtly told me so many months later, in Byelorussia, after the Liberation: why the two of you and not I?" Daniele was resurrecting the "civilian" code of morality that was irrelevant in the camps. Nonetheless, Levi could not convince himself that he was not guilty, and it weighed on him the rest of his life: "Daniele is dead now, but in our meetings as survivors, fraternal, affectionate, the veil of that act of omission, that unshared glass of water, stood between us, transparent, not expressed, but perceptible and 'costly'" (*Drowned*, 80–81).

In the Lager, prisoners were protected by the collapse of the former morality and the ever-present punishment that excused present and future crimes. When the war ended, the old morality, the unconscious conscience, returned insistently as the standard by which they must judge their actions in the Lager.

As well as the psyche's diminishment of concerns about death, the organization of the hierarchy of troubles to put aside all but the most pressing concern, and the relieving of guilt in the Lager because of continuous punishment, the psyche in Auschwitz functioned in other merciful ways. It also blunted the horrors done to others that the prisoners saw daily. This "economy of horrors" is seen in many contexts. People often cannot grasp the full enormity of suffering. To be moved by tragedy, the tragedy has to be personified, an insight that has become familiar in literature and popular culture. For instance, the death of one prisoner, Anne Frank, resonates with the psyche more than deaths tolling in the millions.

This human tendency to an economy of horrors is best illustrated in Andre Schwartz-Bart's *The Last of the Just*. In that work, only the special few can feel the pains of all humanity; the rest of us tend to economize our feelings. We pick and choose the tragedy for which we grieve, and one person or incident becomes emblematic of the occasion. Every day, most of us go about our business without blinking at the statistics of the dead due to old age, disease, war, and natural disaster.[14] The prisoners' situation was serious, because they could not ignore the death and suffering that promised to finally engulf them. They could not capture, nor did they want to capture, the enormity of it all, and they did not tend to focus too long on any one death. There is a compendium of causes for the dulling of the prisoners' senses toward the enormity of the horror, some of which have already been touched upon in this chapter. Diminishment of thoughts of death, the hierarchy of troubles, and the delay of guilt all contributed to the muting of the horror done to others. The death of others receded before the possibility of their own death, and the hierarchy of troubles let the prisoners grasp only what was immediately in front of them. Levi describes the blunting of feelings: "Already for many months I had no longer felt any pain, joy or fear, except in that detached and distant manner characteristic of the Lager, which might be described as conditional: if I still had my former sensitivity, I thought, this would be an extremely moving moment" (*Survival*, 52–53). Pleasure and pain were of a detached, bygone day.

In the Lager, survival called for a willed callousness to others and the need to accentuate selfishness, an account of behavior that parallels Thomas Hobbes's descriptions of everyday life in the state of nature. Levi describes this condition in what he calls one of the laws of the Lager: "That man is bound to pursue his own ends by all possible means, while he who errs but once pays dearly" (*Survival*, 13).

Prisoners' feelings were diminished for those suffering alongside them for other reasons. Levi describes in great detail the prisoners' attitudes towards the *musselmans,* who had descended further than Levi and who were a constant reminder of whom he might become. One hypothesis, perhaps too facile, is that the suspicion Levi and others had that they were already *musselmans*—or well down that path—generating self-hatred that is projected onto the *musselmans*. Also at work is our tendency to think

---

14. We will discuss the consequences of this economy of horrors when it plays a great role in the lives of those, like Levi, who bear witness to the Holocaust.

less of those who are below us in social status. The "living" in the Lager condescendingly looked down on the living dead. The less fortunate deserved what they got, for otherwise they would not be on the very bottom. The consequences of continuous terror led them to an abject existence, but a look at the *musselmans* allowed the "more fortunate" to think that those victims' dismal behavior was the cause of their lower *musselmans* status; they must deserve it. Humans often fall prey to this type of reversal of cause and effect in their thinking.

In conclusion, elements in human nature unexpectedly showed up under extreme conditions to give the prisoners an unexpected margin for survival. Unfortunately for Levi, as with many other aspects of human life, virtues always turn out to be mixed: conscience returned in ordinary life and stalked him for the rest of his days.

7

Choices

I must have by then overcome the most terrible crisis, the crisis of having become part of the Lager system, and I must have developed a strange callousness if I then managed not only to survive but also to think, to register the world around me, and even to perform rather delicate work, in an environment infected by the daily presence of death.

—*The Periodic Table*

That evening I brought into camp the small rods and Alberto a metal plate with a round hole: it was the prescribed caliber to which we had to thin down the rods in order to transform them into flints [for lighters] and therefore bread. . . . We worked for three nights: nothing happened, nobody noticed our activity, nor did the blanket or pallet catch fire, and this is how we won the bread which kept us alive until the arrival of the Russians and how we comforted each other in the trust and friendship which united us.

—*The Periodic Table*

Primo Levi's observations in the Lager led him to conclude that the prisoners had very little latitude for choice and were forced into rigid patterns of conformity: "In reality, in the vast majority of cases, their behavior was rigidly preordained."[1] However, Levi and other prisoners found that even under such harsh and unconditional circumstances of slavery, they could use will and guile. Here we find Levi's ambivalence about existence that

---

1. *The Drowned and the Saved*, 49. Future references will be cited parenthetically in the text.

he expresses in *"Force Majeure."* We can do very little to recover our existence when crushed, yet it is not only possible to help our cause, but it is done daily.

The last chapter examined the unusual capacities the prisoners exhibited during extreme circumstances—capacities that helped prolong some of their lives and, coupled with colossal luck, managed to save a few. This chapter will explore in a preliminary way Levi's ideas about the actual possibilities and ethos of personal choice. The first section describes some methodological concerns that will help us to carry on an intelligent conversation. The second section initiates the investigation of Levi's ideas about choice by looking at his critique of existentialism, postmodernism, and the role of intellectuals in the Lager.[2] The chapter concludes with a discussion of some of Levi's other critical ideas about choice, which stem from his empiricism and some of his other domain assumptions. The theme of choice is not exhausted by this chapter and will be confronted again, especially in the chapters "Purpose and Work," "Optimistic Pessimism," and "A Defense of Modernism."

First, it must be understood that the word *survival* will be used in two senses, each exemplified separately by the English and Italian titles of his first book. The English title, *Survival in Auschwitz,* gives the impression that the work will be about the empirical theme of why some lived and others died in Auschwitz, truly one of the themes of his book. Earlier chapters have described the crushing circumstances the prisoners faced and the role of human nature in their survival. This chapter moves to consider some of the diversity of individual actions prisoners took to keep alive. Survival, in this sense, is staying alive.

Levi's Italian title, *Se questo e un uomo,* translates into "Is this a man," a title that raises the question of whether those who went through the experience of the Holocaust survived as moral beings. Survival as a moral being can be understood in two senses. First, under extreme circumstances, is there anything left of man as a moral being—the one who in the classical sense previously lived in cooperation and harmony with others? His audienced posed a second question about the survival of moral beings, which he felt compelled to answer: Did the prisoners do everything in their power to rebel or escape from their captivity? This chapter will investigate the possibility of moral choice in the Lager in both senses. Did the pris-

2. Levi rarely mentions his antagonist's names, and I will follow suit and not draw attention too far afield from Levi's own ideas.

oners have actual choices in terms of human solidarity, and was there actual room for resistance to the enemy? In sum, this chapter asks if some skills that they brought to the Lager and deliberate choices they made in the Lager could have helped the prisoners to physically survive the experience, and possibly prevented their loss of status as moral human beings. The reader cannot read Levi without turning the question on himself or herself in both senses, physical and moral survival: "Could I have 'survived?'"

The second methodological consideration is that we, as readers, have an impossible task. Putting ourselves in the shoes of another being, *verstehen,* is difficult enough, but it is virtually impossible to put ourselves in the shoes of a prisoner in Auschwitz. To do so, we would have to forget that genocide ever happened, forget what we know of the literature of resistance, and imagine unimaginable pain. Can we withstand physical pain better than mental anguish? In addition, there is a subjective element in us that we cannot fathom beforehand: "Now nobody can know for how long and under what trials his soul can resist before yielding or breaking. Every human being possesses a reserve of strength whose extent is unknown to him, be it large, small or nonexistent, and only through extreme adversity can we evaluate it" (*Drowned,* 60). *Verstehen* is all but impossible, but because the stakes are so high, we must try to answer these questions.[3]

When we try to understand Levi's critique of others who speak out on ideas of choice, we can begin to tease out Levi's preliminary ideas on the topic. This section will examine sequentially his critiques of choice in existentialism, postmodernism, and intellectualism.

As suggested throughout this work, Levi criticizes existential thought when he indicates that heroic acts of choice in the Lager so rarely happened that they are irrelevant to a discussion of Auschwitz. For Levi, choice, even under normal circumstances, is an impossible ideal that causes a good deal of grief. He points out the necessity of establishing a more reasonable basis for understanding the logic of choices.

For instance, he vehemently disagrees with Jean-Paul Sartre's idea that we can usefully distinguish between "good faith" and "bad faith" to judge those who are not making authentic decisions. Levi believes that

3. Here outsiders find themselves in a difficult position. Witnesses to the Holocaust obviously want readers to understand what happened, but witnesses can view readers' presumptions that they understand what Holocaust victims went through as statements of falsehood, acts of hubris.

assuming full responsibility for making sure that we are cleansed of self-deception is an impossible and harmful ideal.[4] Levi tries to fight off the existential and often, simultaneously, the deterministic psychoanalytic influences in thought. He argues against the existentialist's awesome responsibility for good faith on one end of the continuum, and the tendency in social science and modern linguistic criticism to throw out responsibility altogether on the other. Taking the middle ground is always difficult, yet the extremes must be countered.

Levi defines bad faith as follows: "They [perpetrators] lie knowing that they are lying: they are in bad faith." He admits to his revulsion at reading the justifications that the Nazis used. They all used variations of the same themes: "I did it because I was ordered to; others (my superiors) have committed acts worse than mine; in view of the upbringing I received, and the environment in which I lived, I could not have acted differently; had I not done it, another would have done it even more harshly in my place. For anyone who reads these justifications the first reaction is revulsion" (*Drowned*, 26).

This statement also shows the deterministic logic of social science, which blames events on the environment in which a person lives. At first glance, Levi's statement appears to propose that we are clear of mind and we know when we make decisions on the basis of good or bad faith. However, for Levi, reality is more complicated, because the good faith/bad faith distinction is a difficult ideal for most people. It presupposes a mental clarity that we usually can't achieve in ordinary life, and as Levi shows, the distinction was completely destroyed in the Lager:

> Now, anyone who has sufficient experience of human affairs knows that the distinction (the opposition, a linguist would say) good faith/bad faith is optimistic and smacks of the enlightenment, and is all the more so, and for much greater reason, when applied to men such as those just mentioned. It presupposes a mental clarity which few have and which even these few immediately lose when, for whatever reason, past or present reality arouses anxiety or discomfort in them. Under such conditions there are, it is true, those who lie consciously, coldly falsifying reality itself, but more numerous are those who weigh

---

4. Only where Levi specifically mentions someone's name do I also use the occasion to mention the name. For instance, in the prior sections there is an implicit critique by Levi of existential notions, but I will refrain from giving the opponent a face, something that might only be a guess on our part.

anchor, move off, momentarily or forever, from genuine memories, and fabricate for themselves a convenient reality. (*Drowned,* 26–27)

Thus, this process may begin consciously in bad faith as in his example above of the pat rationalizations, or less consciously from a more comfortable set of observations. Whatever the source of the ideas, after many repetitions they become sanitized, because "initial bad faith has become good faith." "Weighing anchor" on the truth has utility: "The silent transition from falsehood to self-deception is useful: anyone who lies in good faith is better off. He recites his part better, is more easily believed by the judge, the historian, the reader, his wife, and his children" (*Drowned,* 27).

Louis Darquier de Pellepoix, a member of the Vichy government who was responsible for the deportation of seventy thousand Jews, is a good example of one of those who "weighed anchor" on the truth. He denied everything. Levi says, "I think I can recognize in him the typical case of someone who, accustomed to lying in public, ends by lying in private too, to himself as well, and building for himself a comforting truth which allows him to live in peace" (*Drowned,* 28).

Men like Darquier cannot be expected to have the capacity to make a tough decision based on good and bad faith, because it is an extraordinary ideal that demands more than most can give. It is a discipline that few practice: "To keep good and bad faith distinct costs a lot: it requires a decent sincerity or truthfulness with oneself; it demands a continuous intellectual and moral effort" (*Drowned,* 28). Keeping from lying takes a deliberate effort of attention.

Levi suggests that people like Darquier and Adolph Eichmann, who came of age before National Socialism, have no excuses for what they did. They are responsible for their acts, and the distinction between good faith and bad faith adds little to explain why people must or must not be held accountable for their actions. They cannot use the excuse of not understanding right from wrong because they were brainwashed by a totalitarian regime. What matters for Levi is not whether everyone is guilty because they didn't hold to the high standard of good faith. Virtually everyone who did evil acts remembers the acts and should be punished, even though they "weigh anchor" on the meaning of these acts and have rationalized to themselves and others what the events mean: "It is generally difficult to deny having committed a given act, or that such an act was committed; it is, on the contrary, very easy to alter the motivations which led us to an act and the passions within us which accompanied the act itself" (*Drowned,* 31).

Thus, Levi does not excuse people from the choices they make; "weighing anchor" on the truth provides no mitigation for their actions. The crimes are real, they happened, people suffered and died, and the perpetrators must be punished. They are crimes against the flesh; the good faith/bad faith distinction is not the standard by which people are to be held accountable, for that distinction does not resolve actual cases.[5] It leaves us with only heroes and saints to be judged against the rest, and most of humanity falls short of the highest standards. The good faith/bad faith distinction would put nearly everyone in the criminal class, providing no useful moral distinction. In particular, the ethos of good faith/bad faith throws unnecessary guilt on the Lager residents.[6]

Levi disagrees on other grounds with existential thought. Unlike existentialists, he does not trust the sovereignty of individual judgment. As individuals we can make and must make judgments on the behavior of individuals, but the sovereign person may not be the best judge of his own behavior. Even if we bother to interrogate ourselves, most of us in the final analysis are not ruthless enough with ourselves. For this reason, we need civilization and discourse with others.

Levi argues that we should be free beings and that our actual choices can be used differentiate us as moral beings, from the saints and heroes to those in the "gray zone" to those clearly criminally responsible. Nietzsche and others made much of the importance of the massive self-assertion so necessary against a social order that tends to destroy choice and with it a creative human life. As with the Cartesian moment, we are the center of existence and must have the will to face down social circumstances that crush us.[7] Existentialists argue that such will is necessary for ordinary persons to resist totalitarian regimes like that of Germany. Those who seek to fight the heavy hand of technology and organization in our lives today use the same argument to bolster their morale.

Levi highly values individual actions, but he believes we must be accountable to others as well ourselves. In contrast to Nietzsche, he emphasizes the hubris in extolling individual choice to the exclusion of everyone

5. Obviously, this does not preclude holding ourselves accountable for good faith and bad faith if we so choose. Levi objects to using the distinction for judging others.

6. In Sartre's early writings, he scorns the psychoanalytic energies necessary to ferret out self-deception.

7. A careful reading shows Nietzsche argued that the individual who spiritualized instincts—for example, hate and lust into competition and love—should be considered exemplars.

else. He warns of the dangers of considering oneself the sole sovereign. Equally dangerous at the other end of the spectrum is falling for the pure virtue of decisiveness in others and in the process ignoring one's own reservations about others. Levi's critique of the precursors to existentialism like Nietzsche, as well as to his successors, like Sartre, is similar to that of the criticisms of Nikos Kazantzakis and Bertrand Russell. Civilization, and not the solitary self, must be the measure of man:

> Neither Nietzsche nor Hitler nor Rosenberg were mad when they intoxicated themselves and their followers by preaching the myth of the Superman to whom everything is permitted in recognition of his dogma and congenital superiority, but worthy of meditation is the fact that all of them, teachers and pupils, became progressively removed from reality common to all times and all civilizations, an integral part of our human heritage which in the end must be acknowledged. (*Drowned*, 106–7)

Nietzsche's voluntary restrictions of self-restraint do not work. In many cases, those who worship the idea of self-assertion and who are ignorant or "weigh anchor" on his calls for self-discipline ignore voluntary restrictions.

Contemporary analyses show the more subtle Nietzsche that Levi understood, the Nietzsche who saw his Zarathustra as one who is tormented by the idea that there is no God or external guidance and understands the tragedy of this predicament. The key is to tragically try for mastery of oneself. If one is successful in mastering oneself and bringing about a revaluation of values, one might cause some suffering, but not treat cruelty as an end in itself. With hindsight Levi saw Nietzsche's Alcibiades, Hitler, a pupil who understood just enough to incorporate the lessons of self-assertion from the master, but who did not pick up the nuances of the master's thought on tragedy and spiritualization.

Levi, an individualist himself, cannot ignore the inevitable tension in his own thought between individual choice and civilization, because he believes the dangers of complete isolation or separation from civilization can be fatal. Also, Levi knows he must face the tension between knowing and doing. Descartes and Hume see in advance the conflict between knowing and doing when they choose to postulate their ideas. However, they fall short of injecting the full consequences of their ideas into the public situation. Nietzsche, in contrast, is for Levi just another intellectual who followed his ideas through to their dangerous conclusions and ignored the dictates of social life.

Thus, although Levi acknowledges the importance of individual freedom, he is wary of existential ideas. The choosing individual cannot be trusted to discipline himself to become that tragic, self-controlled, and in the end generous being Nietzsche envisioned with his Zarathustra. If this being does not perfect self-control, then there is the possibility of another Alcibiades or Dionysus with no directive to live in accord with others. In addition, Sartre's exhortation to freedom does not give us a useful moral measure of man. In extreme situations, it sets a measure for saints and heroes and leaves the rest of us with no measure by which to judge our behavior. Good faith and bad faith are psychologically naïve concepts. Levi shows that most of us are incapable of making judgments about our own motives. When we judge ourselves we tend to weigh anchor on the truth or will ignorance. We are poor judges of ourselves, for true self-judgment is a rare act of courage.

Although Levi is put off by existential thought, as an individualist he shares ideas with many of these thinkers. Life is tragic, there is no God, and individual choice is a key element of our existence. His key difference with them is simply that man alone cannot be trusted.[8] Not only is it rare to fully discipline ourselves to self-control, but those who follow the footsteps of Zarathustra only part way are infused with hubris, not tragedy, and can convince others too easily that they are a present, living God.

Levi also finds himself in disagreement with postmodernists, thinkers who are poised at the opposite end of a continuum of initiative and action. For some postmodernists, man is nowhere to be found, and if he exists, he is incapable of making judgments. Levi mentions no theorists or schools of thought directly in *The Drowned and the Saved,* but he makes clear that he does not want the vagueness of language or the possibility of multiple perspectives to erode the notion of truth and therefore diminish the significance of the Holocaust. Levi is not unsympathetic to the problems of knowing; he simply expresses them in a very different way. We must make choices, but as humans we do not have the appropriate tools and complex reality does not cooperate either to allow us to decide with

8. Levi makes no comment on Sartre's Kantian ethics for the individual, but from Levi's point of view it would appear to suffer, as does Nietzsche's thought, from making the person the sole judge of his or her conduct.

absolute certainty. However difficult choice is—for humans, it is tragic—judgment is necessary.

This section will try to convey Levi's critique of incommunicability in postmodern thought. The final part of this section will show how Levi uses categories of body and mind to give an interesting twist to Michel Foucault's sequence of the punishment of the body and then the reconstruction of the mind as successive stages of modern disciplinary procedures.[9]

Incommunicability was in vogue in the 1970s in Europe: "'Incommunicability' supposedly was an inevitable ingredient, a life sentence inherent to the human condition, particularly in the life style of industrial society: we are monads, incapable of reciprocal messages, or capable only of truncated messages, false at their departure, misunderstood on their arrival." Levi, in light of his personal experiences, takes great exception to its use: "To say that it is impossible to communicate is false; one always can. To refuse to communicate is a failing; we are biologically and socially predisposed to communication, and in particular to its highly evolved and noble form, which is language." He believes that the human condition and industrial society are not absolute barriers to communication: "It seems to me that this lament originates in and points to mental laziness; certainly it encourages it, in a dangerous vicious cycle." The view is frivolous to Levi because we only can afford to hold it if we believe that all views are what Georg Groddeck called "luxury views," ones that make no difference with respect to reality. It is an affectation. If we get out of the habit of trying to communicate, mistrust builds among us.[10] "Except for cases of pathological incapacity, one can and must communicate, and thereby contribute in a useful and easy way to the peace of others and oneself, because silence, the absence of signals, is itself a signal, but an ambiguous one, and ambiguity generates anxiety and suspicion" (*Drowned*, 89).

Thus, in normal society, incommunicability is a frivolous affectation, because we always have time to establish the natural connections to one another through language. In contrast with this "affectation," Levi remembers a time when the failure to communicate happened absolutely and with fatal consequences: "I find it imperative to intervene precisely when I hear people talking about failed or impossible communication. 'You should have experienced ours.'" There are degrees of possible communi-

---

9. Foucault, *Discipline and Punish*, 7–10, 19.
10. Groddeck, *The Book of the It*, 134.

cation with others, and few have ever experienced the total failure of communication with all its brutal consequences: "In today's normal world, which by convention and contrast we call from time to time 'civilized' or 'free,' one almost never encounters a total linguistic barrier, that is, finds oneself facing a human being with whom one must absolutely establish communication or die, and then is unable to do so" (*Drowned,* 89, 88).

This linguistic barrier, the inability to understand one's captors, can lead to death. In the Lager, "one is surrounded by a perpetual Babel, in which everyone shouts orders and threats in languages never heard before, and woe betide whoever fails to grasp their meaning. No one has time here, no one has patience, no one listens to you; we latest arrivals instinctively collect in the corners, against the walls, afraid of being beaten." Prisoners perished quickly if they did not understand the orders of the SS guards.[11] If the prisoners answered the guards, even in a halting German, they could establish some rudimentary relationship. If the prisoners didn't understand the language, the SS became enraged and "an order that had been pronounced in the calm voice of a man who knows he will be obeyed was repeated word for word in a loud, angry voice, then screamed at the top of his lungs as if he were addressing a deaf person or indeed a domestic animal, more responsive to the tone than the content of the message" (*Drowned,* 91). It was learn or die; this is incommunicability to Levi. The German was a bastardized German, peculiar to the Lager. Learning enough German to understand the most rudimentary orders was so important that Levi gave up precious bread rations to have someone teach him to understand the commands.

In contrast, modern problems of communication are a mere annoyance and can be resolved in dialogue. This is Levi's answer to incommunicability. He, along with postmodernists, struggles with the ambiguities of language, but in his own way. For instance, in the same pages where he speaks of incommunicability, he mentions the barrier between the survivor and his children when the latter say that they are hungry, cold, or tired. The children are using words that don't apply to what the survivors felt: "What do you know about it? You should have gone through what we did. In general, for reasons of good taste and good neighborliness, we try to resist the temptation of such *miles gloriosus* interventions" (*Drowned,* 89).

---

11. Levi, *Survival in Auschwitz,* 38. Death comes less from the physical effects of the beating and more from the total confusion and demoralization that comes from the inability to understand and communicate. Future references to Levi's *Survival* will be cited parenthetically in the text.

He addresses this problem formally and suggests that different experiences lead to the development of different vocabularies:

> Just as our hunger is not that feeling of missing a meal, so our way of being cold has need of a new word. We say "hunger," we say "tiredness," "fear," "pain," we say "winter" and they are different things. They are free words, created and used by free men who lived in comfort and suffering in their homes. If the Lagers had lasted longer a new, harsh language would have been born; and only this language could express what it means to toil the whole day in the wind, with the temperature below freezing, wearing only a shirt, underpants, cloth jacket and trousers, and in one's body nothing but weakness, hunger and knowledge of the end drawing nearer. (*Survival*, 123)

The problem is not permanent incommunicability but making oneself understood, even if the existing concepts are not quite up to the task. Instead of words to describe severe deprivation, words that are inadequate to the task, he formulates longer descriptions that try to come closer to the experienced reality. In Wittgenstein's sense, he supplies a broader context for understanding. These descriptions always remain somewhat inadequate, for although Levi finds language indispensable, and comprehensible, it is still an imperfect tool.

In his essays on writing, Levi discusses the difficulties of lucid expression and acknowledges the necessity to be clear so that the text is unambiguous to others: "One should not write in an obscure manner, because a piece of writing has all the more value and all the more hope of diffusion and permanence, the better it is understood and the less it lends itself to equivocal interpretations." Speaking the language of the heart is no excuse, because "he who is not understood by anyone does not transmit anything, he cries in the desert." Occasionally, someone's obscure style is fully reflective of his circumstances and cannot be helped. He puts Paul Celan, a Holocaust poet, in this category and indicates that Celan's obscure writings are not due to the common mistakes with respect to clarity: "Celan's obscurity is neither contempt for the reader, nor expressive inadequacy, nor lazy abandonment to the flow of the unconscious; it truly is a reflection of the obscurity of his fate and his generation, and it grows ever denser around the reader." Levi doesn't deny the allurement of such work, because "[i]t attracts us as chasms attract us, but at the same time it also defrauds us of something that should have been said and was not, and so it frustrates and turns us away." Levi concludes, "If his [Celan's] is a message, it gets lost in the 'background noise': it is not a communication, it is not a language, or at most it is a dark and truncated language precisely like that of a person who is about to die and is alone, as we all will be at the point of death."[12]

Clarity is a personal obligation for Levi: "As long as we live we have a responsibility; we must answer for what we write, word by word, and make sure that every word reaches its target." He expresses a preference for clear writing, which must enter the marketplace with the ideas of authors who write obscurely or defend such obscurity: "Discourse among men in the tongue of men is preferable to the animal whine and it is hard to see why it should be less poetic than the whine. But, I repeat, these are preferences of mine, not standards."[13] In his typical open way, he feels it is necessary to speak one's mind though truth is far from certain. As we might expect, he always leaves the door open to other interpretations: "Whoever writes is free to choose the language or nonlanguage that suits him best, and everything is possible: writing which is obscure for its own author may be luminous and open for him who reads; and the writing not understood by its contemporaries may become clear and illustrious decades and centuries later."[14]

Levi therefore believes the obligation of the writer is to make his thoughts clear to the reader. Communication, unless it is simply to oneself, involves the receptivity of the reader or listener: "My 'perfect' reader is not a scholar but neither is he an ignoramus; he does not read because he has to, nor as a pastime, nor to make a splash in society, but because he is curious about many things, wishes to choose among them, and does not wish to delegate this choice to anyone." Unfortunately, the current explosion of texts engulfs the "perfect" reader. Today "all writing is smothered in a few months by the mob of other writings which push up behind it."[15]

Levi's audience changed significantly over time, due to the surplus of writings and increase of new interests. After all, what is Levi's perspective on the Holocaust to the young? In the beginning, they seriously listened and made up their own minds, but over time they became increasingly blasé and skeptical. Today, the writer has to work harder to reach his audience. There are a plethora of perspectives and explanations and no seeming urgency to act on what we read. Levi's ideas comprise merely one more

12. Levi, *Other People's Trades*, 107, 171, 173–74.
13. Ibid., 174, 175.
14. Ibid., 169.
15. Ibid., 74–77.

perspective along with the surfeit of others. Bewildered, readers—encouraged by postmodern motifs—have a tendency to give up the difficult task of weighing one set of views against all the others. Levi's "perfect" reader who reads, evaluates, and decides no longer exists.

Levi understands the problem of incommunicability, but he feels that it is merely another of the agonies of existence: one must gather courage to write, and the reader must take responsibility for reading intelligently. It is vital for him to get the story across. We must be aware of the consequences of people's uncivilized behavior and attempt to change it. The concluding chapters will deliberate on the political consequences of being unable to capture the discerning reader's attention.

In addition to incommunicability, Levi faces another postmodern critique, one just brushed upon above. There is no firm way to choose among the myriad of stories that are told about the past and future public situation. Fact and fiction bleed together. All becomes discourse, or if you like, story; all writing becomes fiction.[16] Our postmodern world may be described in many stories with no privileged organizing narrative. Each of our many selves operates in separate narratives, with no central self or focal view of the world. In this collage of discourses the "civilized" miss any sense of community or self, but of course these are not to be lamented, because they too are simply part of an older narrative, the modernist perspective. Roughly, this seems to be the set of postmodern ideas Levi is intent on criticizing.

For Levi, existentialism is not knowing and yet choosing through will in the potential service of oneself. Postmodernism is not privileging any ideas and thus not having a firm basis for knowing and choosing. Levi, the tragic pluralist, finds himself between the postmodernist on one side, and the existentialist and the Manichean on the other. His tragic approach shares some of the doubts of postmodernists, but ultimately he retreats from their views because of the lack of a theory of action. Acceptance of postmodern ideas would throw what we know about the Holocaust into confusion.[17]

16. Of course, any story may be weakened. He speaks, as we have said, on the erosion of memory, the denigration of the victim, and the passage of time, among others. Levi has dealt with them, as we have shown, in order to come to what he sees as necessary conclusions.

17. This consequence is also a thorn for postmodernists who do not know what to do when people discuss the Holocaust, for it is always embarrassing to speak of the passionate testimony of survivors as merely another story.

Levi understands the postmodern insights about the intricate links between knowledge and power. He recognizes that in the Lager, the prisoners were Hobbesian beings always looking for ways to fulfill their varied ends and using what they knew against all the others. Yet Levi hopes that in ordinary times, we will be able to gather the courage and distance to flesh out differences between knowledge and power in a public forum.

In his understanding of fiction, Levi finds sympathy with postmodern views and then establishes his difference with them. Initially, postmodern assumptions free the writer from restricting canons by suggesting that everything is fiction, and there is no judging one against other. Levi happily acknowledges that the writer of fiction creates the text and the rules by which he would like to be judged, creating the writer's solitude with his creation and his awesome responsibilities. Levi then finds his difference with postmodernists because he wants to make a distinction between fictional and factual writing. In factual writing, the writer agrees to many conventions of scientific reporting. These rules are perfectly arbitrary to postmodernists, and Levi is inclined to agree, but he sides with modernists in suggesting a community of scholars is necessary but may be supplanted through reasoned discourse.

However, as a pluralist he inclines slightly toward postmodernism when he agrees that different people can view the same events differently. For example, as already stated, he says that survivors have a peculiar position from which to view Auschwitz. Their views can be compared with those who see a greater part of the concentrationary universe, those who see it as co-conspirators, and those who now see it in a greater historical perspective with all the benefits and deficits conferred by the passage of time. The survivor at the bottom sees the Holocaust differently from the privileged prisoners. Levi knows what a difficult task it is for humans to understand and judge events in which they have a powerful stake and how perspectives may be difficult to compare with one another. However, the difficulties must be overcome as well as possible.

Perhaps we can understand Levi's thinking by seeing it through the modernist perspective elaborated by Alfred North Whitehead. Whitehead describes four modes of looking at the world. The first, looking at the world as facts, is a mode where Levi knows there can be dispute, but reasonable people can draw similar conclusions. For instance, it is possible to look at the facts of the Holocaust and come close to agreement on how many people died and where. Matters of fact may give way to new data, but it is clear when the events happened, where they happened, who committed them, and how many died. A community of scholars agrees upon key definitions of concepts. Some may dispute these facts out of naïveté or vicious motives, but we have established methods of thought and observation at our disposal to settle disputes among reasonable people.[18]

Levi is in concert with Isaiah Berlin in arguing that agreements on truth can be established, even with severe differences in culture.[19] Levi is not naïve about the difficulties of the task. We have discussed the difficulties language may present to the analyst, and Levi goes to great pains to show how different groups may see the same events differently. In the end, however, these views can be reconciled with one another. Whitehead suggests that facts are not analytically separate from other ways we have of looking at the world. Levi, along with Berlin and other pluralists, believes that keeping them separate and trying to make choices is difficult, maybe even tragic, but for consequential reasons it must be done.

The second way we see the world is to look for purpose within groups and in individuals. In postmodern thought, purpose is not analytically separate from the other categories, especially the category of fact. Even if an individual or group claims to objectively search for facts, postmodernists believe that ultimately the purpose of knowledge is for reasons of power. Purpose, which infects any inquiry, is brought to light in postmodernists, modern-day successors to Thrasymachus. Not only is it possible that the search for truth masks the purposes of power from other individuals, but most individuals do not even know that they are fooling themselves. Students of the mind like Georg Groddeck and Jacques Lacan have serious doubts as to whether we can understand much about ourselves.

Levi sympathizes with postmodernists and others who find difficulty in understanding purpose in human beings, but at this juncture he seriously parts company with them. The difficulty in understanding motives does not keep us from the basic understanding of the facts, he argues. The discovery of purpose has always been a problem in the search for knowledge about human beings. It is simply the restatement of an old and difficult problem.

The formidable task of untangling the snarl of human motives is basic to understanding. Motives are important in predicting future behavior as well as in affixing responsibility for terrible acts. Levi canvasses the mo-

18. Whitehead, *Modes of Thought*, passim.
19. Berlin, *The Crooked Timber of Humanity*, 70–90. See also Whitehead, *Science and the Modern World*, 82.

tives that Holocaust scholars and others have considered since the war, and he tries to understand which are true motives and which are rationalizations. To shed more light on the subject, he cleverly describes the process of "weighing anchor on the truth," which may be a way of understanding why the perpetrator himself does not know his motives. We can reasonably disagree why something happened: Was it the imperatives of culture, base motives, group processes, or individual evil? As shown earlier, it is even up for debate as to whether the analyst wants to understand evil, because his social science perspective tends to diminish the responsibility of the culprits. Reasonable people can still look at what happened and come to some agreement as to why, as well as the punishment for those who executed the deeds. The pragmatic task of enforcing the law, which may mitigate the consequences for perpetrators or bring reward to heroes, pushes us to understand motives. The raw facts of a case are in a different category for Levi, as well as for Whitehead, and cannot be disputed in the same way as motive. Facts may be theory laden and not simply a mirror of the mind, but these are not new problems, ones we need to give up on. He will not give up on his empiricism. Too great are the dangers to the flesh.

Levi's ideas on purpose and cause are pivotal to understanding his modernist position. Here his critique of postmodernism is most pointed. His most thorough methodological discussion of purpose and cause is in a short essay, "Why Does One Write?":

> It often happens that a reader, usually a young person, will ask a writer, in all simplicity, why he has written a certain book, or why he has written in this way, or even, more generally, why he writes and why writers write. To this last question, which contains all the others, there is no easy answer: not always is a writer aware of the reasons that induce him to write, not always is he impelled by only one reason, not always do the same reasons stand behind the beginning and the end of the same work. It seems to me that at least nine motivations can be identified and I will try to describe them . . . [20]

Levi goes on to list and describe these purposes, for example: the irresistible urge to write, to entertain, to "teach something to someone," to "become rich," or to write "out of habit."[21]

In establishing why he and others write, Levi tries to discern purposes

---

20. Levi, "Why Does One Write?" in *Other People's*, 74.
21. Ibid., 74–77.

and establish which ones are most important. He obviously subscribes to "overdetermination" in establishing the causes of an event: "Overdetermination is descriptive of the fact that a phenomenon may be caused by more than one factor, some being more important than others."[22] Levi notes that his list of nine reasons for writing cannot possibly exhaust all the possible candidates. His essay is rich with ideas about how we decide on causes, for ourselves or for others, often by cutting through self-delusion. Here, as in other places, he shows a great deal of psychological understanding. We can eliminate those causes that seem too self-serving by distinguishing cause from rationalization: "To become famous. I believe that only a madman would sit down to write just to become famous, but I also believe that no writer, not even the most unassuming, not even the least presumptuous, not even the angelic Carroll mentioned above, was ever untouched by this motivation."[23]

We have other ways to try to eliminate alternative causes of events and decide which ones are primary in deciding circumstances. As tied as he is to scientific generalization, Levi also understands the contingent nature of cause when he uses the example of Cleopatra's nose to indicate how history turns on chance. In his example, he raises the question of how different history would have been had Cleopatra been born with a large nose. In terms of chance in his own life, he gives the example of his never having scarlet fever as a child.

In his essay "The Best Goods," Levi reiterates his belief that we can find primary causes in our analyses: "There is one constant in Judaism, which operates in every time and place, and it is the importance which for centuries has been given to education." This is in answer to his own question, "Where did they get this strong voice, which issued from such a small social body?" Toward the end of the essay, where he has discussed educational importance in Judaism, he allows for other causes: "Certainly there have been and are other cements: religion, collective memory, common history, tradition, persecution itself, and the isolation imposed from outside. A counter proof of this is the fact that, when all these factors become attenuated or disappear, the Judaic identity in turn becomes attenuated, and the communities tend to dissolve, as happened in Weimar Germany and is happening in Italy today."[24]

22. Ludwig Eidelberg, *Encyclopedia of Psychoanalysis*, 288.
23. Levi, "Why Does One Write," 77.
24. Levi, "The Best Goods," in *Other People's*, 83, 82, 85.

Cause is overdetermined, but the important causes can be determined: "I believe that, as always in the story of human affairs, there is not a single cause but rather an interlacing of causes; but among these, one seems to me to prevail."[25]

The key for Levi is not that he is correct all of the time, but that to operate in the world we must make such choices; arguing for one's perspective can be healthy for ideas. This reinforces John Stuart Mill's liberal notion that ideas unchallenged tend to grow stale, cliché, and irrelevant. It is the path to making a virtue out of disagreement instead of concluding that choice is impossible. For Levi, the oppositions are now, and have always been, inevitable.

Human explanation always lies beyond our grasp, but reason and language can be used to make reality roughly comprehensible. Alexis de Tocqueville believed that only God could understand the world in its individuality. Human beings need to simplify reality in order to understand it. Along the same lines, Aristotle indicated that a key to understanding politics is not to go beyond what the data tells us; it is an imprecise science. Levi concurs: "What we commonly mean by 'understand' coincides with 'simplify': without a profound simplification the world around us would be infinite, undefined tangle that would defy our ability to orient ourselves and decide upon our actions" (*Drowned*, 36).

Simplification is not perfect understanding, but a task we must forever pursue: "In short, we are compelled to reduce the knowable to schema: with this purpose in view we have built for ourselves admirable tools in the course of evolution, tools which are the specific property of the human species—language and conceptual thought. We also tend to simplify history" (*Drowned*, 36).

Levi's judgment is always measured. Just as we can give up on the chaos of the world and not even bother to understand it, on the other hand we can go too far with our simplifications. As noted earlier, Levi expresses the fear of oversimplification when he stresses the Manichean tendency in man. He points out that good and evil oversimplify the role of those involved in the Holocaust, for there was a vast gray zone of behaviors. Yet, he knowingly walks a tightrope when discussing cause and blame for the Holocaust. He reviles those who blur the distinction between good and evil in the matter of violence and the Holocaust, and he tries to prevent the discourse from degenerating into a mere listing of perspectives. It takes

25. Ibid., 82–83.

firm resolve to settle between a Manichean position on one pole, and on the other pole, a way of thought that allows an equal footing to all discourses. His disciplined pluralism is a more nuanced view of the motives of the participants. Levi recognizes that there are not two or three perspectives as he suggests in the chapter on the gray zone; reality is multilayered, and our job is to disentangle the layers and finally make choices.

Whitehead's last two categories are value and ideals. Levi intuitively understands the interrelationship of Whitehead's categories and the necessity to keep them separate in analysis. In our thoughts and action, purpose can get tangled up with what Whitehead calls "value." We put value on most things of the world, but often this does not correspond with what we see as their purpose. Levi's work is an attempt to understand the facts, discern purposes, and affix value. These tasks invite great difficulty, but they are not insurmountable to the modernist Levi.

Whitehead poses ideals as the final mode of thought that helps define the way we look at the world. Levi, as we have suggested, feels that clinging to certain ideals without any tragic perspective can be extremely destructive. At the other extreme, if ideals and purposes dissolve in a methodological heap and we are left with no guides to action, we become consequences of other's ideals and purposes. We will continue to have something to say about those who hold to irrational ideals or those who abandoned some reasonable basis of choice, rival theories to Levi's courageous, disciplined pluralism.

Existentialism and postmodernism influence Levi a great deal. He cants toward existentialism in stressing the existence and importance of the individual, and toward postmodernism in opening up analysis to a myriad of ways to look at human behavior. However, he believes that the existential and postmodern stances also open up the possibilities for influencing human behavior in very undesirable ways. It is one thing for the existentialist to push the limits of our freedom, but it is another to go as far as to assume that we should be the sole judge of our behavior. Postmodern thought is an affectation if it presumes possible motives for behavior when there is virtually no empirical evidence for existence of these motives. In addition, it opens the door to the cruel but convinced tyrants when we throw up our hands at the difficulties of language and refrain from making choices.

In summary, Levi's scientific method of analysis and his hedonism are squarely within modernism. His pluralism acknowledges the complexities of the world and the difficulties faced by finite man in making determina-

tions of fact, purpose, and value. Rather than agree that one must abandon doing, or at least doing on the basis of knowing, Levi seems closer to
Ortega y Gasset's position of integral truth than to existentialists or postmodernists. Ortega y Gasset writes, "[T]he peculiar property of every living being, the individual difference, far from impeding the capture of truth,
is precisely the organ by which the specially corresponding portion of reality is perceived." He goes on to say: "Integral truth is only obtained by
linking up what I see with what my neighbour sees, and so on successively. Each individual is an essential point of view in the chain."[26] The ag-
gregation of ideas is inductive, and the methods are scientific. Levi and Ortega y Gasset hold to the view that knowledge is intelligible, and although
laced with uncertainties, it is necessary to gather in order to have a basis
for action. Levi pulls back from the possibilities of action for action's sake
or the pure play of different discourses, directions in which his pluralism,
if stretched into postmodernism, could lead him. For Levi, existentialism
and postmodernism are luxury views that we cannot afford in the modern
world.

Levi's scientific analysis and his hedonism carry him to his courageous
pluralism. Defense of the flesh is the imperative that impels him to action.
Acting assumes that we can be responsible, at least in part, for what happens to us. Although our feeling for others is not our strongest impulse,
perhaps we can be taught to care about what happens to others. If not, at
least we can see that their fate is wrapped up with our own, and that it is
in our self-interest to provide for the welfare of others.

Levi clearly questions the judgment of contemporary intellectuals in his
writings, and not only existentialists and postmodernists. He asks the type
of question Isaiah Berlin so nicely asks: Does knowledge of politics guarantee that the possessor will have good judgment with respect to practical
affairs? Both Levi and Berlin answer no.[27] Additionally, in *The Drowned
and the Saved,* Levi asks whether the knowledge of intellectuals helped
them survive better than others in the Lager. His discussion centers on the
definition of the intellectual stated by a fellow Holocaust survivor, Jean
Améry. Améry's intellectual is the disinterested scholar most interested in
knowledge for knowledge's sake: "An intellectual, as I would like it to be
understood here, is a man who lives within a system of reference which is

26. José Ortega y Gasset, *The Modern Theme,* 94–95.
27. See Berlin, "On Political Judgment," 26.

spiritual in the broadest sense. The sphere of his associations is essentially humanist and philosophical. His esthetic consciousness is well developed. By inclination and aptitude he is attracted by abstract thought. . . .
If one talks to him about 'society,' he understands the term in its sociological but not worldly sense" (Améry quoted in *Drowned*, 131).

Levi believes Améry's definition is restrictive in two ways. First, "I
would say it is more appropriate that in the term *intellectual* be included,
for example, also the mathematician or the naturalist or the philosopher
of science." Second, it should be distinguished by a far-reaching curiosity
and not have an arbitrary bias against practicality: "I would propose to
extend the term to the person educated beyond his daily trade, whose culture is alive inasmuch as it makes an effort to renew itself, increase itself,
and keep up to date, and who does not react with indifference or irrita-
tion when confronted by any branch of knowledge, even though, obviously, he cannot cultivate all of them." Although he never formally refers
to pragmatism, Levi's intellectual will apply his knowledge to the pressing
problems of existence and not ignore the flesh in his accounts by remaining wrapped in his own abstractions. Levi suggests,

> [i]n any case, whichever definition one may choose, one can only agree
> with Améry's conclusions. At work, which was prevalently manual,
> the cultivated man generally was much worse off than the uncultivat-
> ed man. Aside from physical strength, he lacked familiarity with the
> tools and the training, which, however, his worker or peasant com-
> panion often had; in contrast, he was tormented by an acute sense of
> humiliation and destitution" (*Drowned*, 132).[28]

In addition, the intellectual had to overcome his confrontation with
brute reality. This was especially difficult for the intellectual of the type envisioned by Améry: "The philosopher too, says Améry, could arrive at acceptance, but by a longer route. He could perhaps break down the barrier of common sense that forbade him to accept a too ferocious reality as
true; he could, finally, admit, living in a monstrous world, that monsters
do exist and that alongside Cartesian logic there existed the logic of the
SS" (*Drowned*, 144).

The manual worker with no illusions could use his skill to survive and
not have to overcome any idyllic dreams. Levi puts forth the most serious
problem for the abstract intellectual in a quote he takes from Améry:

28. The concluding chapters will greatly expand on Levi's views.

> Thus the fundamental spiritual tolerance and methodical doubt of the
> intellectual became factors of self-destruction. Yes, the SS were enti-
> tled to do what they did: natural right does not exist, and moral cat-
> egories are born and die with the fashion. There was a Germany that
> sent Jews and political adversaries to their death because it considered
> that only in this way could it realized itself. And so? Greek civilization
> too was based on slavery, and an Athenian army had set up its bar-
> racks in Melos just as the SS did in the Ukraine. Human victims were
> murdered in unheard-of numbers, so far as history's lights can illumine
> the past, and in any case the perennial quality of human progress was
> but a naiveté born in the nineteenth century. (*Drowned,* 144)

Primo Levi agrees with Améry and feels that intellectuals often abandon the field to evil: "This surrender before the intrinsic horror of the past
could lead the scholarly man to intellectual abdication, furnishing him at
the same time with the defensive weapons of his uncultivated companion:
'It has always been like this, always will be like this'" (*Drowned,* 144).

Levi slyly finds his difference with Améry. The two agree that intellectuals, especially the ones who do not get their hands dirty with realities,
were at a distinct disadvantage in the Lager. Levi, however, believes that
some may have their intelligence attuned to realities. He sarcastically suggests: "Nevertheless, unlike Améry and others, my feelings of humiliation
due to manual work was moderate; evidently I still was not 'intellectual'
enough" (*Drowned,* 133). Levi's analysis of intellectuals is pointedly
aimed at those of the intellectualist tradition subjected to critique by
Dewey and Ortega y Gasset, individuals secure in social status and free of
worldly concerns who have little time for the flesh-and-bone world.

This explains why Levi is appalled by the postmodern shift in thinking.
In spinning their own theories, they too often ignore their own flesh. The
problem with the intellectual who freezes himself out of the action is that
he leaves the field open to those extremely dangerous individuals who espouse certainties. A courageous pragmatism is needed to counter both
those who can't choose and those who choose too easily.

Many of Levi's preliminary ideas on choice have been drawn out
through his discussions concerning existentialism, postmodernism, and intellectualism. Now we will move on to some other scattered insights about
choice. First, there is a practical element in Levi's thoughts, which may be
expressed as follows: If we practice Aristotelian habituation by accus-
toming ourselves to tools that can be used against adversity, can we resist
future terrors? Levi is confident that the understanding of extreme cir-

cumstances, accompanied by testing of our skills and tenacity against adversity, will allow us to better endure. The known is always preferable to the unknown with respect to danger.

For example, the habituation to adversity, the Aristotelian sense of learning, is useful in the face of prospective terrors. As suggested, he felt his hikes into the wilderness with Sandro were useful in teaching him to deal with the unforeseen in the Lager. "He dragged me along on exhausting treks through the fresh snow, far from any sign of human life, following routes that he seemed to intuit like a savage. . . . What mattered was to know his limitations, to test and improve himself; more obscurely, he felt the need to prepare himself (and to prepare me) for an iron future, drawing closer month by month." Levi acknowledges the debt to Sandro: "That is why I am grateful to Sandro for having led me consciously into trouble, on that trip and other undertakings which were only apparently foolish, and I am certain that they helped me later on."[29]

As his experience with Sandro shows, preparing for contingencies can be useful. If nothing else, thorough readiness can give a sense of peace in the face of impending adversity. In a short story by Arthur Conan Doyle, a terrified protagonist finds himself locked in a cage with a leopard. After he does all he can to find the most secure place in the cage—it is not possible to find a spot beyond the reach of the leopard—he finds himself at peace.[30] For these reasons, we like to know what is ahead of us; we try to foresee by putting ourselves in the place of others and simulating responses to the situations they face. Only actual circumstances will give us a measure of ourselves, but preliminary preparations may prove to be useful. Peace of mind among the survivors depends on the choices they made in the Lager. The damning question was for all concerned: "In my own eyes and the sight of others, did I do all that I could do?"

Secondly, can our divided self be reconciled, or better yet, can our better self win out in the choices we make? We have already met with the tragedy of ill-constituted beings, the tragedy of confronting the obstacles of the external world, and the fact that we can never achieve complete happiness. Here Levi adds another tragedy to thinking about our existence, the tragedy of our divided selves. One part of the self remembers the lessons of civilization and believes that living a virtuous life is reward in itself. The other self wants to give in to extreme pain for more comfort and

29. Levi, *The Periodic Table*, 45, 48.
30. Doyle, *Tales of Terror and Mystery*, 101.

a better chance at survival. Uniting one part of the self to our "better self" is hard enough when terrible circumstances are not dragging us down. In the Lager, it was virtually impossible.

In Western thought this is the tragedy of ideals, Tocqueville's fugitive perfections, or Hobbes's strivings of power after power. In Hindu philosophy, it is called *dukkha,* the continual striving that can never be satisfied. William James calls the inability to satisfy the self the "habit of inferiority to the full self." For those with a conscience, guilt over the lack of courage, the failure of nerve, is stowed and does not fade.

In the extreme conditions Levi talks about, the side of the self that resists doing the "right thing" has much aid from brutal circumstances. What bedevils Levi is that in times of peace, when privation fades from the mind and it is easier to comply with the dictates of conscience, the public often applies the morality of peacetime to the actions that took place in terrible times. If we recur to an example from the previous chapter regarding guilt, this full dynamic can be seen at work. In short, an acquaintance of Primo Levi spots him taking clean water out of a pipe with no intention of sharing it with this acquaintance, but only with his friend Alberto. After liberation, this acquaintance asks Levi, "Why the two of you and not I? It was the 'civilian' moral code surfacing again" (*Drowned,* 80). Levi wonders: "Is this belated shame justified or not? I was not able to decide then and I am not able to decide even now, but shame there was and is, concrete, heavy, perennial" (*Drowned,* 81). This shame is so devastating, because there is no overcoming it. Metaphorically in *"Force Majeure,"* shame attaches to the civilian in the alley. He is crushed by the boot and never recovers. The rational arguments that counter shame—for instance, that virtually none resisted the terror and that almost nobody shared in the Lager—are ineffective against shame. Nor was the realization that the Lager brought on a fatalism that affected all the prisoners any consolation: "[I]t is obvious that whoever is too weak, or naked or barefoot, thinks and feels in a different way, and what dominated our thoughts was the paralyzing sensation of being totally helpless in the hands of fate" (*Survival,* 155). When the morality of ordinary times returned to become the standard for judging behavior in the Lager, nothing worked for the survivors to abolish the shame.

William James describes the psychological circumstances in ordinary life that make it difficult to live up to the ideal of the full self and hence leave guilt in its wake:

> Stating the thing broadly, the human individual thus lives usually far
> within his limits; he possesses powers of various sorts which he ha-
> bitually fails to use. He energizes below his *maximum,* and he behaves
> below his *optimum.* In elementary facility, in co-ordination, in power
> of *inhibition* and control, in every conceivable way, his life is con-
> tracted like the field of vision of an hysteric subject—but with less ex-
> cuse, for the poor hysteric is diseased, while in the rest of us it is only
> an inveterate *habit*—the habit of inferiority to our full self—that is
> bad.[31]

James's man is full of strivings that will go unfulfilled, whether it is to
be a "better person," a more diligent worker, or a more accurate recorder
of events. James then asks to what do beings owe their escape? "Either
some unusual stimulus fills them with emotional excitement, or some unusual idea of necessity induces them to make an extra effort of will. *Ex-
citements, ideas, and efforts,* in a word, are what carry us over the dam."[32]

He goes on to suggest that "habit neurosis" constricts our lives, and
that we all suffer from it to a degree: "Turning from more chronic to acuter
proofs of human nature's reserves of power, we find that the stimuli that
carry us over the usually effective dam are most often the classic emotional
ones, love, anger, crowd-contagion or despair. Despair lames most people,
but it wakes others full up."[33]

Culture influences this aspiration for ideals and the despair over their
fugitive nature. Alexis de Tocqueville stresses the cultural root of ideals
where he perceives the striving for self-perfection as an integral result of
living in a democratic culture. The more equality is advocated, the more
individuals strive against their neighbors and themselves to succeed at
endeavors that would distinguish them from others. The fact that man
improves has been with us from our beginnings, but in aristocracies we
have a different notion of personal progress than in democracies: "Not,
indeed, that an aristocratic people absolutely deny man's faculty of self-
improvement, but they do not hold it to be indefinite; they can conceive
amelioration, but not change." In a democracy there is the notion of infinite possibilities and men continually pursue fugitive perfections: "Aristocratic nations are naturally too liable to narrow the scope of human

31. James, *The Writings of William James,* 674.
32. Ibid., 674.
33. Ibid., 676.

perfectibility; democratic nations, to expand it beyond reason."[34] Finally, this penchant for ideals may be subject to cultural influences, but it may also have deeper roots. Even in Eastern countries, where practice exists to overcome the self and its personal ambitions, the striving self is extremely difficult to uproot.

In the Lager, the guilt from not living up to the full self clearly leaves permanent scars. Even in ordinary life, the satisfaction of this self does not make for unbridled happiness. New obstacles always crowd in to be conquered. The self does not long enjoy glory and peace. As the concluding chapters will show, Levi argues that we must modify our belief in perfection with the understanding that to approach one's ideals is an agonic struggle.

For Levi, in contrast to others, the choice itself is not the agony, but rather the inability of the present acting self to carry through the actions in order to satisfy the fugitive perfections. We have no Aristotelian essence, but a set of ideas that we want to live by. Choices, although difficult, can be made. In Aristotle's terms, knowing must be habituated through acting. Yet under extreme circumstances, learning through habituation evaporates. Levi's personal agony of not meeting civilized standards despite good reasons why he could not is symbolized in his conclusion about the survivors: "The worst survived, that is, the fittest; the best of all died" (*Drowned*, 82). In his play on Darwin, the fittest are the good, and they don't survive.

The battle of the self is tragic for Levi on two levels. We fight a losing battle with our bodies, fate, and others. Also, as suggested above, we lose the battle with ourselves in trying to deal with these obstacles. Overcoming outside obstacles builds strength, but inevitably we lose many of these battles. The losses are tragic and double, for we suffer the additional humiliation of losing, which we express to ourselves.

This chapter concludes with some other important ideas Levi had about choice. Levi adds tragic complications to the ideas of existentialists, postmodernists, and intellectualists on the subject, but with his customary ruthlessness toward knowing, he indicates further that especially in drastic situations, it may be that no moral systems or moral choices are possible. Again, we come upon that split brought on by *force majeure,* where people are utterly destroyed and, at the same time, go on with their strug-

34. Alexis de Tocqueville, *Democracy in America,* 2:34, 35.

gles. This ambivalence in Levi is found in a conversation with another prisoner, Steinlauf, who by keeping himself clean devises a way to survive the indignity of the Lager and retain a modicum of self-respect. Levi has a discussion with Steinlauf about the virtues of washing:

> I suddenly see Steinlauf, my friend aged almost fifty, with nude torso scrub his neck and shoulders with little success (he has no soap) but great energy . . . and without preamble [he] asks me severely why I do not wash. Why should I wash: Would I be better off than I am? Would I please someone more? Would I live a day, an hour longer? I would probably live a shorter time, because to wash is an effort, a waste of energy and warmth. Does not Steinlauf know that after half an hour with the coal sacks every difference between him and me will have disappeared?" (*Survival*, 40)

Steinlauf volunteers his rationale for washing. Prisoners have one power, which they should not give up: "The power to refuse our consent. So we must certainly wash our faces without soap in dirty water and dry ourselves on our jackets. We must polish our shoes not because the regulation states it, but for dignity and propriety. We must walk erect, without dragging our feet, not in homage to Prussian discipline but to remain alive, not to begin to die" (*Survival*, 41).

At that moment, Levi rejects Steinlauf's advice and uses it to question whether Steinlauf's system is more useful to prisoners than following the less articulated Hobbesian principle of "obey orders or forfeit your life": "No, the wisdom and virtue of Steinlauf, certainly good for him, is not enough for me. In the face of this complicated world my ideas of damnation are confused; is it really necessary to elaborate a system and put it into practice? Or would it not be better to acknowledge one's lack of a system?" (*Survival*, 41)

In retrospect, Levi understands Steinlauf's rationale. In the Lager were many posted signs telling the prisoners to wash their hands before eating and warning about hygiene. He thought they were part of the diabolical humor he had heard about, but he later interpreted these signs to be right, but for different reasons than the Germans had for posting them. "But later I understood that their unknown authors, perhaps without realizing it, were not far from some very important truths. In this place it is practically pointless for purposes of cleanliness and health; but it is most important as a symptom of remaining vitality, and necessary as an instrument of moral survival" (*Survival*, 40).

Levi is responding to Steinlauf on two levels. First, people crushed by overwhelming force rarely respond heroically to adverse situations. He explores the gray moral area in his writings because this is where most people fall when they respond to adversity. This refers back to his critique of existentialists on grounds that the gray zone is nonexistent for them. Existentialists tender their claims that choice is either/or; the world is populated either by heroes or stinkers. Levi knows that there are a few heroes, but the rest of us should not be judged by such an impossible ideal, and yet—can we give up the ideal altogether? Later we will see that his liberalism does not depend upon the liberal response, which is in agreement with the Sartrean ideal: If you want to convince me of anything, you have to be a hero or a martyr. Levi calls no one, including himself, to sainthood, martyrdom, or heroism. His liberalism calls for a minimalist approach to action.

On the second level, Levi does not want to give up the ideal of choice altogether, even though in Auschwitz, given the physical and psychological deprivation, it was so difficult for humans to exercise choice. Initially, in his response to Steinlauf, he indicates that if survival is the goal, stoic resignation to circumstances is a more rational strategy than willing what you cannot will and exhausting a good deal of needed stores of energy to resist by defiantly bathing. Given the irrational universe, the prisoner will try to learn the new rules of navigation instead of holding fast to the old rudder of resistance.

In retrospect, however, Levi gives a positive nod toward Steinlauf's strategy. Expressing his ambivalence—scorning Steinlauf's strategy while in Auschwitz and approving it retrospectively—Levi raises a critical question we have all asked ourselves at some time, usually when we have to convince ourselves to take the stoic route. When the odds are against us, do we take the path of least resistance and call it a rational choice? Is choosing not to wash the intelligent choice for survival, or simply a rationalization for taking the easier route? Even if we take the easier route and it works out, we tend to question our moral courage. To counter this conclusion about ourselves, we marshal empirical evidence that the stoic route was correct, but usually we cannot entirely convince ourselves. Levi has no final answers to these questions, but he draws the issues sharply so that we know what the parameters are when we choose.

Finally, although most of what happens to prisoners is a matter of chance, they still have the responsibility of knowing and choosing. Levi gives his ideal of this process in an essay where the protagonists, space explorers, operate in conditions of drastically less compulsion than those in the Lager, but a similar logic governs both. In "The Moon and Man," Levi is as rapturous about man as he ever gets, yet he cannot see his task in any other way than heroically trying to overcome the tragedies of our existence. Here is his ideal: "Our world, in so many of its aspects sinister, provisional, diseased, and tragic, has also this other face: it is a 'brave new world' that does not recoil before obstacles and does not find peace until it has circumvented, penetrated, or overwhelmed them." Its heroes are "not that of the pioneer, the hero at war, the lone navigator." He sees a new type arising from space exploration, one who is "daring to challenge the unforeseen, but a daring to foresee everything—a quality even more courageous."[35] This sums up much of his personal philosophy, which is forged out of his experiences: understand and challenge the unforeseen. Be prepared through education, both formal and informal, for the adversities of existence, and, almost paradoxically, be open to what opportunities, however slim, the unforeseen brings.

This chapter, through its critique of existentialism, postmodernism, and intellectualism, establishes some of Levi's basic parameters on the theory of choice, which will be refined in ensuing chapters. Postmodernism extends the options we have for looking at the public situation, but Levi tries to insure that we do not abandon the necessity of choosing on which positions to act. Existentialism extols choice and emphasizes the tragic circumstances of man, ideas that Levi can agree with. However, he believes that existentialism puts unrealistic demands upon a person with its vast distance between heroes and stinkers. As well, Levi refines the way we think about individual choice, which will be featured in "A Defense of Modernism." Levi agonizes over the relationship of the individual to the collective with respect to making choices, but he ultimately comes down on the side of the individual. For him, the individual is the center of responsible decision-making; he must reflectively review the experience of others before making his choice. Levi has a much different definition of intellectuals than Améry's intellectualist, contemplative conception—Levi believes that philosophy must be life philosophy, a conclusion that puts him squarely within the pragmatic tradition. He feels the imperative to make choices even though decisions are very difficult to ground and make. The consequences of history teach us that we have no other choice but to

35. Levi, "The Moon and Man," in *"The Mirror Maker": Stories and Essays by Primo Levi*, 90.

try to anticipate and meet future circumstances, or leave them in the hands of others. Finally, in his dialogue with Steinlauf he uncovers the phenom-enology of choice and indicates one of the true agonies of choosing: the almost impossible moral feat of understanding whether we are choosing the correct path or rationalizing the easiest alternative, especially in ex-treme circumstances.

8

Purpose and Work

The aims of life are the best defense against death: and not only in
the Lager.

— *The Drowned and the Saved*

Work played a central role in Levi's life, both in the Lager and in ordinary
life. In the Lager, toiling as a slave had a virtual monopoly on his energy
and thoughts. In ordinary life, his work as a chemist occupied a great space
in his active world, and after he retired as manager of the paint factory,
his work as a writer was never far from his thoughts. For Levi, understanding the nature of work comes close to understanding the core of purpose in life. Although a separate book should be written on Levi's relationship with work, we will have to be satisfied with condensing his
thoughts into this chapter.

The free pursuit of the good life through work comes close to expressing Levi's ideal, but of course this leaves out the trenchant ironies we
would expect from him.[1] First, we will describe sources, constitutional and
cultural, for our penchant for work. Second, we will focus on Levi's conception of work and its place in his life philosophy. Third, we will focus
on work in the Lager and the consequences of the total perversion of this
work by the Germans. Fourth, we will look at individual strategies of work
devised by Levi and others that helped to forestall their demise. Finally, we
will investigate Levi's ironic comments on work and see if work can provide us with purpose in life.

1. From Plato through Freud, philosophers have spoken about the centrality of love and
work. Levi says very little about love in his works, preferring to speak about work. As we
have noted, he does speak of friendship a great deal.

In "The Sixth Day," a short story discussed earlier, bureaucrats who work for God are asked to design man distinct from other animals, and they are given four main characteristics as parameters. One is language, and a second is "a certain degree of preference for social life," both characteristics discussed in previous chapters. The other two parameters evoke work: "a particular aptitude for the creation and utilization of tools" and "fitness for life under conditions of extreme labor"; Levi fully believes these are inherent capacities in man.[2] Again and again in his writings, toolmaking, tool utilization, and the ability to use tools in extreme circumstances emerge as keys to our survival. They are givens in our nature, but due to modifying environmental influences, they are found to different degrees in individuals.

The penchant for work is an end in itself, but at times it may take on an added urgency because work is often performed in service of another end, the will to live. The will to live is the topic for discussion between the main characters, Anna and Walter, in the short story "Westward." Walter acknowledges the existence of the survival instinct: "This is the rule, that each of us human beings but also the animals, and . . . yes, also the plants, everything that is alive struggles to live and does not know why. The why is inscribed in every cell, but in a language that we cannot read with our minds." But as with all things human, Walter admits that there are exceptions to the rule: "But also those in whom the message is clear can have gaps. Individuals without love for life can be born; others may lose it for a short or long time, perhaps for all the life they have left; and finally . . . here, perhaps I've got it: also groups of individuals may lose it, epochs, nations, families."[3] It is obvious from the above statements that Walter believes humans possess instinctual forces that can be modified by culture.

Levi's conception of work is a key component in his life philosophy. Work is the constant cooperation, but more often competition, between man and materials, an unending struggle. By and large, work is a losing struggle with the materials and serves as a metaphor for the struggles with existence. Levi conveys in *The Periodic Table* "the strong and bitter flavor of our trade [chemistry], which is only a particular instance, a more strenuous version of the business of living." Levi began this battle in school with the elements on the Periodic Table, and he continually struggled with them

---

2. Levi, "The Sixth Day," in *"The Sixth Day" and Other Tales,* 92.
3. Levi, "Westward," in *"Sixth,"* 128, 129.

all his working life: "It is the spirit that dominates matter, is that not so? Was it not this that they had hammered into my head in the Fascist and Gentile *liceo?* I threw myself into the work with the same intensity that, at not so distant a period, we had attacked a rock wall." From this early spirit of conquest, which brought him up against the problems of chemistry and the difficulties of life, he concluded that life is tragic. Chemical events "give you the impression of fighting an interminable war against an obtuse and slow-moving enemy, who, however, is fearful in terms of number and bulk; of losing all the battles, one after the other, year after year; and to salve your bruised pride you must be satisfied with the few occasions when you catch sight of a break in the enemy front and you pounce on it and administer a quick single blow."[4]

Levi's analysis of his struggles with chemistry, his metaphor for all work, plays a major role in his writings. They are individualistic struggles between man and nature. He "would deliberately neglect the grand chemistry, the triumphant chemistry of colossal plants and dizzying output, because this is collective work and therefore anonymous." Levi is more interested in work as a metaphor for the individual life of struggle rather than analyzing work as collective with man as a cog in a machine: "I was more interested in the stories of the solitary chemistry, unarmed and on foot, at the measure of man, which with few exceptions had been mine: but it had also had been the chemistry of the founders, who did not work in teams but alone, surrounded by the indifference of their time, generally without profit, and who confronted matter without aids, with their brains and hands, reason and imagination."[5]

Individual confrontation with materials brings him many defeats, and with his solitary labors, the defeats are personal. He describes in detail several confrontations with matter, where he is responsible for identifying the source and cause of problems. For example, in *The Monkey's Wrench,* the narrator, a chemist very much like Levi, tells the main protagonist, Faussone, a welder, about his responsibility for finding out why the paint inside a tin did not stand up to anchovies. Levi acknowledges getting the test results from the woman who worked in the canning factory; she had assured him that she would repeat the test, but she was confident that she would get the same results. He began to feel cramps in his stomach. Faussone responds to Levi's story by indicating that in those same situations he

4. Levi, *The Periodic Table,* 203, 154.
5. Ibid., 203.

also suffers: "That's right. I get a pain here, on my right side: I think it's my liver. But for me a man who's never had a negative test isn't a man; it's like he was still at his first communion."[6]

Levi's idea of work is Socratic: work may occur within a system of power, but the aim of work is not profit or power but wrestling with raw materials using knowledge. It is the manipulation of materials to get the best results, as it is for Socrates' trainer to get the best out of his horses. For Levi, it means doing well by the man or materials that are the object of his work. He is not utopian, for he knows that working in the way he wants inevitably includes interactions with bosses, coworkers, and hard-to-please clients. However, dealing with bosses and coworkers is not part of the work itself, which consists of the manipulation of matter.

Other trades can quickly turn sophist in nature; the only goal becomes manipulating others to make money or gain power. Salesmanship often turns from setting up a deal, which is mutually beneficial, to using knowledge of people's weaknesses in order to make as much money as possible. In Socratic terms, work can turn from love of the object and making it better to exploitation of the object. Mordo, Levi's early companion on the trip home from Auschwitz, compartmentalized trading and intellectual work by doing one in the day and the other at night. Selling for Mordo was pure sophistry, whereas Levi believed that even in a trade so easily given over to sophistry one could sneak other virtues in, as did Cesare: "Cesare was full of human warmth, always, at every moment of his life, not just outside office hours like Mordo Nahum. . . . One of them was free, the other was a slave to himself; one was miserly and reasonable, the other prodigal and fantastic. The Greek was a lone wolf, in an eternal war against all, old before his time, closed in the circle of his own joyless pride; Cesare was a child of the sun, everybody's friend." It was not because Cesare was always fair to his customers: "Not that Cesare is much concerned about acting legally; but he likes a sense of style, gamesmanship, putting one over on the next man without making him suffer."[7] In conformity with our earlier analysis, Levi introduces another necessary element into work, one in accord with his hedonism: There should be no unnecessary pain.

For the most part, Levi is content to comment on professions like chemistry, welding, and writing, where he sees the primary relationship as the confrontation between man and materials. Even the author, who must be

6. Levi, *The Monkey's Wrench*, 148.
7. Levi, *The Reawakening*, 64, 65, 66.

attuned to his audience, finds that his central battle is with words on a page. It is clear, however, that in all work there must be the Socratic loving care for the objects of work, whether they are materials or man. Humans, whether at the core or periphery of work, must be treated well. Work should incorporate many virtues of living well with others, even though people may be subsidiary to the major purpose.

Levi, a nominal socialist, was criticized in Italy for being in a privileged profession after the war and refraining from protesting against the general alienation of labor. Yet Levi provides a model of non-alienated labor, and he understands that many others were not so fortunate as he was in their work situations. To the dismay of some of his critics, he chooses to direct his activism in different directions, trying to make sure that genocide is not repeated by waging a relentless campaign of remembrance and advocating civilized modern liberal virtue.

Levi further explores the virtues of work in *The Monkey's Wrench*, where the chemist and Faussone agree on the advantages of work:

> We agreed then on the good things we have in common. On the advantage of being able to test yourself, not depending on others in the test, reflecting yourself in your work. On the pleasure of seeing your creature grow, beam after beam, bolt after bolt, solid, necessary, symmetrical, suited to its purpose; and when it's finished you look at it and you think that perhaps it will live longer than you, and perhaps it will be of use to someone you don't know, who doesn't know you.[8]

In addition to the satisfactions and frustrations of doing work, good work also has a serendipitous outcome: It is useful for man because it maintains his dignity. Faussone expresses this idea succinctly: "The fact is that after I felt sure of myself as a welder, I felt sure of myself in everything, even the way I walked."[9] Levi also recounts the importance of the dignity conveyed by work in Auschwitz. In the Lager, good work was even more vital than in ordinary life because all other sources of dignity had been stripped away: "He [Chajim] is Polish, a religious Jew, learned in rabbinical law. He is about as old as I, a watchmaker by profession, and here in Buna works as a precision mechanic; so he is among the few who are able to preserve their dignity and self-assurance through the practice of a profession in which they are skilled" (*Survival*, 47).

8. Levi, *Monkey's*, 53.
9. Ibid., 124.

Work is of overwhelming importance to Levi, but like William James, also a philosopher of work and effort, there is more to life than work and some of the peripheral joys attached to it. Levi agrees with Plato that the artisan does not live the fullest life. Work is extremely important, but in his opening essay in *The Periodic Table,* Levi looks back on his relatives who worked due to social pressures but did not have the fullness of life, and he compares them to the element argon and other inert gases: "The little that I know about my ancestors presents many similarities to these gases. Not all of them were materially inert, for that was not granted them. On the contrary, they were—or had to be—quite active, in order to earn a living and because of a reigning morality that held that 'he who does not work shall not eat.' But there is no doubt that they were inert in their inner spirits, inclined to disinterested speculation, witty discourses, elegant, sophisticated, and gratuitous discussion."[10]

In order to have a full life, intellectual life, as Levi defines it, is necessary. Levi conveys the importance of work and its role in the alleviation of pain, and he finds it imperative that curiosity extends beyond work to the pursuit of an active imagination and a full civic life. Life joins the work of Plato's artisan and Aristotle's man of practical reason. Levi recognizes the importance of participation in civic life in the tradition of Plato's philosopher king, but he prefers it to be carried out in the style of the modern pragmatic democrat.

Since work is so important to Levi, one of the Germans' most unforgivable crimes, short of mass murder, was to strip work of all of its dignity and convert it into an affliction. Work is a way to achieve purpose, no matter how provisional. The perversion of work is to force people to do work not of their choosing and make that work a great hardship—a condition that can happen in ordinary life as well. When he was working for a business using his chemistry skills, he did not like his work on phosphorus, but management insisted he do it: "Just as much as the analysis of nickel in the rock had exalted me, elemental in my previous incarnation, so was I humiliated now by the daily dosage of phosphorus, because to do work in which one does not believe is a great affliction."[11]

In the Lager, the idea of work was mocked as the prisoners were compelled to work at tasks not of their own choosing under brutal and hu-

10. Levi, *Periodic,* 4.
11. Ibid., 120.

miliating conditions. In his first recollection of Auschwitz, the perversion of the idea of work is already obvious: "The journey did not last more than twenty minutes. Then the lorry stopped, and we saw a large door, and above it is a sign, brightly illuminated (its memory still strikes me in my dreams): *Arbeit Macht Frei*, work gives freedom" (*Survival*, 22). The sign was an ironic portent of the coming perversion of work. The "work was purely persecutory, practically useless for productive ends: to send the undernourished to dig up turf or cut stone served only a terroristic purpose" (*Drowned*, 121). In the earliest days of the Lager, before the demand for "productive slave labor," most labor was purposeless, seemingly designed just to humiliate the prisoners. This was done even though the Germans understood the importance of the need to have a purpose and to do a job well: "Even the Germans, however, had understood it, although in previous experiments they made people do grossly useless tasks, like shoveling dirt from here to there and then back again, or digging trenches and then filling them up. As I said before, when they began to feel the scarcity of manpower they gave up this tormenting use of labor. Work [when he was in Auschwitz] was still very hard, but not pointless."[12]

The task was no longer to push around dirt, perhaps, but to build a wall or lay a pipe. Still, the tasks were not of one's choosing; their work could only help the enemy, and there was no compensation: "Work was not paid; that is, it was slave work." The work served someone else's demonic ends, the work was crushing, the work was done in horrible conditions, and it was meant to be a punishment: "At any rate, for Nazi and Fascist rhetoric, in this the heir of bourgeois rhetoric, 'work ennobles,' and therefore the ignoble adversaries of the regime are not worthy of working in the commonly accepted meaning of the word. Their work must be afflictive: it must leave no room for professionalism, must be the work of beasts of burden." Work was "persecutory": "To humiliate, to make the 'enemy' suffer, was their [the SS's] everyday task; they did not reason about it, they had no ulterior ends: their end was simply that" (*Drowned*, 120, 121).

Despite the transformation of work into an affliction, the prisoners took on parts of four possible attitudes toward work. First, the fundamental way that the prisoners survived "persecutory labor" is described earlier in reference to those who functioned "beneath life." Essentially, it was to exist only in the present moment and attend to the work of affliction at hand. It is an inversion of the process Taoism describes when the individual vol-

12. Ferdinando Camon, *Conversations with Primo Levi*, 49.

untarily lives in the present moment and his or her thoughts spontaneously occur. In Zen, humans may be best off living life as a dog, immersed in the present moment. This is a free state reached through the most demanding self-discipline. Through the mercy of the hierarchy of troubles, the prisoners found themselves attending to the present circumstances and not thinking about much else. Of course, as in Zen, the perfect moment rarely comes, and other thoughts intrude, but the prisoners stayed mostly in the present moment. By force of circumstances, and no small mixture of will and resignation, the prisoners got through the day by focusing on the task before them.

To live beneath life and survive in the camps, the prisoners first had to survive the existential meltdown and then manage the problems that intruded all at once by sorting them out, one by one. This meant a massive adjustment for men who were used to working as free men. To survive in the state beneath life while working, they had to begin to understand the orders of their oppressors and follow them as good Hobbesians who are faced with the prospect of "work or die." Their inclinations toward work determined if they would have any chance at all of survival: "We already know in good part the rules of the camp, which are incredibly complicated. The prohibitions are innumerable: to approach nearer to the barbed wire than two yards; to sleep with one's jacket, or without one's pants. . . . The rites to be carried out were infinite and senseless" (*Survival,* 33–34). Part of survival was understanding the language so that prisoners could absorb the rules of the new universe. In addition, they were not to try to understand the motives behind these rules or anything else about the organization and actions of their captors. They had to grasp that "there is no why here"—that is, to learn a whole new epistemology, no easy task.

Though beneath life most of the time, they did learn to look out for themselves. Disposition toward work is partially innate and partially learned; many responses are reflexes, but some are calculated in that little free time available to the mind. The prisoners had to learn the preparations necessary to survive the work itself, as well as the ways of making the work itself a bit more tolerable. They had to learn anew how to care for themselves, how to supplement the starvation ration, and how to dress to avoid what we now call hypothermia. These are intentional preparations and actions, which if not taken, led to a quicker death: "We have learnt that everything is useful: the wire to tie up our shoes, the rags to wrap around our feet, waste paper to (illegally) pad out our jacket against the cold." At work, concern about the cold did not cease: "By now it would be impossible to be wetter; I will just have to pay attention to move as little as possible, and above all not to make new movements, to prevent some other part of my skin coming into unnecessary contact with my soaking, icy clothes." Other strategies were necessary for dealing with the cold: "Whoever does not die will suffer minute by minute, all day, every day: from the morning before dawn until the distribution of the evening soup we will have to keep our muscles continually tensed, dance from foot to foot, beat our arms under our shoulders against the cold" (*Survival*, 33, 131, 123).

To survive, prisoners had to understand that rewards and punishments for work had been reversed. For instance, the captives had to learn that the whip, the instrument of degradation, was also used as an encouragement by the Kapos in this upside-down world: "I bite deeply into my lips; we know well that to gain a small, extraneous pain serves as a stimulant to mobilize our last reserves of energy. The Kapos also know it; some of them beat us from pure bestiality and violence, but others beat us when we are under a load almost lovingly, accompanying the blows with exhortations, as cart-drivers do with willing horses" (*Survival, 67*).

Also, to provide for their vital needs, it was often necessary to unlearn virtue in order to steal, and to guard against the theft of one's few possessions: "We have learnt, on the other hand, that everything can be stolen, in fact is automatically stolen as soon as attention is relaxed" (*Survival*, 33). These and many other new skills and ways of thinking were necessary to survive the pains and humiliations of work.

In addition to living in this Hobbesian state "beneath life," and when possible scrounging for their self-interest, prisoners had to think of their work in four other ways. First, they could still take pride in their accomplishments, even though the task was done under compulsion and to the advantage of the enemy. Levi finds many instances of this in the Lager, and he also notes that it was a theme in a major box-office hit: "Those who saw the famous film *The Bridge on the River Kwai* will remember the absurd zeal with which the English officer, prisoner of the Japanese, strives to build an audacious wooden bridge for them and is shocked when he realizes that the English sappers have mined it." For Levi, thinking of work as artistry is a way of surviving beastly work, but he also notes with irony that under compulsion, "love for a job well done is a deeply ambiguous virtue" (*Drowned*, 123).

In *The Drowned and the Saved*, Levi mentions the same phenomenon of artistry under duress. In Alexander Solzhenitsyn's *One Day in the Life of Ivan Denisovich,* Levi recalls, "Ivan, the protagonist, sentenced though guiltless to ten years of forced labor, finds satisfaction in building a wall according to the highest stands of his trade." Lorenzo, Levi's benefactor in Auschwitz, turned to observe that the wall was perfectly straight, and Levi reflects on how deep his ethos of work ran. Lorenzo worked "not in deference to orders but out of professional dignity." It was not Lorenzo's war, but when the Germans "set him to build protective walls against the aerial bombs he built them straight, solid, with well-staggered bricks and as much mortar as was required" (*Drowned,* 122).

In Camon's *Conversations with Primo Levi,* Levi suggests that "work can be a salvation, if you're able to perceive that the work is useful. I remember one of my fellow workers (the one who didn't want to steal, remember?), he wanted us to do a good job so as to be able to feel some gratification at the end of the day."[13] Sometimes by habit, or by deliberate calculation, artistry becomes a basic motivation of work, even in the most perverse of circumstances.

The third inclination toward work is to sabotage it by cutting corners. Most of the time sabotage by prisoners occurred less to keep their dignity than to keep up whatever strength they had left. They would malinger in the latrines, move slowly at work when the task was onerous, and do as little as they could, short of severe punishment. Levi often held this disposition, and when others worked harder than they needed to, he was brought to anger. Those who worked at full tilt in the Lager were like Soviet Stakhanovites or Schmidt, the pig iron worker in Frederic Jackson Taylor's proud tale of the laborer who set the bar high for those who would do the same work routines in the future. They force laborers, whose work is compared to theirs, to work to exhaustion. In addition, the Stakhanovites and the Schmidts are doomed in the Lager. Levi says:

> He [Kraus] works too much and too vigorously: he has not yet learnt our underground art of economizing on everything, on breath, movements, even thoughts. He does not yet know that it is better to be beaten, because one does not normally die of blows. . . . He still thinks . . . oh no, poor Kraus, his is not reasoning, it is only the stupid honesty of a small employee, he brought it along with him, and he seems to think that his present situation is like outside, where it is honest and logical to work, as well as being of advantage, because according to what everyone says, the more one works the more one earns and eats. (*Survival,* 132)

13. Ibid., 48–49.

Fourth were those who were "mad" and actually enjoyed the working circumstances in the Lager. In this category Levi mentions only one example, Elias the Dwarf. He not only worked hard at whatever task he was given, but he enjoyed the labor: "His fame as an exceptional worker spread quite soon, and by the absurd law of the Lager, from then on he practically ceased to work." Although Levi does not say it explicitly, Elias is for society the reverse of the canary in the coal mine. If the Eliases of the world thrive, then we must look at what is wrong with the world. In ordinary life, "Do we not see individuals [incipient Eliases] living without purpose, lacking all forms of self-control and conscience, who live not *in spite of* these defects, but like Elias precisely because of them?" (*Survival*, 97–98).

In sum, four attitudes toward work had survival value in the Lager: beneath life in the present moment with a Hobbesian attitude toward work; preserving artistry in doing a meaningless task; sabotaging work; and, at least for Elias, flourishing in slavery through the defect of madness.

It is worth exploring some of the individual work strategies that surfaced in an environment where there appears to have been little room for anything but conformity: "Many were the ways devised and put into effect by us in order not to die: as many as there are different human characters" (*Survival*, 92). Simultaneously, when the prisoners were crushed by *force majeure* and living as Hobbesians, they often became ingenious in using their guile to forge rudimentary strategies for survival. Even under the harshest conditions of conformity, short of the *musselmans* stage, there was still some room for discretion.

Levi gives us some memorable portraits of those prisoners who had been virtually crushed by inexorable outside forces, yet devised ways to traverse the narrow interstices to give chance a chance. Studying them allows us to understand how for Levi, life philosophy is an individual task, as James suggests, influenced by others, but limited by one's own disposition.[14] Behavior is the outcome of human nature under extreme circumstances, prior knowledge applied to present circumstances, and the ability to reflect on an upside-down world during those moments of limited intuition and introspection.

Levi's character sketches are of people who had scratched out ways of

14. This work is a testament to the will, guile, and luck that allowed Levi to survive. Here is the place to describe the very different and yet useful strategies of others he observed personally.

surviving that ranged from the crudely reflexive to the carefully rationalized. "We will try to show in how many ways it was possible to reach salvation with the stories of Schepschel, Alfred L., Elias and Henri." Schepschel's story is typical for many of those who tried to make it, without a
lot of conscious thought, in the Lager. His task was to make sure he ate,
and so he scrounged for ways to supplement the given starvation ration:
"Schepschel is not very robust, nor very courageous, nor very wicked; he
is not even particularly astute, nor has he ever found a method which allows him a little respite, but he is reduced to small and occasional expe-
dients, '*kombinacje*' as they are called here." For example, he stole a
broom and sold it, set aside food to hire a cobbler, and adapted his skills
as a saddler to make braces out of electric wire. Like most, he did not go
out of the way to do evil to others, but he gave in to the pressures from
time to time to save himself: "When the opportunity showed itself, he
[Schepschel] did not hesitate to have Moischl, his accomplice in a theft
from the kitchen, condemned to a flogging, in the mistaken hope of gain-
ing favour in the eyes of the *Blockältester* and furthering his candidature
for the position of *Kesselwäscher,* 'vat-washer'" (*Survival,* 92, 93). He
muddled through, kept from the very worst by innate goodness or prior
training, but he was not averse to giving in to authority to save himself.

Elias, with Shlepschel, was on the un–self-conscious end of the continuum, a great distance from those who thoughtfully calculated their strategies for survival. Levi suggests that "he is the most adaptable, the human
type most suited to this way of living." Levi wonders whether it was because he was mad, an atavistic throwback, or simply a product of the camp
itself. Physically, he was indestructible, and mentally there seemed to be
no purpose, resistance to any work, or attachment to anyone or anything.
He stole, fought, cheated, and finally brutalized those under him for the
day, and all without moral hesitation. Levi concludes that he was a combination of all three: mad, an atavistic throwback, and a product of the
camp itself (*Survival,* 97).

Two others, the engineer Alfred L. and Henri, had more carefully rationalized plans for survival than Schepschel and Elias. Alfred L. for example, through deliberate self-control, gave up the chance for the most
soup in the present as part of his plan for a "better future." Alfred L. had
been a respected director of an important chemical factory, but in the Lager
he was stripped of everything like everyone else: "His plan was a long-
term one, which is all the more notable as conceived in an environment
dominated by a mentality of the provisional; and L. carried it out with

rigid inner discipline, without pity for himself—or with greater reason—for comrades who crossed his path." Although physically wasted like everyone else, Alfred L.'s plan was to hold himself aloof and keep himself looking as neat and composed as possible so that he would not be confused with the masses. This way he waited his turn for jobs, which he finally got and made his life a bit easier: "He took every care not to be confused with mass; he worked with stubborn duty, even occasionally admonishing his lazy comrades in a persuasive and deprecatory tone of voice; he avoided the daily struggle for the best place in the queue for the ration, and prepared to take the first ration, notoriously the most liquid, every day, so as to be noticed by his Blockaltester for his discipline" (*Survival*, 94).

Henri, only 22, had the most complete ideas on how to survive the Lager. He cut off every tie of affection; he willed coldness, an insensitivity that had come naturally to Elias, so as to put all his resources toward survival: "According to Henri's theory, there are three methods open to man to escape extermination which still allow him to retain the name of man: organization, pity and theft" (*Survival*, 98). This turns out to be a sophisticated theory of conduct, but the only method that needs some elaboration here is pity. For Henri, pity was useful to make those who had something he wanted feel sorry for him. This, in addition to theft, was his chief method of procurement. Each of the above work strategies involve different degrees of calculation, but they all share the necessity to transcend the laws of work and decency born of ordinary times. At the end of his discussion of the four prisoners, Levi makes clear his disapproval of their strategies: He has no wish to see any of them again.

Elsewhere in his writing, Levi describes with more favor those who devised survival strategies but did not lose all sense of character in the process. These characteristics are less related to an atavistic expedience or a planned move to de-civilize, as was characteristic of the above-mentioned four, but more related to striving to retain some attitudes and behaviors as good in themselves. Lorenzo, the Italian laborer, gave Primo Levi and, as it turned out, many other Italian prisoners goods at great risk to himself: "Alberto and I were amazed by Lorenzo. In the violent and degraded environment of Auschwitz, a man helping other men out of pure altruism was incomprehensible, alien, like a savior who's come from heaven." Nor did Lorenzo do it because of praise he might get. In fact, "he was a morose savior, with whom it was difficult to communicate."[15]

15. Levi, *Moments*, 155.

Alberto, as previously described, lived with as much cheerfulness and inventiveness as was possible in the situation. He did not put in for special work details, but preferred to make it through without privileges. In fact, until his death in the tragic final march back toward Germany, he conserved better physical and mental stamina than most.

In some ways, another acquaintance of Levi's, Rappoport, was close to Schepschel, Elias, Henri, and Alfred L., but in Levi's eyes, deserved more praise. Polish by origin and perhaps 35, Rappoport, who had received a medical degree from Pisa, embraced traces of the morality of survival that Levi found so absent in Schlepschel, Henri, Alfred L., and Elias. Like the four of them, Rappoport easily shed the vestiges of civilization to survive: "He lived in the Camp like a tiger in the jungle, striking down and practicing extortion on the weak, and avoiding those who were stronger; ready to corrupt, steal, fight, pull in his belt, lie, or play up to you depending on the circumstances. He was therefore an enemy, but not despicable or repugnant." Where he greatly differed from the others was in the way that he framed his circumstances. He had lived a full life, but what counts for Levi is that Rappoport self-consciously understood his vital life in this admirable way:

> While I could I drank, I ate, I made love, I left flat gray Poland for that Italy of yours; I studied, learned, traveled and looked at things. I kept my eyes wide open; I didn't waste a crumb. I've been diligent; I don't think I could have done more or better. Things went well for me; I accumulated a large quantity of good things, and all that good has not disappeared. It's inside me, safe and sound. I don't let it fade; I've held on to it. Nobody can take it from me.[16]

This accounts for the fact that "Rappoport's vitality, which I would have admired under other circumstances (and in fact admire today), appeared out of place and insolent." The twenty months that he had been in the Lager had not tipped the positive balance in his life: "To tip the balance, it would take many more months of Camp, or many days of torture. Actually (he caressed his stomach affectionately) with a little initiative, even here you can find something good every so often." Rappoport concluded this conversation with Levi by saying that he may die, but neither the camp nor the Nazis would ever get the best of him: "'So in the sad event that one of you should survive me, you will be able to say that Leon

16. Ibid., 20, 23.

Rappoport got what was due him, left behind neither debits nor credits, and did not weep or ask for pity.'"[17]

Finally, we will look at the broader framework of purpose and work and whether work gives our life meaning. Can work ultimately provide us with purpose in life? Levi believes that work is an imperative that serves our ultimate need for survival. But there is Levi's ironic twist to consider: Are life and work ultimately meaningless, despite our seemingly natural affinities with them?

Even in ordinary circumstances, Levi mentions how vitally important purposes are to the life of the individual: "The aims of life are the best defense against death: and not only in the Lager" (*Drowned*, 148). Almost everyone (as we remember in "Westward," Levi made some exceptions) operates according to a purpose or purposes, something that is defining of human behavior. Every culture tries to give an account of the origins of purpose and guide it in avenues believed to be useful to that culture. Socrates' recollection, Gabriel Marcel's spirituality, and Hegel's history evince origins and direction. Even in Eastern thought, where egoistic purpose is looked upon as undesirable, purpose is looked upon as a given of nature. *Dukkha*, the constant striving after striving, must be worked against. Levi believes with Hobbes that the aims of life, which attach to a variety of objects, are inherent in man.

In the Lager, the important questions about life were rarely asked because the prisoners were forced to live beneath life. They didn't ask: Is work an end in itself? Is work a means to an end? If work is a means to an end, what end? They were immersed out of necessity in the task before them as Hobbesian beings or in the somnambulist state of a *musselmans*. In the Lager, man appears to have been stripped of any purpose, but Levi shows how, except for the *musselmans*, purpose didn't completely die. Given the overarching purpose of survival, clinging to the Hobbesian contract was virtually the only viable sub-purpose available to the prisoners: your work or your life. Also, to survive, the prisoner's sub-purpose was to maintain constant defensive vigil on life.

Martin Buber, in his short story "The Master of Prayer," indicates possible meanings of life. There is wisdom, power of words, beauty, joy, death (living life with a view to a higher moral code), and honor.[18] In the Lager,

17. Ibid., 22, 23, 24.
18. Buber, "The Master of Prayer, in *The Tales of Rabbi Nachman*, 126–27.

deliberation on these or other justifications of life would be exceptional. Of these aims, the most one can say is that from time to time Levi got satisfaction in knowing and observing them in the Lager. Buber's scheme can be used only in hindsight, for the prisoner's attention was fixed on the work in front of him, not the why of it. The quote above, "The aims of life . . . " is preceded in Levi's text by a statement not about higher purpose, but about sub-purposes, the more mundane defensive actions necessary to keep one alive: "I almost never had time to devote to death. I had many other things to keep me busy—finding a bit of bread, avoiding exhausting work, patching my shoes, stealing a broom, or interpreting the signs and faces around me" (*Drowned,* 148).

The hierarchy of troubles kicks in and purpose becomes staying alive; the most immediate threat remains foremost on the mind. The hierarchy is simplicity itself to deal with the oppressive immediacy of life: "The conviction that life has a purpose is rooted in every fibre of man, it is a property of the human substance. Free men give many names to this purpose, and think and talk a lot about its nature. But for us the question is simpler. Today, in this place, our only purpose is to reach the spring" (*Survival,* 71). Man is suffused with purpose. It was not contemplation and justification of a higher purpose that sustained individuals in the Lager, but unthinking pursuit of the absolute necessities for survival.

Once again we confront the theme that runs all through Levi's works. "*Force Majeure*" presents the picture of the individual crushed by the boot of the experience, and yet, he persists. In the Lager, the prisoner was not yet devoid of purpose; he was trying to survive, a slave to a discipline of work not of his own choosing. We see examples of initiative on the part of prisoners that involved a degree of self-awareness and self-control. In Ka-Be and at other rare times when not suffering from pain and exhaustion, the prisoners thought beyond pure survival and wondered if they could minimize the compromises with their former being.

When Levi asks what philosophies sustain people best in abject circumstances, he begins to ask larger questions about life and purpose. Jean Améry believes that intellectuals' ideas cave in to pressure quickly. Their intellectual doubt, so prized, leads to self-destruction. Améry says: "And what if those who proposed to annihilate him were right, based on the undeniable fact that they were the stronger? Thus the fundamental spiritual tolerance and methodical doubt of the intellectual became factors of self-destruction. Yes, the SS were entitled to do what they did: natural right does not exist, and moral categories are born and die with the fashion" (*Drowned*, 144).

Elie Wiesel also comments on Améry's discovery: "I believe it was Jean Améry who noted that the first to bow to the oppressor's system and to adopt its doctrines and methods were the intellectuals." Wiesel continues: "On the other hand, how many secular humanists and intellectuals renounced their value system the moment they grasped its futility and uselessness? Sobered, disoriented, and disillusioned, some allowed themselves to be seduced by the ideology of cruelty. The number was significant." All intellectuals were not seduced: "Not the Rabbis and Priests, who, after all, were intellectuals too. With a single exception, no rabbi agreed to become a Kapo. . . . All preferred to die than serve death."[19]

Although a nonbeliever, Levi agrees with Wiesel that religious beliefs and other strong beliefs served those in the Lager well:

> Alongside this latent propensity of the agnostic intellectual [who justifies existing power], Améry observes what all of us ex-prisoners observed: the non-agnostic, the believers in any belief whatsoever, better resisted the seduction of power, provided, of course, they were not believers in the National Socialist doctrine. . . . When all is said and done, they endured the trials of the Lager and survived in a proportionately higher number. (*Drowned*, 145)

Levi cannot shake the idea that being a sensitive intellectual is a hindrance to his own survival: "I know that I am not made of the stuff of those who resist, I am too civilized, I still think too much, I use myself up at work" (*Survival*, 103). Yet, Levi's scientific detachment, analysis, and curiosity about many things, no matter how mundane, are important survival tools. They give him the ability of that new space pioneer who can foresee the world as it unfolds and anticipate danger and select opportunity.

Most of the strategies mentioned above involve either saving shards of old ideas or throwing out the old civilized virtues and replacing them with simple expediency.[20] Except if the prisoner was a "prominant," he could hardly contemplate a justification for survival or formulate new means

19. Wiesel, *All Rivers Run to the Sea: Memoirs*, 85, 86.
20. Levi's views on purpose make an interesting comparison with the views of another Holocaust survivor, Viktor Frankl, who makes purpose central to his existential analysis.

that would be useful for survival. Yet, in the Lager, almost everyone was in-fused with purpose: Work to stay alive. Tactics of staying warm, scroung-ing for life-sustaining scraps, and avoiding a bad beating dominated the prisoners' days. Broader purposes usually could not be sustained from their former lives and were replaced by an unlearning of civilized virtues. The meaning of life was a given—to stay alive—and the means to life were circumscribed by the brutal existence. Lack of freedom compelled clarifi-cation: Obey or die.

Now the larger questions Levi asks about life, purpose and work, can be addressed. All the terrors of the Lager suspended major questions about purpose. The order, "Do as I say now or die!" quickly put off existential questions about life. Not having to answer such difficult questions might be some relief; in Auschwitz, existential angst was completely superseded by the privations. Unfortunately, as clear as it was in the Lager to under-stand and act on the few options available, the prisoners suffered guilt from being forced from their civilized alternatives, and they suffered from that guilt for the rest of their lives. Most of all, it took away that most cherished privilege—to be miserable in one's own free ways.

Questions about death and the meaning of life come at us for three rea-sons: First, in extreme circumstances like the Holocaust, the enemy de-grades work, and for some slaves, their defenses melt away. Work no longer serves as a veil over the abyss; despair penetrates the Hobbesian state. Hobbesians become *musselmans* who give up and die under these circumstances. Second, in ordinary life, we have time for death. Work is not necessitated by survival, and even if it can be endured, work no longer serves as a veil over questions of purpose. Boredom, often caused by the temporary abatement of defensive life or the completion of a major pro-ject, causes us to ask questions about death and purpose. Third, intellec-tuals can induce this state by methodical doubt. For Levi, work may sim-ply be a veil to protect us from the more serious questions of life and death.

Existential questions vexed Levi during a hiatus in his journey home from Auschwitz. He and many others were temporary dependents of the Russians at the "Red Barn." Levi and other refugees no longer had to scrounge for the essentials of life. He missed work and variety, those use-ful veils so important to human consciousness, while staying at the Red Barn. This hiatus, in contrast with the imperatives of the Lager, tem-porarily relieved him from a pure defensive life, and existential questions surfaced.

Levi indicates that perfect happiness is not to be had because of the tragic nature of life itself, and we can only cover that tragedy by interposing activities of any kind to mask ourselves from ourselves. Levi, in enforced idleness at the Red Barn, was watching an absurd play: "Perhaps because, under the grotesque appearance, one perceived the heavy breath of a collective dream, of the dream emanating from exile and idleness, when work and troubles have ceased, and nothing acts as a screen between a man and himself; perhaps because we saw the impotence and the nullity of our life and of life itself, and the hunch-backed crooked profiles of the monsters generated by the sleep of reason."[21]

Levi never attempts to shield himself from the tough questions about life, and he thoroughly understands that he can undermine happiness when he uses reason to try to understand these questions. Defensive life and perhaps even the few higher pleasures serve as a shield from very uncomfortable thoughts that we induce or that invade us in periods of boredom and intelligent questioning. Levi does not deny the pleasures that free work gives him, and one must include on that list the respite from such agonizing existential questions. In truly utilitarian fashion, the intellectual satisfaction of exploring the question of purpose is pitted for Levi against the joys of doing our provisional work, which allows us to forget the question of why we are doing it.

We are purposeless beings who feel we have purpose, except when we look too closely into the matter and find ourselves purposeless. The veil is not too terrible for Levi, because he has no trouble remembering the abyss and would like to be able to forget it for just a moment or two. On the other hand, those of us who can forget the abyss need some incentive to continually return to it because of its importance in understanding life.

21. Levi, *Reawakening*, 159.

9

Optimistic Pessimism

> They [chemical events] give you the impression of fighting an interminable war against an obtuse and slow-moving enemy, who, however, is fearful in terms of number and bulk; of losing all the battles, one after the other, year after year; and to salve your bruised pride you must be satisfied with the few occasions when you catch sight of a break in the enemy front and you pounce on it and administer a quick single blow.
>
> — *The Periodic Table*

Primo Levi is an "optimistic pessimist," and this oxymoron will make clear much of his life and thought. His optimism must be seen against the backdrop of a tragic existence. Levi addresses what death means, what adversities we face, and how we respond to adversity. With this sequence of questions explored, he confronts the world with his pessimism. Against a backdrop of pessimism, he counterposes his optimism.

Levi speaks of optimism frequently but usually only briefly, and these utterances are scattered throughout his works. There is probably more misunderstanding of his optimism than any of his other ideas. Miryam Anissimov in a fine biography, *Primo Levi: The Tragedy of an Optimist,* makes a reasonable assumption, given Levi's frequent use of the concept of optimism, that he is indeed an optimist. The death of an optimist in the title is meant to be ironic, because Levi is believed to have taken his own life, not usually thought of as the act of an optimist. In his article "Memories of Hell," Istevan Deak refers to Levi as a pessimist.[1] We will attempt

---

1. See Anissimov, *Primo Levi: Tragedy of an Optimist,* 12; Deak, "Memories of Hell," 39. Writes Deak: "Todorov [*Facing the Extreme: Moral Life in the Concentration Camps*], however, finds many exceptions to the laws of the jungle in concentration camp literature

to understand what Levi means by "optimism" and "pessimism" and his use of the idea of "optimistic pessimism" to bring together his thoughts on knowing and action.

Traditionally, analysts have thought of optimism on three levels: first, ideas of death; second, evil on the level of existence; and third, sentiments toward overcoming the adversities of existence. A key figure in this tradition is Gottfried Leibniz, who gives an argument for why being is good, further arguing that we can be optimistically disposed toward the circumstances we face in our lives. In his "Theodicee," he explains that God chose this world because it is the best of all possible worlds; Christianity is rational, and creation itself is reasonable. This world is the greatest collection of divine attributes possible. Evil necessarily participates in existence and shows us the greatness of the Creator. Death may lead to a better chance for the good in the afterlife and is not a necessary evil.

For Leibniz, therefore, the problems of living in this world can be overcome. This sentiment of optimism is a step into practicality when one assesses death and evil as positive and feels a good possibility for success in this world. Leibniz begins with the metaphysical proposition about good and evil in the world and proceeds to an empirical assessment of life chances, given the world of good and evil. Levi attempts to answer the two questions as well, but with different results. Nature provides Levi with the data of whether being is good, and it gives us the chance to calculate possible success against adversity. Like Leibniz and others, he contemplates the role death plays in our existence.

Schopenhauer and Leopardi bring a different perspective to questions of optimism and pessimism.[2] They look at the question from the point of view of lived existence and determine that man, as constituted, is no match for existence. Existence and practicality collapse into one judgment about the world: We are finite beings who are inadequate to existence. For Schopenhauer, the will of the world is expressed internally in the person and resembles *dukkha*, insatiable desire. Unlike his Eastern counterparts, Schopenhauer holds out no hope that we can subdue our strivings and thereby cherish actual achievements instead of being humiliated by unfulfilled de-

---

and points out that Primo Levi and other pessimists themselves performed quiet acts of compassion and heroism."

2. Levi, in *The Drowned and the Saved*, shows himself to be familiar with the pessimistic views of Schopenhauer and Leopardi. See *Drowned*, 70. Future references will be cited parenthetically in the text. For Schopenhauer and Leopardi, see Schopenhauer, *The World as Will and Representation*, vol. 1, and Leopardi, *Essays and Dialogues*, both passim.

sire. Striving is a subjective state gathered through introspection, but in Schopenhauer's world, it is invariant in intensity in man. Schopenhauer's only way out obviously is not through some form of optimism, but in the flight into aesthetic contemplation, where desires can be satisfied in the imagination. He renounces the will to live in order to lose himself in imagination. Existence, challenged by our will to live, is a corpus of endless temptations that can never be fulfilled. The flaw is within our being, because we cannot satisfy ourselves; we are inadequate to life because of our incessant desires. Both the outside world of temptations and our insatiable will are seen through the prism of lived existence. In sum, we are beings who cannot be satisfied.

For Giacomo Leopardi, life also makes its demands, and again these are seen through lived existence. We can grasp no coherent conception of happiness as an attainable goal, for the world is not within the control of the will. As with Schopenhauer, so it is with Leopardi: The world is not synchronized to our efforts. Again, with respect to life, we are insufficient beings. In reconstructing Levi's views on optimism and pessimism, we will borrow from the ideas of all three, Leibniz, Schopenhauer, and Leopardi.

Analytic philosophers tend to discount the study of optimism and pessimism on the grounds that assumptions about existence are metaphysical assumptions with no basis in truth; optimism and pessimism are purely statements of sentiment. Levi, ever the life philosopher, knows he is making assumptions, and he carefully leaves the proper tracks so that readers can find alternative sets of assumptions on which to conduct their lives if they so desire. To contemplate lived existence, it is necessary to come to some conclusions about death and the problematic aspects of the world, as well as to understand and direct our vitality. Primo Levi treats the first two dimensions, death and problematic existence, as having their subjective elements, which influence greatly the conduct of life. There are also empirical questions to answer in deciding the problematic aspects of the world, which include our own natures. The third element, our vitality, makes it imperative that we act in this life. On biological grounds, a leap into practicality may be unavoidable, for contemplation will not suffice. The leap into practicality will involve a calculation of strength relative to the adversities we face. In this analysis of vitality, Levi disagrees with Schopenhauer: Contemplation cannot be set over and above the flux of life to quell our restless will to live.

Before pushing on into Levi's ideas on optimism and pessimism, most of which were forged during the Holocaust, we should recount his recollections about the optimism of his youth. Only as a youth could Levi be considered an optimist in his thoughts about life and death, the goodness of being, and the possibilities of extracting that good. When Levi thinks back to his youth as a free man, he remembers that he thought little about death. Death was merely something that happened to others. He also felt that being was good, and that he would be able to take full advantage of the good: "I used to think of many, far-away things: of my work, of the end of the war, of good and evil, of the nature of things and to the laws which govern human actions; and also of the mountains, of singing and loving, of music, of poetry. I had an enormous, deep-rooted, foolish faith in the benevolence of fate; to kill and to die seemed extraneous literary things to me."[3]

Levi's youthful faith relied not on belief in God or on careful calculation of his chances of success based on his unique personal circumstances, but rather on the exuberance of youth, vaguely resting on the benevolence of fate. His early beliefs in science, some of which he carried through life, rested on the optimistic premise that we can uncover the laws of the universe if we proceed methodically with our studies. In his youth, science was a way of knowing and conquering recalcitrant matter: "Like Moses from that cloud I expected my law, the principle of order in me, around me, and in the world. I was fed up with books, which I still continued to gulp down with indiscreet voracity, and searched for another key to the highest truths: there must be some key, and I was certain that, owing to some monstrous conspiracy to my detriment and the world's, I would not get it in school."[4]

Levi would use science, but he would not follow the well-trodden path of his pedantic teachers: "I will understand everything, but not the way *they* [his teachers] want me to. I will find a shortcut, I will make a lock-pick, I will push open the doors."[5] In essence, he believed that we are immortal, that we can know everything, and, ultimately, that we can do anything. In William James's terms, the young Primo Levi was a happy soul. His scientific optimism continued through life, although, as he got older, he was no longer as certain that nature would yield its secrets. He also came to understand that the world was becoming disenchanted with the consequences of some scientific discoveries. Only in his youth was he a pure optimist.

3. Levi, *Survival in Auschwitz*, 143. Future references will be cited parenthetically in the text.
4. Levi, *The Periodic Table*, 23.
5. Ibid.

In his later years, Levi's optimism became tempered by his knowledge of death, the existence of evil in the world, and the restricted possibilities of action. In accordance with Leibniz's analysis, each of these themes can be separately analyzed. To begin the exploration of death, a recurrence to existential thought is necessary. For most existentialists, death is the certainty, the one limiting condition of our existence; the fact that our lives are finite colors all of our views. Levi agrees. Death is a fundamental fact not to be ignored in the contemplation of lived existence. As suggested earlier, he wishes he had the consolations of religion, but he cannot will himself to believe. He finds himself alone in the universe, and death is final.

As a fundamental fact, death, for Levi, takes on a number of important social meanings. Death's power over us is contained in our reactions to it. For Leibniz and legions of others, death may take us to a better place; it can be a good. However, because death is finality for Levi, we have to search for purpose on Earth. Life must contain its own meaning without relying upon an afterlife to bail us out, but he has doubts about life containing meaning. As explained in the last chapter, purpose and work shield us from the possibility that life is meaningless.

For Levi, death is tragic because we have a vital, almost universal urge to live, and we comprehend that our lives are so short. As we have seen, a hedonistic calculus is the final judge of what is good in the world. In terms of hedonistic calculations, death is the ultimate pain or terror of life. Levi suggests that we have a better idea of what is bad than what is good, and for the most part, people think of death as bad. Thoughts of death terrify. As a result, no one should be able to breach our freedom and cause our death against our will. We are to choose if we wish to live or die, and even if there may be no meaning in the universe, it is up to us to explore and not for anyone else to decide.

This raises the question of whether death in utilitarian terms is ever considered a good for nonbelievers. Death is a fact, most often horrifying, but it can have different social meanings, some positive.

First, as suggested earlier, Levi and Eli Wiesel feel that in horrific situations death sometimes can begin to look good. (We will speak of this at greater length in the epilogue, which confronts the circumstances of his death.)

Second, thoughts of death heighten humility and allow us to think more deeply about the meaning of existence. Keeping our finitude in mind may keep us from taking on the role of a god, a role that more often than not spares nobody from our cruelty when we play out our ambitions. Levi reminds us of the importance of the influence of death on our humanity when he suggests that to some extent, we are all like Chaim Rumkowski, the pathetic, self-important lord over the Lodz ghetto: "Like Rumkowski, we too are so dazzled by power and prestige as to forget our essential fragility." Even if, from time to time, we forget about death and forget the lessons in humility, eventually we are brought back to these thoughts at the end: "Willingly or not we come to terms with power, forgetting that we are all in the ghetto, that the ghetto is walled in, that outside the ghetto reign the lords of death, and that close by the train is waiting" (*Drowned*, 69).[6]

Finally, we can argue endlessly about whether we can go long stretches without thinking about death, or whether death is always on our mind and we must repress it. For Levi, death seems to be a constant backdrop, but it can be driven from consciousness by work or slavery to abysmal conditions. Work seems to suspend the existential questions about death, and thoughts of death are mercifully tempered by extreme circumstances where victims find themselves beneath life, necessarily immersed in activity just to survive. This raises the question for Levi: "Is it useful sometimes to forget about the idea of death, for without anesthesia, life is overwhelmed with pain?" Death was ever present to Levi because of his experience in Auschwitz. He could never forget the lessons of death, nor could he escape the pain of those thoughts for long. He wished for some momentary relief, though he knew death would never be far from his thoughts. On the other hand, Levi believes that those who rarely think of death because their hubris leads them to believe in their own infallibility and immortality need strong reminders about their own finitude.

If Levi believed in another world, death would still cast its shadow on this life, for it would tell of another place with its own rewards and punishments. Since he does not believe in an afterlife, death is an important fact for Levi, but it is one that takes its meaning from the pleasures and pains of this life, his good and evil.

For Levi, once he was past his youthful optimism and death had cast an inevitable shadow over his life, there was no turning back. He agrees with James that once we become "sick souls"—not an altogether bad state—there is no way to become again "happy souls." The key for Levi is that

---

6. Elias Canetti, in *Crowds and Power*, comes to the opposite conclusion. Thoughts of our own mortality may simply bring pleasure from the fact that we are still alive and others pass on before us, or that they are now suffering in pain.

only the individual, and not others, should be able to make choices about his or her life or death.

The second dimension of optimism and pessimism, the idea that being is good, is inextricably tied to the discussion of death. However, in our discussion of being as good, we primarily will examine Levi's pessimism about work and meaning in the world, our ill-constituted beings, our being crushed by *force majeure,* and the preponderance of pain in this world.

As Levi casts a steely glance at the world, he sees no God and hence no purpose. Work is a diaphanous veil that barely hides the meaninglessness of the world, and the other veil, religion, is not accessible to him. In addition, thoughts of death bring to the transient world an overwhelming amount of pain. A cold look at the universe thus shows no evidence of an external source of good and evil, and existence appears to be one carnivorous cycle of pain and pain. He has no theodicy to explain away any of the pain; the world is a venue for pain shadowed by death.

Furthermore, we are ill-constituted beings subject to the fates and the whims of others like ourselves. With respect to the fact that we are ill-constituted beings, we can wrest temporary victory from existence, but we are not constructed to win any permanent victories. We are on the losing end of the struggle to overcome ourselves.

Force majeure may be so powerful in existence as to render any attempts to overcome it virtually impossible. This is certainly the case with the trauma of the Holocaust that Levi so carefully describes:

> I intend to examine here the memories of extreme experiences, of injuries suffered or inflicted. In this case, all or almost all the factors that can obliterate or deform the mnemonic record are at work: the memory of a trauma suffered or inflicted is itself traumatic because recalling it is painful or at least disturbing. A person who has been wounded tends to block out the memory so as not to renew the pain; the person who has inflicted the wound pushes the memory deep down, to be rid of it, to alleviate the feelings of guilt. (*Drowned,* 24)

Because none of these defenses is completely successful, Levi and others confront the abyss daily. Jean Améry expresses the same sentiments. The Gestapo tortured him because he was active in the Belgian resistance, and then they deported him to Auschwitz because he was Jewish: "Anyone who has been tortured remains tortured. . . . Anyone who has suffered torture never again will be able to be at ease in the world, the abomination of the annihilation is never extinguished. Faith in humanity, already cracked by the first slap in the face, then demolished by torture, is never acquired again" (Améry quoted in *Drowned*, 25).

As a metaphor, *force majeure* raises the questions of the difficulties of life and how life leaves indelible footprints on our chests. Whether the traumas of childhood or the events of adulthood—most often objectively lesser horrors than the Holocaust—how can we overcome such betrayal? Of course, in Levi's terms, the standard is the hedonistic one: Can we ever overcome the unhappiness we carry within us because of guilt and fear, and face life with a "clean slate"? This question, of course, has bedeviled psychoanalysts ever since cure did not follow automatically from bringing trauma to light and "working through" became the operative "cure." Can we ever overcome the betrayal and the circumstances that caused it? William James agrees that after such instances we can never again become happy souls. In James's terms, we are left as unhappy souls with a tragic sense of life, and we can never live as in the past when we were happy souls.

Levi's hedonism suggests that the good is primarily the absence of pain; only the fugitive possibility of positive pleasure dangles in front of us. For the most part, existence is pain and its infrequent absence. In his empirical assessment, existence tends to be dominated by secularized evil, pain. Levi rarely talks about pleasure as an achievable positive good because the hierarchy of troubles dominates our lives, both in times of objective horrors and ordinary times. Pleasure is felt as a contrast to pain when our top concern disappears through luck or our own efforts. However, before we can savor the pleasure, the next trouble down on the hierarchy begins to dominate our thinking so that there can never be complete happiness.

The hierarchy of troubles is part of our constitution, making it difficult to "enjoy" life. For instance, he accuses Leopardi of excessive optimism about the good times in contrast with the bad times. Leopardi—as well as some of Levi's contemporaries, expressing themselves in literature, poetry, and films—speaks of the joys of liberation. In disagreement, Levi suggests that "[i]n the majority of cases, the hour of liberation was neither joyful nor lighthearted. For most it occurred against a tragic background of destruction, slaughter, and suffering." Joy was tempered by the tragedies men faced when the hour of liberation came and the troubles surfaced, which had mercifully been buried in the extreme times: "Just as they felt they were again becoming men, that is, responsible, the sorrows of men returned: the sorrow of the dispersed or lost family; the universal suffering all around; their own exhaustion, which seemed definitive, past cure; the problems of a life to begin all over again amid the rubble, often alone" (*Drowned*, 70–71).

Even in ordinary life, we are ever alert to the newest pain or danger that may confront us. This is part of our fate as ill-constituted beings, and this is how Levi's pessimism outdoes Leopardi's: Liberation from war is not the end to all troubles.

Schopenhauer's pessimism lurks in Levi's thoughts, but he also goes beyond Schopenhauer in showing the rich texture of our impossibility. We are ill-constituted beings who have been crushed by *force majeure*, purposeful beings whose activity simply masks the fact that there may be no purpose behind what we are doing. If we satiate our desires—merely a temporary interlude to more troubles—we become bored. Work and purpose only partially cover the pain we suffer in this life. However, where Schopenhauer sees redemption in art, Levi leavens his own Schopenhauerian pessimism on existence with his optimism about our ability to respond to adversity.

The third dimension of optimism or pessimism is the leap we make into practical life to establish a response—or make no response—to death and existence. What is our attitude and response to the good or the bad we believe is existence? It is this mood toward adversity that people often refer to when they say a person is an "optimist" or a "pessimist." If we view the structure of life and the possibility of death positively, then we are assumed to be "optimistic," beings capable of overcoming adversity.

Levi's pessimism with respect to death and the existence of evil makes the calculations about life after the leap into practicality more problematic than they were for the young, optimistic Levi. Optimism is easy when the gods and fate are lined up on our side, when we believe there is little evil to overcome, and that being is good; it is tougher for the mature Levi, who must struggle with life and death, to come to understand that death is a finality, and accept that in life there is a preponderance of pain, his secularized evil.

Where is the room for optimism? Levi is burdened by the dead weight of existence. We do not have the beginning optimism of a Leibniz that the world is the best of all worlds. Levi's meaningless world is populated by ill-constituted beings, many of whom have been crushed by *force majeure* and live in a preponderance of pain over pleasure.

The opening for Levi's optimistic response to the world of adversity comes through his hedonism, where he believes that we have an obligation to decrease pain in the world even though we ultimately fight a losing battle against it. Before progressing to a discussion of this optimism, which leavens or modifies his pessimism, we need to more thoroughly discuss existence as the house of pleasure and pain and the implications of the varying levels of misery.

Earlier discussion has suggested that there are vastly different levels of pleasure and pain depending on life circumstances. One of the horrors of Auschwitz is the realization of how much pain humans can inflict on each other, and how life can be taken away by others for no reason. This torture and death is condemned by Levi and nearly everyone in the world, and in Levi's sense, we all become hedonists, despising pain and death. We do not know the good necessarily, but we know the bad.[7] This is one of the reasons postmodernists squirm so badly when conversation turns to the Holocaust. We seem to agree on the truly bad stories, and in consequence postmodernists shrink before attacking collective stories about evil.

Levi suggests that his survival in Auschwitz hinged on some glimpse of the possibility of a world other than the Lager, a world where friend and foe alike might coexist and where inflicting pain is not the norm. As illustrated earlier, Levi could have assumed a permanent Hobbesian Hell, but when he sees the example of Lorenzo and his generosity in the face of danger, the possibility of another world, his former world, and his chances of survival are buoyed.

The world may be meaningless, and it is certainly full of pain, but one surety is that we can reduce some pain in the world. In this sense, we live in the world like Huxley's *Brave New World,* not Orwell's *1984.* This is the opening for the optimism in Levi's optimistic pessimism. Perhaps we can increase the good as well, but decreasing the bad seems always to be first on the agenda for Levi, the optimistic pessimist.

Levi fully recognizes Schopenhauer's insight about the world as will, but he does not share the pessimistic response of using the aesthetic imagination to secure desires. Once we decide to keep living, we encounter all the greater and lesser pains (evils) that we should, and do, seek to alleviate. Levi realizes this is a leap into practicality in a world that, he suspects,

---

7. The key is how long we remember this insight, and why there are exceptions, issues that will be treated in the next two chapters.

would reveal only the abyss if stripped of the veil of work and purpose. Nonetheless, we have no choice, for we are purposeful beings with a moral imperative: We ought to alleviate pain, and it is possible, at least for short periods of time, to do so.

Freedom and knowledge in the assessment of life are foundations for his hedonism. Levi suggests that circumstances are always better when we are free to be miserable in our own ways, as opposed to being under someone else's imposed jurisdiction of pain. Also, being may not be good, but in life there is certainly the terrible and the just ordinary bad; therefore, we must actively seek to reduce pain. The frustrations of pain will always be there, but as Levi explains, they are variable, and there are also some momentary victories in dealing with them.

If life is to be lived with the minimum of pain, optimism is a useful mood. In his essay "Spears Become Shields," Levi speaks of the overall importance of optimism: "I believe that a certain amount of optimism is required, without which one doesn't accomplish anything and one lives badly. 'There's no longer anything to be done' is an intrinsically suspect statement and of no practical utility; it serves only as an exorcism for him who utters it; that is, it isn't of much use." This is as much a critique of Schopenhauer's pessimism as it is an endorsement of his optimistic pessimism. Our actions can relieve pain and death: "I don't mean to say by this that nuclear holocaust is impossible: the forty thousand bombs ready to be used do, unfortunately, exist, almost all of them stored in the United States and the Soviet Union. They are a dangling sword, but there is still something one can do, the sentence has not yet been pronounced."[8] The desire to live creates a natural optimism of chances when we calculate existence. Life is a strong force.

Once we survey death and existence, we can decide what constitutes a satisfactory level of action. What does it mean, in William James's terms, to be "a match for life"? We know what the adversities of existence are and now the questions can be asked: What measure of success against adversity will bring us satisfaction? Do we set out to defeat all evil, make modest inroads into it, or pronounce ourselves successful if we can wrestle with evil even if we constantly lose ground to it? Or should we fight when we have the chance of winning and in other cases stoically not will what we cannot will? Optimism is the subjective bar of satisfaction that

8. Levi, "Spears Become Shields," in *"The Mirror Maker": Stories and Essays by Primo Levi*, 103.

we establish for success, combined with the perceived ability to satisfy that standard. This establishes our mood toward existence. In other words, in addition to making the first two calculations about death and the pleasures and pains of existence, we are left with the subjective determination of what should be a satisfactory success for us in our advances toward pleasure and against adversity. Nikos Kazantzakis, for example, does not tell us what standard to choose, but he makes it clear the types of standards we can hold ourselves to. On the page facing the prologue of *A Report to Greco*, he reports on "Three Kinds of Souls, Three Prayers":

1) I am a bow in your hands, Lord. Draw me, lest I rot.
2) Do not overdraw me, Lord. I shall Break.
3) Overdraw me, Lord, and who cares if I break!"[9]

In his discussions of the Holocaust, Levi indicates we have variable tolerances for pain and adversity. He does not set out a standard for success, other than indicating that in his case, a response to life should be slightly overbalanced toward pleasure, often in the Epicurean form of alleviation of pain. In hedonistic terms, his life is good if satisfaction outweighs dissatisfaction. In the Arunde tribe in his story "Westward," individuals can choose to die if their subjective pains outweigh their pleasures:

Each of them was taught from infancy to evaluate life exclusively in terms of pleasure and pain, factoring in, of course, also the pleasures and pains the behavior of each individual caused his fellow men. When in the judgment of each individual, the balance sheet became permanently negative, when, that is, the citizen felt he suffered and produced more sorrows than joys, he was invited to an open discussion before the council of elders and if his judgment was confirmed, the conclusion was encouraged and facilitated.[10]

Everyone has a different threshold of pain and a different measure of success. Pleasure may be keeping up with adversity, knowing you are battling with adversity, or willing what you can will and not willing what you cannot.

Ultimately, we calculate the difficulties that confront us against the expectations of the inroads we expect to make against adversity. In this sense,

9. Kazantzakis, *Report to Greco*, 16.
10. Levi, "Westward," in *"The Sixth Day" and Other Tales*, 132–33.

Levi does not assume we all have the same tolerances for adversity, either in expectation or capacity to deal with it. In contrast, Schopenhauer's pessimistic conclusions about death and existence are capped off by the equally pessimistic possibilities of action. Action, for him, is always a losing process, and the only way to deal with adversity is in the active imagination. Levi is pessimistic about death and existence, but his response to adversity is optimistic: We must make inroads into the pain of existence.

As described above, Levi believes our attitude toward life as a whole must be optimistic. Yet, he knows that the mood of optimism or pessimism is a mix of empirical observations, metaphysical assumptions, contingency, eros, expectations, and selective attention. Within the general framework of optimistic pessimism, in a specific situation, the empirical evidence may not give us accurate assessments of our chances. We can rationally calculate our chances of success, but ample room still exists for mood. One person can be optimistic and another pessimistic; moving toward optimism or pessimism can be a pragmatic choice. However, mood is a quarrelsome companion: Only under certain circumstances can we control mood, and not let it control us.

Optimism can help people survive extreme circumstances like those encountered in the Lager, and it can be useful in the struggles of everyday life. It is a matter of finding some good, any good, in circumstances where pain and suffering is overwhelming. Levi shows how what we will call "small change optimism"—the anticipation of receiving the little "goods" in life—provides sustenance when he is on the bottom. This is how small change optimism works for Levi: "It is lucky that it is not windy today. Strange how in some way one always has the impression of being fortunate, how some chance happening, perhaps infinitesimal, stops us crossing the threshold of despair and allows us to live. It is raining, but it is not windy. Or else, it is raining and is also windy: but you know that this evening it is your turn for the supplement of soup, so that even today you find the strength to reach the evening" (*Survival,* 131).

These fortuitous events first appear as luck to him. Yet, his small change optimism is grounded in empirical fact as opposed to more utopian wishes about the future. When he reflects upon his "luck," his empiricist temperament kicks in, and he sees them as real breaks and tangible benefits, not some future fantasies. Small rewards always emerge; tangible benefits would always be on the horizon in the short run. For Levi, this small change optimism turned out to be life-saving. However, it is conceivable that others, who did not survive when they were on the bottom, looked at the miseries and the small "goods" conferred by circumstances differently than Levi. Good fortune may have appeared insignificant with respect to the many miseries they suffered, may have been looked at as an ironic joke or, more likely, as without significance. We can easily see this idea of pessimism among those we encounter in ordinary life who look to existence to confirm their pessimism. Every misery confirms their bad luck. This view also looks empirically correct by its proponents; jokingly, it is given the moniker "Murphy's Law."

We may also find grounds for the appearance of small change optimism when people are subjected to intolerable conditions. If most of the time they are wondering if they can simply continue, small respites and favors that crop up must seem like miracles. For example, "when you really seem to lie on the bottom—well, even in that case, at any moment you want you could always go and touch the electric wire-fence, or throw yourself under the shunting trains, and then it would stop raining" (*Survival,* 131). Small change optimism is closer to empiricism, perhaps, than other forms of optimism, and Levi is not about to purge it from his nature.

Levi is also willing to go with his optimism when circumstances can't be calculated precisely as to their outcomes. Other times Levi knows that optimism of a certain kind might be useful, but he is unwilling to change his views of the universe for ones he believes are manifestly false. Truth and optimism can clash. Levi observes that those who believed in God or some other larger purpose, like communism, for instance, had the best chance of survival in the Lager. He sees them as optimists who felt there was a reason for their suffering. Like Leibniz, they believed evil has some meaning in the greater scheme of things. In addition, with God or some other large force, they were not alone in the universe. It was easier for them to consider that they were, in William James's terms, "a match for life." In his service to truth, however, he cannot will himself to believe in God for pragmatic reasons. James's advice about the "will to believe" would have been rejected.

Levi believes his sources of weakness and his strength come from within himself. He alone should be optimistic or pessimistic. He expects no help from the religious viewpoint, and since he knows he doesn't believe, he could never celebrate in the added superiority or hubris this viewpoint would give him with respect to others. Perhaps he agrees with Shelley that we should believe in a kind of optimism in which we are our own gods. Yet, Levi sees his aloneness in the universe as no particular advantage—

he would like to believe—but he never tries to will optimism when it goes against his fundamental ideas.

Other forms of optimism, which don't resemble small change optimism, are destructive to the psyche, and this becomes obvious in the extreme conditions of the Lager. The optimism described above is to cherish the short-term benefits and ignore the costs of living from day to day. Optimism in this sense means that the next day will bring some benefits, that luck is with you. That is acceptable to Levi. But when optimism becomes the belief that the general tenor of life may change abruptly from the awful to the good, optimism turns sour for those in the Lager. Great expectations are dashed, and the consequences are grave. All semblance of rational calculation disappears: "We had an incorrigible tendency to see a symbol and a sign in every event," Levi writes. For example, "According to our character, some of us are immediately convinced that all is lost, that one cannot live here, that the end is near and sure; others are convinced that however hard the present life may be, salvation is probable and not far off, and if we have faith and strength, we will see our houses and our dear ones again" (*Survival,* 77, 36).

In the Lager, most prisoners fluctuated wildly between the two moods: "The two classes of pessimists and optimists are not so clearly defined, however, not because there are many agnostics, but because the majority, without memory or coherence, drift between the two extremes, according to the moment and the mood of the person they happen to meet" (*Survival,* 3).

The swings can be destructive because the highs can cause hopes to be dashed, and of course, the lows can cause people to give in to existence. Levi presents an excellent example of avoiding such wild swings in moods by invoking his small change optimism: "It [the chemical exam] seems to have gone well, but I would be crazy to rely on it. I already know the Lager well enough to realize that one should never anticipate, especially optimistically. What is certain is that I have spent a day without working, so that tonight I will have a little less hunger, and this is a concrete advantage, not to be taken away" (*Survival,* 107). Small change optimism focuses on more immediate benefits, and we can count upon their appearance, but the same is not true of optimism about the sweeping changes, which are born of rumor or fantasy.

Additionally, absolute adherence to the extremes of optimism or pessimism is of no use to practical life: "More precisely: there exists a tendency, irrational but observed over the centuries, and well in evidence in situations of danger, to carry the probability of a terrible event close to its extreme values, zero and one, impossibility and certainty." Optimism, which depends upon the induction of feelings, may sway us to the more probable, but grasping at certainty is going too far. It is not only a violation of empiricism for Levi, but as he suggests, it has hurtful consequences for the individual: "And yet we should reject our innate tendency toward radicalism, because it is a source of evil. Both the zero and the one lead us to inaction: if the future damage is impossible or certain, the 'what to do?' ceases."[11]

Extreme pessimism, however paralyzing in normal productive life, does have its uses in conditions of extreme slavery. There, pessimism accords with the fact that except for small change optimism, nothing changes, and if it does, it is always for the worst. In the following example, an optimistic rumination proves to be a useless expenditure of energy:

> "When things change, they change for the worse" was one of the proverbs of the camp. More generally, experience had shown us many times the vanity of every conjecture: why worry oneself trying to read into the future when no action, no word of ours could have the minimum influence: We were old Häftlinge: our wisdom lay in "not trying to understand," not imagining the future, not tormenting ourselves as to how and when it would all be over; not asking others or ourselves any questions. (*Survival*, 116)

In other words, don't will what you can't will because the effort consumes psychic capital, a commodity in short supply. Levi sees worrying functioning in the same way that British psychoanalyst Adam Phillips does: Historically, the term *worry* is an active verb, and worry is an active process that expends a large amount of energy.[12] In the Lager, when the prisoners anticipated some kind of liberation, the possibility of psychic exhaustion caused by optimism arose: "We all said to each other that the Russians would arrive soon, at once; we all proclaimed it, we were all sure of it, but at bottom nobody believed it. Because one loses the habit of hoping in the Lager, and even of believing in one's own reason. In the Lager it is useless to think, because events happen for the most part in an unforeseeable manner; and it is harmful, because it keeps alive a sensitivity which is a source of pain" (*Survival*, 171).

11. Levi, *Other People's Trades*, 103–4.
12. Phillips, *On Kissing, Tickling and Being Bored*, 50–51.

This last quote includes the additional insight that true optimism in these circumstances is not possible, because at bottom hope depends upon the general belief in our own reason, and that belief has been destroyed. Paradoxically, optimism can only come about when the use of reason is suspended with regard to specific prospects.

In addition to the many ways that optimism proved useful or useless in the Lager, for the most part the insistent hierarchy of troubles and their dogged presence in the mind crowded out most thoughts of optimism and pessimism. Prisoners operated beneath life: "The fight against hunger, cold and work leaves little margin for thought, even for this thought. Everybody reacts in his own way, but hardly anyone with those attitudes which would seem the most plausible and the most realistic, that is with resignation or despair" (*Survival*, 124–25).

Levi's perspective on life is an optimistic pessimism. He is pessimistic because we are faced with death, which he sees as tragedy. Levi's attitude toward death is indicative of how we can approach the evils of existence. We must try to rally against them, but ultimately it is a losing proposition. Evil is the preponderance of pain, and we will suffer much pain in our lives for three reasons: it is impossible to achieve happiness, we are ill-constituted individuals who usually make more than less pain, and we have been crushed by *force majeure*.

Levi's optimism, which modifies his pessimism, is based on the idea that we can make some inroads against pain in this life. His method of choosing calls for small change optimism, which gives us the vitality to continue and holds closely to his empiricism. We will continue to encounter his optimistic pessimism when we discuss his ideas on public life, which are based on his tragic sense of life, hedonism, and optimistic pessimism. Much is wrong with the public situation, and it may well overwhelm us, but we have no choice but to try to do something about it.

Defense of Modernism

10

Civilized Liberalism

"Everything is arcane/but our pain," to quote Leopardi once more:
the certitudes of the layman are few, but the first is this: suffering
(and inflicting suffering) is acceptable only if rewarded by the
avoidance of greater suffering to oneself or others.

— Other People's Trades

And one must take into account a definite cushioning effect exercised both by the law, and by the moral sense which constitutes a
self-imposed law; for a country is considered more civilized the
more the wisdom and efficiency of its laws hinder a weak man from
becoming too weak or a powerful one too powerful.

— Survival in Auschwitz

Primo Levi embraces the modern insight that we are all strangers and that
we commence thinking about others from the standpoint of our own individuality. His political philosophy develops from the perspective of an out-
sider who becomes engulfed by Auschwitz and comes to understand both
the fragility and importance of solidarity with others. The Holocaust reinforces the difference with others Levi felt when he was a youth studying for
his degree in chemistry. Levi's return, after the Holocaust, to others is literally from an individuated state with the clear realization of his aloneness.

Adam Phillips grasps this modern temper when he writes, "Our life will
be what we can make of feeling left out. That experience, which takes so
many forms, is the raw material."[1] This is especially true for Levi, who be-

1. Phillips, *Monogamy*, 114.

199

lieves exclusion is a primary political question. Upon his return from the Holocaust, Levi, basically a shy man in the service of his chemistry and science, felt compelled to witness to what he saw and speak out about what social arrangements could be made to minimize the possibilities of another Holocaust. Politics is a return to others, and he was compelled to write and talk about how strangers can get together. Levi understood that we can never become one with others, but we have to try. As Georg Simmel suggests, even if we try to identify completely with another, we are not identical in interests to the other person, and we remain alone. This raises several questions for Levi: Can we join together in political arrangements that allow us to live together? Can these modern arrangements work through time to prevent the Holocaust from happening again? Is it possible that the social and political arrangements we call "modernism" are the cause of the Holocaust in the first place?

Levi's intellectual life began with the idea that he was an individual, slightly alienated from other students, afraid of women. Only his bonds to science and his chemistry education were secure. The war plucked him from his lonely individualism, causing him to re-evaluate his stance toward other people. The Holocaust did nothing to dissuade him from the idea that solidarity is fleeting, especially in times of scarcity. Yet, the idea that he could live the rest of his life free of attachments was a "luxury view" for someone who had been deported to the Lager. He could not be Jean Améry's detached philosopher, because he optimistically hoped to stave off, at least for a time, the overwhelming collective violence in this world.

A key to Levi's political philosophy is that his writings support modernism. His view goes against the conventional, casual wisdom which argues that the Holocaust proves modernism is a failure.[2] Levi argues otherwise: We have known what the right behavior is all along, and the simple problem is that the Germans were not educated to the good. In a finite world of ill-constituted human beings, it is unfair to hold modernism as an infallible position and then decide it is completely discredited by the

2. See Zygmunt Bauman, *Modernity and the Holocaust*, for a thorough discussion of the relationship of modernity to the Holocaust. As we shall see, Levi is a firm supporter of modernity, but he is not unaware of some of its more dangerous features, like technology and bureaucracy. In the end, he does not see any turning back to a premodern world, nor any reasonable alternative to modernity.

Holocaust.[3] Does Auschwitz prove that modernism contains its own seeds of destruction and inevitably leads to fascism? No more than we can deem fascism responsible for the restoration of democratic governments in Western Europe, because incipient democracies succeeded fascism in Europe. Can we say fascism is the cause of democracy because of the fatal flaw that Bertrand Russell points to in fascism: that the ceaseless rhythm of power over power is doomed in the end to fail?[4]

Levi would not minimize the horror of Auschwitz by saying that fascism is only a blip on the graph of modernism and now Western civilization is on the right course. The Holocaust was a ghastly, consequential event, and levelheaded analysts must come to some understanding about its causes. More specifically, is modernism the cause? Is modernism's failure caused by the weakness of liberal democracy? For Levi, strong civic education can work. As Russell predicted before the war, the U.S. and Britain would not succumb to fascism because they had too long a history of representative government. Education of our recalcitrant souls is the key to staving off fascism for Levi as it is for Russell.

Levi sees the origins of violence in human nature. The tenuous cure for strife lies in the education to modern political arrangements. We are self-aggrandizing beings who under pressure quickly lose all solidarity with others. In harsh circumstances, the propensity for hierarchy and subordination, rather than disappearing, becomes dominant, even in situations where the stakes are minimal. When Levi thinks about nature, he sees violence as a constant and the norm, and although he won't give in, his hopes for any civilization are low. Modern political arrangements, as do any political arrangements, have the tragedies of being human built into them. For Levi, these tragedies cause the miseries of the world, and there is no permanent cure. All of this is an expression of his tragic optimistic pessimism.

Levi's optimism is that we can maintain the thin film of civilization through education. His optimism informs his politics with the idea that people can be educated against their basic propensities. He knows genocide has occurred before Auschwitz and has occurred afterward, but education, however weak it may be, is the only barrier to its recurrence. Fighting against mass murder is an important part of his overall campaign to

3. Levi is careful in his strong defense of modernism not to trivialize the systematic deaths of so many people.
4. See Russell, *"In Praise of Idleness" and Other Essays,* 82–120.

minimize pain and maximize pleasure in our lives. At first, it appears this is an antinaturalistic ethics, for human nature's tendencies, according to Levi, are toward destructive behavior. However, evidence exists that we are initially educable to cooperation and exchange, even though their hold on us is tenuous.

Education is the only counter for Levi to our ill-constituted selves, and it does work in some situations. Garth Wood is correct in saying that virtually all of us are civilized to some degree, and to do ill, we have to rationalize to overcome our education.[5] There may be exceptions, like Elias, but most of us have some degree of education that must be overcome before we can hurt others. As suggested earlier, throughout his writings Nietzsche marshals arguments against the herd society and the human tendency to put down massive self-assertions, yet he admits that he may be arguing to defeat the dominant trait of humans: their conformity to conventional standards. For Nietzsche, civilization, and not the will to power, may predominate. The rare exceptions are the sporadic Napoleons and others who create new values in society. For Levi, this overcoming of civilization is all too common, but at least education has a fighting chance.

The conflict between atavism and education may be expressed in a slightly different way. Modernism fails if people think that striving for liberty and equality will settle problems of existence. Liberty and equality are ultimately tragic concepts. Liberty has no answer to the question, "Liberty to do what?" What is our liberty for? If we don't have liberty, does liberty provide its own raison d'être? What happens if we do have it? Does having liberty hamper the development of fraternity? Equality has that same element of tragedy, for if we achieve equality, then we are truly unhappy, for nobody wants to be equal. We want freedom and equality at the same time. Tocqueville understands the tragedy of liberty and equality and sees the many ways they clash with each other in practice. For example, liberty for the few can be achieved on the backs of abject equality of others, which gives us a mass society and all its vices.[6]

If we define modernism as the secular movement to build a liberal political system that promises to bring the good, then we have to understand that built into any human endeavor is the possibility of failure. The project is virtually impossible because of our cold reason, our irrational passions, and many other contradictions we embody. In addition, the tragedy

5. Garth Wood, *The Myth of Neurosis*, 141–46.
6. Tocqueville, *Democracy in America*, 1:264–80.

of modernism manifests the contradiction that the freedom it demands will always be incompatible with the rational structures built up during the same period of time: the embodiment of the conflicting demands of the individual and the group. It is built into the structure of all situations, but only in democracies are people encouraged to understand and act as if these differences are reconcilable. In democratic politics, the conflict between freedom and civilization is highlighted in Joseph Schumpeter's inquiry into whether a democratic civilization is free to vote for those whose program for rule is to vote out the democratic constitution and arbitrarily institute another form of government.[7]

For Levi, as for Freud, civilization is a thin veneer. Freud suggests in a letter to Albert Einstein that he is surprised that given human nature there is not more violence in the world. Levi is careful to suggest that human weakness is not an excuse for the Holocaust, which it would be for the pessimist. The challenge to the optimistic pessimist is to stop the brutality rather than accept it. Modernism is simply our best chance as tragic beings, and education of a particular kind for Levi, one that emphasizes the utility of recognizing pain and avoiding it, is our only course.

Levi's call for a civilized education runs counter to many other educational ideas that speak in praise of violence and destruction. One of the defining characteristics of humans is how easy it is for us to rationalize violent acts. It is one of our proclivities that distinguishes us from other animals. William James recognizes this all too well in his essay "The Moral Equivalent of War," where he identifies a war-regime that chooses to teach the manliness of war and heroism. This group, which makes up a large contingency of citizens in most civic cultures, cannot be reasoned with on the grounds that pain and inequality are evils and must be limited. Instead, the war-regime must be cleverly addressed in terms they will understand and accept. They cannot be convinced of the virtues of peace, but they might accept the moral equivalent of war as a replacement for the overwhelming destruction of modern warfare. Ernest Becker provides the psychological underpinnings of the war-regime in suggesting that some manage the fear of death by painting evil as the face or faces of people different from themselves.[8]

Modern liberalism devolves down to a method, one best described by James Madison in Federalist #10. Liberalism is not dependent on the as-

7. Schumpeter, *Capitalism, Socialism, and Democracy,* 242.
8. James, *"Pragmatism" and Other Essays,* 289–301; Becker, *Escape from Evil,* 48–50.

sumption of good will and a peace party that can convince the recalcitrant to be of good will. In Madisonian democracy, we are free to press our claims, and yet we strive for some kind of equity because we know our claims will differ. We are not talking about truth anymore, but about power. We decide through decisions, rules, and arrangements that pit power against power. This is the American cure for our ambivalence where we want liberty and equality at the same time. Decisions are partially taken out of our untrustworthy hands.

Can we make the psychological argument that modernism relies on a tragic sense to make democracy work—for instance, Madison's view that there is no truth and we cannot even trust ourselves? If we rely on this Madisonian insight for our political arrangements, is the idea that ambition must be made to counteract ambition an effective counter to the possibility that a mass public will grow to believe that truth is a big Truth in the grasp of one great person?

Levi relies on process for making choices in modern politics, a process similar to Madison's, where limitation of power is the good and there is no necessary historical dialectic leading to tyranny. In systems with Madisonian arrangements, powerful interests will do less harm, a goal that is an integral part of Levi's hedonism. In "Westward," Levi's story describing the mores of a hedonistic tribe, "[e]ach of them was taught from infancy to evaluate life exclusively in terms of pleasure and pain, factoring in, of course, also the pleasures and pains the behavior of each individual caused his fellow men."[9] As we shall see, democratic politics is the modern answer for the limitation of pain, one that suits Levi.

Levi's political nerve is never more evident than when he defends liberal democracy with his eyes open. He knows that freedom can sweep every idea in its wake, and that is one of the tragedies of modern thought. As Raymond Aron found out in France, defense of democracy is not glamorous, and it is often looked at as plodding.[10] However, democracy renders less harm than other political arrangements. Levi, too, understands that the exciting is not necessarily the good: "It is better to content oneself with other more modest and less exciting truths, [than from charismatic leaders and prophets] those one acquires painfully, little by little and without shortcuts, with study, discussion, and reasoning, those that can be

9. Levi, "Westward," in *"The Sixth Day" and Other Tales,* 132.
10. Allan Bloom, *Giants and Dwarfs: Essays, 1960–1990,* 256, 257, 267.

verified and demonstrated."[11] "Modest truths" is another minimalist concept, which is parallel to Levi's idea of small change optimism. They are less glamorous than great truths and big bucks optimism, but they are forged from careful observation and brutal experience.

Levi is not naïve in his understanding of the fundamental weaknesses of a democratic society. As with man, society also is laced with tragic flaws. Where he differs from many believers in liberal democracy is that he does not subscribe to their idea of unbridled progress, but rests his argument on his optimistic pessimism. The belief in progress caused many to see the Holocaust as the death knell of modernism, because the opposite of progress seemed to result. Levi understands that new ideologies are fueled by hope in progress, but just as quickly they can be trashed when those high hopes are not fulfilled. The optimistic pessimism of a Levi holds steady on its views of liberal democracy: failures are the all-too-human failures.

Earlier, we documented Primo Levi's views about the state of nature, which evolved from his experiences in Auschwitz. In *Survival in Auschwitz,* he documents the first social contract made by the survivors in his barracks. For political philosophers, the state of nature and the subsequent social contract are hypothetical states that give us insights into human nature free of social entanglements. Out of the necessity for some sense of order or design, the social contract arises to remove man from the state of nature. Contracts may vary from the absolutist solution of Thomas Hobbes to John Lockes's "accord," which allows individuals to keep certain basic rights. John Rawls revives this tradition with his idea of the original position and the type of agreement that would have to be drawn up to insure a minimum set of protections for those in the state of nature who cannot predict how they would fare in the new polity.[12]

When Levi conceptualizes about the state of nature and the first contract, his discussion does not involve hypothetical situations but the actual description of the Lager reducing man to the state of nature and the description of an actual social contract after the SS abandoned Auschwitz. He is an inspiration to thinkers who might otherwise have a tendency to ignore actual matters of the flesh in order to weave their own hypothetical fears into a description of human nature and into the social contract.

11. Levi, *The Reawakening,* 215.
12. Rawls, *A Theory of Justice,* 17–22.

Levi's terms, of course, are utilitarian, knowing what the bad is, not some ultimate justification for the good. In the end, for Levi enlightenment virtues guarantee a minimization of the bad.

Levi's civilized liberalism succeeds and Rawls's liberal theory of justice appears weaker because Levi bases his thoughts on the flesh and not on hypothetical calculation. Levi describes his own pain and the terrors of living "beneath life," not some hypothetical state of nature. There is no original position for Levi and no natural conservative inclination for people uncertain about their future status to look for a contract to cushion their fall if they happen to land at the bottom. In the short story "The Hard Sellers," bureaucrats try to persuade a worker from another planet to be born on Earth. While the bureaucrats do their best to play up the Earth's virtues and ignore its flaws, the worker cannily understands earthlings' miseries and flaws. Given the possibility of a guaranteed safe place on the planet, Levi's character rejects Rawls's security. He is willing to take his chances in the world with all of the other people being born and forgo the chance for a head start with a privileged position: "You yourself said that each man is his own maker: well, it is best to be so fully, build oneself from the roots."[13]

Those who get together to make up Rawls's social contract would be members of what James describes as the peace party and not those of the war-regime. Rawls simply ignores the latter in his calculations, for they would most likely assume they would be winners in any new polity. Levi faces an uphill battle to educate the war-regime that pain should be minimized and that pain is not simply an unfortunate artifact of heroic, successful endeavors. Looking for the good and ignoring the bad describes the disposition of the war-regime, a significant force in society, but the war-regime must be educated to understand the importance of the bad in terms of pain. For Levi, relief of pain is not a precondition for social organization, but part of the educational process that is carried on after the social contract is agreed upon. Civilization is a consequence, not a precondition, of the social contract.

The elaboration of the "bottom" in Auschwitz and the subsequent social contract are the baseline assumptions for Levi's political liberalism. Both the state of nature and the actual contract after liberation are very much intertwined with his conclusions about the ill-constituted nature of man and his optimistic pessimism; it is of one piece. We will explain Levi's

13. Levi, "The Hard Sellers," in *"Sixth,"* 160.

modernist interpretation of the state of nature and the social contract briefly before we undertake a more extended analysis of the two.

First, life in Auschwitz, in Levi's understanding of the state of nature, is cast entirely in terms of modern discourse, ideas of freedom, solidarity, and equality. The Hobbesian Hell of Auschwitz, cast in the language of pleasure and pain, describes a situation where the virtues of modernism have disappeared and would look very good to the survivors if they could catch a nostalgic breath. Any attempt to cast these circumstances in a discourse other than the modern one faces great difficulties. To say that "hell" is just another discourse, or that we may play with other discourses, is difficult to sustain in the face of the Hobbesian Hell of the Lager. There is always a free play of imagination, but moving too far from the experience of pain in describing Auschwitz too obviously resides close to delusion. Modernism is appropriate discourse for expressing the horror and the experience and holds out the possible promise of return from pain. Levi understands, of course, that modernism is laced with tragic problems.

Second, Hobbesian Hell and the social contract allow Levi to use the traditional democratic discourse of politics, including ideas like freedom, solidarity, equality, and civilization. Most of these ideas were willfully forgotten in the Hobbesian world of the Lager, but with the cessation of the war, many of these political virtues were restored. However, Levi no longer believed in the progress of democracy, and he returned as an optimistic pessimist to a world shot through with contradiction. In comparison with the hell of the Lager, ordinary life may at first glance appear to be a utopia, but Levi returned with his eyes open. Perfect happiness can never exist in this world, either.

The remaining pages of this chapter will first examine Hobbesian Hell with respect to the loss of modern virtues of civilization: solidarity, equality, freedom, and responsibility. Second, we will describe the emergence of a social contract in Levi's barracks at the time of the liberation of Auschwitz. When Levi looks at the bottom, Hobbesian Hell, his analysis is in terms of loss. The fragile fruits of modernity quickly are lost to the horrors of man against man. Lost is the social contract, which guarantees some stability and continuity with others, plus the benefits of cooperation and friendship. Freedom, obviously, is snatched away as well. Swept away in the brutality and scarcity of the Lager was civilization and its correlate, responsibility, part of which is to insure that the burden of those worse off is lightened. It is difficult to disagree with this assessment and not feel like we are playing an insincere game with someone else's pain.

At the bottom, the prisoners were not party to any social contract. Status at birth was normally the reason for their being in the Lager, and their captors toyed with their lives. At worst, Hobbes thought that individuals would get together to give up their sovereignty to a potential ruler for the promise of peace, but in Hobbesian Hell no possibility of agreements existed; there is no social dialogue. The traditional paternal guarantees of ancient regimes were nonexistent, and there certainly was no joint participation in important decisions as there had been in the good times of modernity. Not only was it not a world familiar to the prisoners, through habit or through mutual consent, but they were not privy to the logic of the Lager's social organization. There was no "why" there; it was an alien world with no known rules of behavior. No words like *challenge, mystery* or *adventure* were apropos, because these terms presuppose a chance to return to ordinary life. There was no room for some revival of classical heroism as a substitute for the continuities of contract and solidarity, for as Levi points out, the best, the heroes, did not survive. The hero acted and was dead within minutes.

The contract Hobbes envisions, in which the sovereign turns out to be an autocrat, would seem like paradise. With no contract, those who constituted the mass, the prisoners, remained in a state of nature. Modernism begins for Levi with the idea of the contract, and he makes it clear why the contract is preferable to the predatory state of nature aggravated by deliberate scarcity. Even the traditional stability would have been preferable to the state of nature, but for Levi there is a yearning for contractual existence that would provide at least a chance for the modern virtues of civilization: solidarity, liberty, equality, responsibility, and the optimistic pessimism toward progress.

In the state of nature, the lack of these virtues is felt as a loss, and they were lost quickly in the Lager. Many definitions of civilization can be found in Levi's work, but they generally describe attempts to overcome ourselves as ill-constituted beings. First, civilization is a series of institutional arrangements in which the individual, in a noncoercive situation, can maintain dignity, hence identity. Plato's division of labor in the *Republic*— although made to work with the help of a lie, the myth of the metals— was one of the first attempts. Everyone would have a place for himself and his talents in Plato's world. In contrast, in the Lager, without a social contract, dignity was virtually unattainable. Talents were abused, personal morality was compromised by murderous scarcity, and the Lager was a death machine. The Salonica Greeks were among the few able to maintain a bit of dignity by resolutely maintaining a bargaining market in the Lager. They did so by ignoring the terror, instability, and the camp wisdom to forget prior virtues:

> That this wisdom [of the Salonica Greeks] was transformed in the camp into the systematic and scientific practice of theft and seizure of positions and the monopoly of the bargaining Market, should not let one forget that their aversion to gratuitous brutality, their amazing consciousness of the survival of at least a potential human dignity made of the Greeks the most coherent national nucleus in the Lager, and in this respect, the most civilized.[14]

Dignity, or the ability to hold to one's beliefs without being forced to abandon them, is one of Levi's definitions of civilization.

Levi goes along with Jean Améry's idea that dignity is necessary for life, and that is precisely what the Nazis took away: "And yet, in order to live, an identity—that is, dignity—is necessary. For him [Jean Améry] the two concepts coincide. Whoever loses one also loses the other, dies spiritually: without defenses he is therefore exposed also to physical death." In Améry's youth, he first identified himself as a German and subsequently as an intellectual. After his capture, the Germans defined him as a Jew and a slave laborer. He had never thought of himself as a Jew and prided in the fact that as an intellectual, he was above manual labor. According to Améry, a forcible loss of identity can be devastating, but a manual laborer forced to toil for others might not suffer as much indignity:

> At any case, whichever definition [of an intellectual] one may choose, one can only agree with Améry's conclusions. At work, which was prevalently manual, the cultivated man generally was much worse off than the uncultivated man. Aside from physical strength, he lacked the familiarity with the tools and the training, which, however, his worker or peasant companion often had; in contrast, he was tormented by an acute sense of humiliation and destitution. Of *Entwurdigung,* that is precisely: lost dignity.[15]

14. Levi, *Survival in Auschwitz,* 79. Future references will be cited parenthetically in the text.

15. Levi, *The Drowned and the Saved,* 128, 132. Future references will be cited parenthetically in the text.

Levi detects the almost universal tendency in the Lager for prisoners to madly scramble for any material scrap or miserable position that may give them even the slightest edge over others. Améry's subtle, smug intellectual was replaced in Auschwitz by the trampling of one by another to find some meaningless scrap or sinecure to elevate one's status. A civilized society, in contrast, allows for a free, rule-governed jostling for position in the social and political order.

If we combine his thoughts on civilization, Levi first defines it as rules to ensure the dignity of one's place or role in the political system, rules that should do away with the sharpest tendencies toward hierarchy as well as those of coercion. This makes way for a second element in his definition of civilization. In several places he says that civilization is where we try to insure that those at the bottom are helped by the social and political systems. Levi indicates that equalization of dignity must take place at the top as well as the bottom. Here he is speaking of the enlightenment virtue of equality: "And one must take into account a definite cushioning effect exercised both by the law, and by the moral sense which constitutes a self-imposed law; for a country is considered more civilized the more the wisdom and efficiency of its laws hinder a weak man from becoming too weak or a powerful one too powerful" (*Survival,* 80). In contrast, in the Lager, coercive hierarchy was the dominant social organization.

Levi is aware of the tragedy of equality in normal society, where equality may clash with liberty and our hierarchical tendencies. Equality, according to Levi, is something we must teach, but for him it has the logic of a commandment. The teaching of equality is necessary because the human tendency is to break the commandment. We preach equality to convince ourselves, but we do not ultimately believe in it. This is one of our key agonies.

Levi acknowledges the difficulty of the battle for equality when he posits the idea that civilization is caring for the less fortunate, yet the evidence from the camp is that we abandon others under stress and have a natural propensity toward advantage. What is so devastating is not that people finally gave in to terror and abuse at the Lager, but how easily civilization collapsed in the earliest stages. As suggested, support of equality is not a naturalistic position for Levi; it is fighting an uphill battle through education. His liberalism, based as it is on the flesh, is grounded in pain and optimistic pessimism, not on the Rawlsian idea that if we did not know our future prospects we would not want to take our chances in life, but insure preferential treatment for those at the bottom. There is no assumption that in the state of nature each person would opt for a system of advantages for those at the bottom. In fact, Levi knows that his position is a hard sell. Few are convinced the worst could happen to them, and fewer would do something in advance to prevent the worst from happening to others.

Perhaps Elie Wiesel expresses Levi's idea of civilization most poignantly when he speaks of his father's generous obligation to feed the hungry. Before Auschwitz, his father always made available a pot of soup for those less fortunate. One of the servants asks him, "How can I tell which ones are really hungry?" Wiesel's father says that one should feed them all, for it is more important not to turn down even one person who is hungry: "'Don't try,' my father said. 'I'd rather feed someone whose pockets are full than send someone away on an empty stomach.'"[16] Today, more emphasis is on policing the weak so that they do not take advantage of the strong in charitable situations. In other words, more emphasis is on not being cheated by the gonif than being charitable to those who need it. Inner strength manifested by the privileged does not come easily. As Nietzsche points out, the "strong" must be secure enough in their own person to allow themselves to be taken advantage of from time to time.

A major fall from civilized modernism in the Lager was the loss of freedom. A prerequisite to action is the ability to think of alternatives, and for the most part this ability was lost in the Lager. As discussed earlier, the attack on bodies was an attack on minds, for one could only concentrate on the pain of the present moment. The days belonged to the prisoners' captors, and except for the occasional respite at Ka-Be, they had little time for contemplation. Even on the occasions when there was a bit of rest, weariness made it difficult to concentrate on anything. Nor did the nights belong to the prisoners. Their dreams were repetitive and insistent. They woke up dreaming of eating food, being shouted at by people speaking another language, or telling the story of what happened to them to an indifferent audience. Hobbesian prisoners functioned by doing what they were compelled by their captors to do, and the pathetic *musselmans* were beyond any kind of thought at all. Their minds and their bodies belonged to their captors.

As well as their inability to conjure alternatives, even if they could, they were extremely limited in their ability to act. When they arrived at the camps, the prisoners already were exhausted and degraded by the experience. Only the very few chose to act as heroes and commit suicide, for that

16. Wiesel, *All Rivers Run to the Sea: Memoirs*, 15.

takes strength, a rare commodity in the Lager. Once the choice was made to live, they moved beneath life into the Hobbesian mode.

Nobody was in the Lager by choice, and they remembered enough to know that if they had their choice—perhaps with the exception of Elias—they would not choose to be in the Lager.[17] However, they were powerless to change their circumstances. Given the overwhelming force around them, and with their freedom to think of alternatives gone, their future was in the hands of fate, or for the religious, God. The *musselmans* were beyond caring.

For Levi, freedom runs concurrently with responsibility. In *The Drowned and the Saved,* the tortuous conditions of the Lager diminish the prisoners' responsibilities for their actions, putting even the worst of them only in Levi's gray zone. To be a man is to be responsible (to make free choices and be accountable for them). The opposite, in this context, were the *musselmans,* who were the living dead with regard to making choices. With two key enlightenment virtues gone in the Lager, freedom and responsibility, man was greatly diminished.

When the hour of liberation was upon the prisoners, it was not a time of joy for the liberated, because they felt rekindled responsibility for themselves and others: Could they find their families? Could they find food on their own? Could they make their way back home? These thoughts came "[j]ust as they were again becoming men, that is responsible" (*Drowned,* 70). As they emerged from the Hobbesian jungle, the problems of the jungle were replaced by life problems, which were formerly submerged in their hierarchy of troubles. Yet, though life after Auschwitz still remained defensive, it was infinitely better to have it in the full blush of freedom. He expresses this idea in *Survival in Auschwitz,* after having a good day and a bit of leisure to think: "[W]e feel good, the Kapo feels no urge to hit us, and we are able to think of our mothers and wives, which usually does not happen. For a few hours we can be unhappy in the manner of free men" (*Survival,* 76).

Along with the exercise of freedom, which can cause pain, the obligations to freedom and responsibility run counter to his ordinary hedonism. As Levi indicates, responsibility is not always pleasurable, but it is an obligation, an imperative. Levi confirms the grave and painful responsibility

17. Elias was perhaps the lone exception to all those who, if they got their bodies and hence their minds back even ever so briefly, craved for their prior freedom. He, in contrast, seemed to enjoy and thrive in his captivity. Elias is perhaps a testament to the idea that it is virtually impossible to find a universal social law.

to responsibility. In *The Reawakening,* when he is asked to comment on the conditions for those interned in the camps of Stalin's Russia, he says: "I do not want to, nor can I evade the duty which every man has, that of making a judgment and formulating an opinion."[18] The issue for Levi is not that we must formulate opinions, but that we cannot help doing so. If we encounter others, it is impossible to evade judgments, because "to recuse all judges is not only presumptuous but useless. Useless because every turn in life, every human encounter, involves a judgment delivered or received, so it is a good idea to get used to receiving and delivering judgments when one is young, when it is easier to contract habits."[19] We cannot stop ourselves. What is important, however, is that we must accept our responsibility by speaking out about and acting upon these judgments, especially when they involve matters of pain to ourselves or others. Freedom to think or act was totally lacking in the Lager, but once we have that freedom, it comes coupled with the responsibility to act through speech or deed. So once again, freedom and responsibility are in the service of Levi's hedonism.

In Levi's mind, we are obligated to help others as well as ourselves, even though helping others is a lost sentiment in much of human behavior. His social ethic is strong and comes from his background in Judaism, and it is consistent with his hedonism. One person is not enough to stand up to evil. He or she, as an individual, is faced with freedom or death. Defense must be collective.

In Isaiah Berlin's terms, Levi's freedom is the negative freedom, freedom from the power of others.[20] We should be able to fight against the pain caused by others and enjoy the luxury of dealing with the ordinary pains of a free society. Except in extremely rare instances, Auschwitz drove away the modern virtues of freedom and responsibility through a regime of fatigue, terror, and gratuitous violence.

Levi does not overly indulge himself in the more abstract and subtle problems of freedom that occur to people with a surfeit of possibilities. Rousseau's concerns with positive freedom and the possibility to force people to be free within the democratic context of the general will, and the more individualized version, the idea that God is dead and that everything is possible, do address Levi's concern that there may be a good. However,

18. Levi, *Reawakening,* 208.
19. Levi, *"The Mirror Maker": Stories and Essays by Primo Levi,* 99.
20. Berlin, *The Proper Study of Mankind,* 194.

these proclamations are far too radical for Levi. His freedom is coupled with the desire to minimize harm for pain of the flesh. Heroism is not heroism if it involves the diminution of others.

Levi's freedom is not the dissolving of false consciousness, but the freedom to decide on the basis of an open forum, free from physical coercion. The problem of false consciousness is a problem in societies where there is severe terror in the way of free expression. In free societies, he does not worry himself about the problems of false consciousness that may restrict what we say and do, whether it is a result of Tocqueville's tyranny of the majority or the tacit wishes of a ruling elite. Education is the remedy for false consciousness, and the individual bears a great deal of the responsibility for knowing. The problem of knowing in a free society is ultimately one of self-restriction; educating the dupes is a secondary problem.

For Levi, all of the virtues of the modern civilized world—civilization, solidarity, equality, freedom, and responsibility—were lost in Auschwitz, with devastating consequences. All analyses of the Holocaust that do not see these virtues as a loss seem like irresponsible play, or worse, cruel self-indulgence. Of course, Levi knows that once established, modernist virtues are problematic. In ordinary life, modernist values conflict, for instance, freedom versus equality, and freedom versus solidarity. We must struggle to put up with these and other modern problems. As discussed, where Levi parts with modernism is the distancing of his views from the idea of progress by substituting the more subtle idea of tragic optimistic pessimism.

We now turn to Levi's description of the social contract. In the last days of Auschwitz, he participated in and witnessed an actual contract, one that serves as his "ideal" of government. It is found in the concluding chapter of *Survival in Auschwitz,* "The Story of Ten Days." Here, he describes the transition from the horror of slavery and death to the return to the status of free men. It is the return to modernity, the slow dawning of civilization —solidarity, equality, freedom, and responsibility. "Government" begins with the free exchange that takes place among the eleven in Levi's barrack of Ka-Be, who were left for dead by the fleeing SS. It is the establishment of a rudimentary social contract.

The sick in his barracks were not, as in the hypothetical situations crafted by contract theorists, coming from a state of nature without some knowledge of prior contracts. Rousseau reminds us that in a state of nature, individuals would not have the language skills presupposed in John Locke's writings. In the Lager, however, prisoners had knowledge of a contract prior to their enslavement. In their own languages, through gesture and a limited shared vocabulary, they communicated the terms of a new contract. It returned them to the status of "man," a recognizable bond with a group of individuals who shared a barracks. For Levi, this experience was formative.

As we have seen, this was not Levi's first experience of social organization in the Lager. Prior to these last ten days, Levi had experienced the exchange of the markets that sprang up even under the coercive heel of the Nazis. More important, Levi's earliest contract in the Lager was his us-ism with Alberto. However, the major social contract was this one from Levi's last ten days in Auschwitz. After the SS cleared out and before the Russians liberated the Lager, the only ones of the eleven left in Ka-Be capable of helping themselves were Levi and two French political prisoners: Arthur, a slight peasant, and Charles, a robust schoolteacher. The Germans had abandoned the central heating plant: "I was thinking that we would have to find a stove to set up and get some coal, wood and food. I knew that it was all essential, but without some help I would never have had the energy to carry it out" (*Survival*, 158). The three agreed to cooperate to find the basics of warm shelter, food, and clothing that would sustain them: "Charles and I finally found what we were searching for: a heavy cast-iron stove, with the flue still usable" (*Survival*, 159). It took both of them to load it on a wheelbarrow, and Levi brought it back to the barracks while Charles tended to Arthur, who was unconscious from the cold.

It is easier to survive with the cooperation of others, yet the brutality and scarcity of Hobbesian Hell allowed only for occasional us-ism and fleeting alliances. Us-ism under the horrors of the Lager was less prevalent than what Elias Canetti calls the "sting": when authorities are oppressing those under them, the oppressed will do it to others rather than cooperate with each other.[21] Voluntary contracts flourish more in conditions of freedom. With the easing of the terror, the three in conjunction with the others in the barracks gradually became a society. The brutal organizing force of the SS was gone, with only the shadows of fear left, and although scarcity still prevailed, civilization commenced. Levi brought the stove into the barracks, the broken window was repaired, and everyone started to relax: "Towarowski (a Franco-Pole of twenty-three, typhus) proposes to the others that each of them offer a slice of bread to us three who had been working. And so it was agreed." This was the beginning of the contract: the sys-

---

21. Canetti, *Crowds and Power*, 315–16.

tem was the barracks of eleven, bound by a system of gratitude through exchange: "The stove, our creation, was here, and spread a wonderful warmth; I had my bed here; and by now a tie united us, the eleven patients of the *Infektionsabteilung.*" Levi notes that this was a startling development: "Only a day before a similar event would have been inconceivable. The law of the Lager said: 'eat your own bread, and if you can, that of your neighbour,' and left no room for gratitude. It really meant that the Lager was dead." He continues: "It was the first human gesture that occurred among us. I believe that that moment can be dated as the beginning of the change by which we who had not died slowly changed from Haftlinge to men again" (*Survival,* 159–60).

Levi's utilitarian contract is forged when the conditions are ripe; coercion does not rule their world any more. The political system includes the happiness of others as well as insuring the happiness of oneself. Levi uses the last fragment of Hillel's statement about our commitments to others as the title of his only novel, *If Not Now, When?* He is aware of what precedes the second part of Hillel's aphorism, "and if I am only for myself, who will be for me?" Concern for others is intertwined with our own welfare, much as it is in Levi's relationship with Alberto. This is the utilitarian basis for friendship joined with an induction of feelings. This is civilization, and this is what was lost in the Lager.

In other words, the extension of our own welfare to concern for the welfare of others is easy in ordinary times and fragile under extreme circumstances.[22] It takes massive self-control in the face of real adversity to think of anyone but oneself. The failings of modernism are the failings of human nature: Under very demanding conditions, civilization is exposed as a fragile veneer. One option, and not a good one, according to Levi, is to abandon the tragic quest for modernism in the face of human weakness. However, Levi has experienced in full the consequences of the disappearance of modern civilization, suffered greatly from it, and hence, is not willing to let go of it easily in the future.

Civilization will not raise all of us to great heights; its more unpretentious goal should be to protect us from pain. Levi thus aims for a lower level of the good through the alleviation of pain, a much more modest goal than those proposed by most utopian schemes. Even in Levi's heroic strug-

22. Perhaps a continuum exists from extreme circumstances to ordinary times to good times, with solidarity disappearing at each extreme.

gle of us-ism, there is Aristotle's sense that we are held together by self-interest as well as induction of feelings. Humans may demand more of themselves, but little hope exists of more being accomplished. In this way, he falls in with those content to forsake the higher good for the more realistic chances, something that characterizes the thought of Locke, Tocqueville, Berlin, and Aron, to name a few. Except for the occasional heroic moments, the best we can hope for is Levi's version of what Tocqueville calls "self-interest rightly understood," which he considers the operating principle of Jacksonian democracy he observes in America.

The higher ideals will be virtually unattainable due to a lack of consensus. Levi agrees with Isaiah Berlin that when his ideals are fanatically held, the leader will make them happen, "for the people's own good," in spite of their objections.[23] In his chapter "The Gray Zone" in *The Drowned and the Saved,* Levi expresses his preference for utility over abstract belief. He describes the relationship between Biebow, the administrator of the Lodz ghetto, its contractor for slave labor, and Chiam Rumkowski, the self-pronounced prince of the ghetto: "Biebow, a small jackal too cynical to take race demonology seriously, would have liked to put off forever the dismantling of the ghetto, which for him, was an excellent business deal, and to preserve Rumkowski, on whose complicity he relied, from deportation. Here one sees how often a realist is objectively better than a theoretician. But the theoreticians of the SS thought otherwise, and they were the stronger. They were *grundlich* radicals: get rid of the ghetto and get rid of Rumkowski" (*Drowned,* 66).

The ghetto, contra to the interests of the Germans in waging war against the allies, was emptied, and the Jews of Lodz were sent to their death. Here we must remember Edmund Burke's warnings about the dire future directions the French Revolution would take when abstract ideals were implemented and practices long held were swept aside.[24]

Levi has accounted for our atavistic tendencies toward violence and glanced at the abyss, the source of his pessimism. But abject pessimism without the leavening of optimism is repugnant to him, because such pessimism can become a self-fulfilling prophesy. "It has obscenely been said that there is a need for conflict: that man cannot do without it. It has also been said that local conflicts, violence in the streets, factories, and stadi-

23. Berlin, "On Political Judgment," 30.
24. Burke and Thomas Paine, *"Reflections on the Revolution in France" and "The Rights of Man,"* 75.

ums, are an equivalent of generalized war and preserve us from it, as petit mal, the epileptic equivalent, preserves from grand mal" (*Drowned*,
200). He rejects these arguments (the moral equivalents of the big war as
little wars) and argues that with a firm resolve, again of education and political will, we can stave off atavistic violence:

> These are captious and suspect arguments. Satan is not necessary:
> there is no need for wars or violence, under any circumstances. There
> are no problems that cannot be solved around a table, provided there
> is good will and reciprocal trust—or even reciprocal fear, as the pres-
> ent interminable stalled situation [cold war] seems to demonstrate, a
> situation in which the greatest powers confront each other with cor-
> dial or threatening faces but have no restraint when it comes to un-
> leashing (or allowing the unleasing) of bloody wars among those "pro-
> tected" by them. (*Drowned*, 200)

Here he concludes that the imperative that allows for exchange is agreement to disagree. But Levi realizes this is a moral injunction and not an
empirical fact when he mentions in the next breath, "[T]he greatest powers confront each other with cordial or threatening faces but have no restraint when it comes to unleashing (or allowing the unleashing) of bloody
wars among those 'protected' by them, supplying sophisticated weapons,
spies, mercenaries, and military advisers instead of arbiters of peace"
(*Drowned*, 200). This is a fine example of his ruthless honesty and his optimistic pessimism. We must prevent war at all costs, yet as ill-constituted
beings, we often fail at the task.

Levi shows us that the best hope for civilized conduct lies with the modest contract of communication and utilitarian exchange. Civilization as the
prevention of pain seems a paradise of sorts; one should never wish the
Lager on anyone. The negotiation and exchange that keeps us from expe-
riencing the worst should not be expected to deliver us to the best. The
"best," prescribed for us by others, is dangerous. Nor can civilization be
expected to deliver us from ourselves. When we return to civilization, we
are not free of all our problems, because we are tragic beings.[25] Our atavistic side lurks, civilization is rich with contradictions, and the hierarchy of
troubles always throws a new concern our way. Levi uses Auschwitz as a
metaphor for life and demonstrates that politics cannot completely over-

25. See Michael Weinstein, *Culture/Flesh: Explorations of Postcivilized Modernity*, for
a brilliant elaboration of this theme.

come the basic contradictions of life.[26] "Willingly or not we come to terms with power, forgetting that we are all in the ghetto, that the ghetto is walled in, that outside the ghetto reign the lords of death, and that close by the train is waiting" (*Drowned,* 69). We are tragic beings, but an understanding of our own finitude and coming to terms with the limits of what we can expect of human institutions are part of the education process that may blunt some of the worst of our atavistic tendencies. We can, and should, expect no more from politics.

In other words, Levi is optimistically pessimistic; he is pessimistic about the ultimate ability of civilized modern liberalism to sustain itself, but it remains his best hope. As we have seen, he is also a minimalist: One way to sustain a fighting chance for this world is to maintain modest expectations for liberalism. Minimalism, which is analogous to Levi's personal modesty, runs all through his civilized liberalism and shares an affinity with the temper of the writings of Madison, Berlin, and Tocqueville. His minimalism includes his preference for "modest truths" as a way of knowing, "small change optimism" as a basis for acting, his suspicion of heroic ideals, and his tragic sense. All of these are embodied in his modest ambitions for a civilized liberal politics.

26. In an interview, Levi indicates that it is permissible, within stringent guidelines, to use the Holocaust as a metaphor. See Ferdinando Camon, *Conversations with Primo Levi,* 20.

11

A Defense of Modernism

More often and more insistently as that time recedes, we are asked
by the young who our torturers were, of what cloth were they
made. . . . [T]hey were made of the same cloth as we, they were
average human beings, averagely intelligent, averagely wicked: save
the exceptions, they were not monsters, they had our faces, but
they had been reared badly.

— *The Drowned and the Saved*

Levi thoroughly believes in modernism, but he has very modest expectations about the role of politics in life. Political arrangements contain the
basic tragedies of existence, as does every form of social organization, and
they cannot be expected to overcome themselves. He believes in modernism because arguing for the virtues of civilization incorporates the best
hope, at least temporarily, for shielding ourselves from pain. We can only
be optimistically pessimistic about the achievement and maintenance of
these virtues.

The modest aims he puts forth—understanding what the bad is and insuring that it does not happen—presents us ill-constituted beings with our
best chance to prevent the worst horrors of life, the ones we commit on
each other. Some blame the Holocaust on the origins of Western thought,
enlightenment virtues, or the contradictions in modernism. Levi does not
find a golden age in Western civilization or in any other cultures. He is not
nostalgic; we must consider the return to modernism, but in returning he
has his eyes wide open. Our ill-constituted ways keep dragging us down,
and we must fight the tendency to give in to the worst in us. It is a world
where we struggle for a "brave new world" on the backdrop of "1984."

This chapter will look at politics, as Levi does, from the minimalist per-

Before World War II, people asked whether a Spartan mentality could be more effective in war than the democratic mentality, with its free flow of information. The inevitable war looked to be a replay of the Peloponnesian War, this time with the crueler, more hateful elements on the Spartan side. In World War II, democracies ultimately triumphed, answering the doubts about discipline in free societies. However, in the aftermath of the War, new questions arose about modernism and its democratic institutions. Does knowledge lead to the unraveling of democratic regimes? Does knowledge gained under the umbrella of freedom lead to all possibilities, including some that are deleterious to the nation or its neighbors? Levi is a staunch defender of modernism and the free flow of thought, and we will delineate here his major lines of defense.

First, Levi assumes the rightness of the idea of civilization in which no individuals should sit too high or too low with respect to their neighbors. It is easier to convince people in the abstract that this position is correct than it is to get them to act against some of their major inclinations and support this position in actual circumstances. Stories of flesh and blood can help. The idea of civilization must be defended vigorously because it has such a tenuous hold upon us.

Second, if disseminated ideas do not conform to these generally accepted ideas of civilization, these ideas must not be suppressed or their presenters intimidated or arrested. No banning of ideas can be allowed, no matter how distorted. They should be discussed around a table and argued out fully. As suggested earlier, Levi sharply criticized the idea of heroic individualism that has become part of the free flow of ideas in democratic society. In addition, he took on the views of those who felt there was no way to discern truth in an open society, that all knowledge is power. One of the problems with both positions is that they abandon the process of discerning knowledge through dialogue.[15] First, the heroic individual dispenses with bourgeoisie life and lives a creative life of action free of guilt and responsibility to others.[16] Second, those who feel knowledge and power are synonymous are irrelevant and weak in dialogue against the certainties of heroic individuals and other absolutists who "know" the truth of being. In the end, however, from the perspective of civilization, Levi felt that all, regardless of their views, should argue questions of life, pain, and

15. The purpose here is to state Levi's ideas, not provide criticism or correctives when warranted.

16. As discussed previously, this is less Nietzsche's position than those who read into him the cruel freedom they want to espouse.

good, and not fight for them as outsiders to civilized life. Modernism is to be the framework of thought and action.

Third, modernism has let the genie of technology loose, and there is no putting it back unless we inadvertently bomb ourselves back to the Stone Age. This has made the modern world a more dangerous place. As stated earlier, though science and technology do not automatically represent human progress, pragmatically, there is no way of halting it. More important, science and technology for Levi flow from that which makes us most human. We should not restrict our toolmaking nature in order to "save ourselves."

Fourth, the knowledge shared in what we call "third world" nations is no more protective of what Levi calls "civilized virtues" than in civilized countries where the virtues make up a large part of the discourse. In fact, he points out that third-world countries have no active civic cultures to prevent would-be tyrants from taking power and acting on murderous impulses. Education to civilized virtues does not automatically lead to the practice of those virtues, but a population exposed to them has more of a chance to defend itself against malefactors than countries that do not espouse them at all. However superficially these civilized virtues are held, they remain a protection for those beneath the social contract, which far exceeds no protection at all.

Fifth, his quarrel is not with modernism, though he realizes that technology has raised the stakes involved in decisions today. The problem is that we are ill-constituted beings who are always inches from war. Whether the Peloponnesian Wars, the Crusades, or the wars of the twentieth century, human beings divide along lines of race, gender, class, or some other perceived difference to pursue what they want at the expense of others. Blaming modernism is historically incorrect and unhelpful. No clever dialectic is at work within modernism to bring out daimonic forces, a "Heroic criminal," or free-flowing skepticism, each of which can ultimately doom the modern world. These forces can be fought within modernism, and if civilization is strong in a country, it can resist them over time. We may inevitably succumb to our ill-constituted beings, but we can fight to prolong the good years through education.

Sixth, for the most part Levi assumes that the virtues of civilization and the reduction of pain are the modest good we can agree upon. He is not looking to propose a grand theory and its elaborate defense. Scattered throughout his texts are passionate defenses of modernism. He feels that he works best at taking clear snapshots of fascinating aspects of existence

by writing concise reports on his observations—the type he was used to making about his findings in chemical experiments.

There is a methodological reason why he might not have worked on the level of a grand social science theory. He understands that to blame modernism or any other structural factor for Auschwitz is to excuse the individual's responsibility for his or her actions. In this peculiar way, social science, whether it explains the actions of individuals or groups, can lead the analyst to see acts as predetermined and thereby diminish the role and responsibility of the actors. The cause, for Levi, can always be found in the study of human nature and prevented by reason. In the social sciences, in contrast, there is the penchant to explain everything away. The social scientist in him leads him to such explanations, but the moralist in him firmly believes that we must refuse to explain away evil.[17] To sum up, in his writings, Levi effectively supports the ideas of civilization, modernism, and knowing as our best hopes against our worst nature, rather than seeing these ideas as partners to our demise.

This second section will show that in a democratic society the free flow of information is plentiful and diffuse. But does this dilution of information, an artifact of modernism, cause the crucial ideas of civilization, pain, and danger to be lost? Is too much knowledge still a good thing, or is the proliferation of information the road to the destruction of memory? Upon his return to postwar Italy, Levi expended much of his energy describing what happened, and why we should prevent it from happening again. His message appeals to our sense of a defensive life in which we try to prevent pain and fear by upholding civilization. Levi faces an uphill battle in a democratic political system, where historical memory is traditionally not very good, and where today so much competition exists for an audience's attention due to the proliferation of stories. The Holocaust is one of a multitude of lessons to be learned and remembered. With so many competing ideas and events, is there any reason to keep the Holocaust in mind and reinforce its lessons? This raises the question of the permanence of ideas on the public agenda, the equivalent of backsliding on one's personal agenda. Does modernism fail on the grounds that little permanent learning takes place? Perhaps modernism may even accelerate forgetting. Today, we

17. There is a wonderful circle here because modern science's penchant for explaining away evil weakens a society's attack on evil. Yet, to use any explanation of modernism as showing a weakness against evil forces should be taboo.

can add the proliferation and democratization of fears in democracy as additional structural conditions that hasten the forgetting of details and the lessons of tragedy.

Grabbing and holding the citizen's attention is not a problem in an authoritarian state.[18] In his interview with Ferdinando Camon, Levi was asked what mechanism could set off an entire nation like Germany. Levi answered that in his opinion, "[T]he means was propaganda. It's the first case in history in which an especially powerful and violent man, a tyrant, found himself in possession of the spectacular weapon of mass communications."[19] In an authoritarian state, one can direct information in whatever direction one wants. Education can be very pointed and directed, and with modern means, it can be used to soften people up to carry out the best—or, more likely, the worst—of aims.[20]

Much of Levi's work is about forgetting. Previously, we dismissed the idea that there was some dialectic afoot that endangers modern democratic philosophy. Here we will address a question implicitly raised by Levi: Is forgetting important lessons democracy's crucial flaw? Ultimately we will conclude, as might be expected, that frailty of memory is simply one more human flaw for Levi that must be overcome.

Alexis de Tocqueville indicates that one of the possibilities in a democracy is the excess of individualism, which causes members of the community to withdraw into themselves, "so that after he has thus formed a little circle of his own, he willingly leaves society at large to itself." Unless there are checks on individualism, our connections with the past are severed: "Thus not only does democracy make every man forget his ancestors, but it hides his descendants and separates his contemporaries from him; it throws him back forever upon himself alone and threatens in the end to confine him entirely within the solitude of his own heart."[21] Individuals are severed from others and hence have no connection to collective history. Forgetting begins, if remembering even took place.

In democratic political systems, success of a particular idea may cause it to go into eclipse with respect to meaning, and it loses its vitality. John

18. Recent information about the former Soviet Union indicates that information could be difficult to avoid, but seeing or hearing is not the same as believing.

19. Camon, *Conversations with Primo Levi*, 40.

20. We will not get into the raging debate here about whether Germans were "willing executioners."

21. Tocqueville, *Democracy in America*, 2:395–97.

Stuart Mill suggests that "[w]e often hear the teachers of all creeds lamenting the difficulty of keeping up in the minds of believers a lively apprehension of the truth which they nominally recognise, [*sic*] so that it may penetrate the feelings, and acquire a real mastery over the conduct. No such difficulty is complained of while the creed is still fighting for its existence."[22] With respect to the Holocaust, one often hears that it is old news, that we have more pressing problems. In line with Mill's concerns about the vitality of ideas, ideas about the Holocaust can lose their freshness and ability to persuade.

Ideas lose their vitality for many other reasons. On the psychological level, ideas discussed in a democratic society may lose their vitality when discussion becomes repetitive, with little infusion of new ideas. The psychoanalyst Adam Phillips indicates that with the constant repetition of a word, we lose our bearings. For example, in concluding a chapter on "Obstacles," he states: "I wrote this essay to show that obstacles are the clue to desire, that the word is full of meaning. But I have an uneasy feeling, which we probably all remember from childhood, and which may be pertinent to the subject at hand; the feeling that comes when one endlessly repeats a word only to be left with an enigmatic obstacle as to its sense."[23] Ideas rarely disappear out of outright defeat as much as from exhaustion.

Ortega y Gasset suggests another reason for forgetting when he recognizes that generation is a key sociological unit in progressive societies. Each generation takes in its singular experiences and finds a place for them in the age cohort's unique perspectives. Events so important to previous generations do not have the same novelty for the newer generation as contemporary ones; they are viewed as merely part of the inert ideas of present society. For instance, for today's generation, "the Holocaust," "the Kennedy years," or even "the Reagan years" are not components of vital experience. Progressive thought in a democracy gives primacy to the young and their ability to "keep up" with change. Younger generations may have heard of the Holocaust, but they often view it as part of the irrelevant world of their mothers and fathers.[24]

In addition to the forgetting or the lack of learning that takes place in a modern democratic state, we can explain some other structural condi-

22. Mill, *"Utilitarianism," "On Liberty," "Considerations on Representative Government,"* 108.
23. Phillips, *Kissing, Tickling, and Being Bored,* 98.
24. Ortega y Gasset, *The Modern Theme,* 11–18.

tions that make it difficult for an important story to be heard.[25] Unfortunately, with freedom of speech comes the proliferation of stories. The overload of information tends to make skeptics of the audience, which, in turn, give most stories little or no credence. There are also so many stories floated that yours most likely will be obliterated quickly by the danger du jour.

These tendencies are illustrated if we extend the narrative in Levi's short story *"Force Majeure"* beyond where the sailor has crushed the Italian in the alley, into the future, where the victim might try to educate the public to his tragedy. Perhaps, if he recovers enough, he can speak out and ask for reforms so that the tragic humiliation is not repeated for him or for others. The Navy must have education programs on decency, and the schools must teach children tolerance. Perhaps something can be done about the dangerous alleys. They could be widened with a number of exits built into them, and streetlights could be added.

However, with the free flow of information and the passage of time, there are other competing fears. This is so even if we stretch Levi's illustration further to indicate that thousands, if not millions, get killed periodically in the unavoidable alleys. The slaughter takes place only periodically, and in those in-between times, the issue is not on the public agenda. Perhaps the sea is polluted and something must be done before the residents become sick from eating fish. The dikes must be shored up before large numbers of people die in a flood. Viruses may be imported in the thriving port. Random crimes are occurring with greater frequency in red light districts. How does the narrator's fear compete with all the others?

In the relatively free nations of the "global society," potentially tragic stories proliferate. There seem to be an infinite number of stories expressing individual and collective fears, making the audience skeptical and very selective of information. Any single message is difficult to communicate, and public interest is even more difficult to sustain. In the past, in democratic societies, the aristocratic distinction between the best and worst sources of public information prevailed, but now the lines between reliable and unreliable information are blurred. Because the public is bombarded by information from increasingly discredited sources, perhaps there is no truth any more—simply more or less exciting stories. Information is now abundant without much peer review, and even lesser standards of reporting are now coming from some of the more "reliable"

25. Throughout his book *The Holocaust in American Life*, Peter Novick talks about the attempts in the United States to keep the public's attention on the Holocaust.

sources. Competition is now unabashedly for audience rather than for truth. This proliferation is leading to the democratization of stories: Each one has the same credence. The public sees a postmodern society in the wash of the overload of information; they become skeptical, and it takes an overwhelming effort to engage them. The problem is circular: The more the public withdraws from active involvement, or moves from source to source, the more "news" becomes a marketing problem.

We have a "popular culture of tragedy." People are educated so much to the proliferation of dangers, potential dangers, and tragedies that television viewers who pay the most attention to television have the most fears about life. The multiplication of fears today is the public equivalent of the hierarchy of troubles, only this public hierarchy is at the very least always neurotic, distorting the objective hierarchy of troubles that we can glimpse when we do our own reduction to the bottom. The implications of the proliferation of fears is severe for those who are trying to educate about serious dangers, whether they be future Holocausts, nuclear war, diabetes, or cancer. Superficial daily reports of tragedy or incipient tragedy bombard the public; media sources tell people what fears they should have and saturate and therefore desensitize them to other fears. Often lost in these stories is the actual or potential pain, suffering, and death that has taken place. Levi, in a newspaper column entitled "The Wine of the Borgias," tries to get beyond the headlines to understand the facts and implications of the adulteration reported in the newspaper about Austrian wines. What were the serious consequences? "The matter of the Austrian wine, at least for the moment, seems more a crooked deal than a tragedy. There is talk of only one death, and its connection to the wine that was drunk is very dubious." The actual human anguish is often lost in the stories, and we have little historical memory of similar but more egregious crimes. Levi reminds us that "[i]n 1937, its [the same agent, diethylenic glycol] incautious use in a medicine in America caused the death of sixty people who had ingested approximately ten grams a day over several consecutive days."[26]

The seriousness of the problem is overwhelmed by the dramatic value of the events. The "new" is given preference to the historical dangers, and drama has priority over serious lingering problems. A continuous drama can be text for a succession of programs that can hold the attention of the public as a series of cliffhangers. The serious, the important, does not necessarily coincide with the prevailing news items. In more traditional soci-

26. Levi, "The Wine of Borgias," in *"Mirror,"* 132, 133.

eties, the past may be told and retold as a warning, as part of an intricate moral tapestry, whereas in a democratic society, attention rests on the bizarre, new dramas where the fundamental attraction is novelty.[27] Democracy likes novelty, and novelty buries history.

Contemporary drama interfused with novelty can hold and keep the public's attention for at least a little while; the bizarre keeps us amused.[28] Perhaps the proliferation of stories with novelty at the center distracts a willing public from the "real" cares of existence. At the same time, there is no quest for truth beyond the story. The poor memory in progressive democracies, and the proliferation of stories of the bizarre, create a difficult environment for someone like Levi, who tries to teach the significance of the lessons of Auschwitz and keep the events vital to a wide audience.

However, forgetting in a progressive democratic society does not always have negative consequences. One of the useful aspects of forgetting in a democracy is the forgetting of grudges, which does not happen in a more traditional or aristocratic political system. Often democracies can get on with business because past prejudice and hatred can be taken to belong to another generation, or they are simply of no concern to someone with an individualistic bent. Nikos Kazantzakis's novel *Freedom or Death* provides a vivid illustration of the difficulty of forgetting in a traditional society. On Crete, occupied by the Turks, there is a friendship stemming from childhood between the leading Turk in the community and the charismatic leader of the Cretans. As much as they are literally blood brothers, there is a tacit pact to forget the past. They have not forgotten these grudges, but simply put them aside. For instance, the Turk's uncle killed the Cretan's grandfather. It does not take much tinder to lead to war in these circumstances, but in a modern society, grudges belong within generations and often do not carry across them.[29]

Thus, despite the salutary aspect of forgetting past hatreds, forgetting in progressive democratic societies poses a threat to those trying to warn against significant dangers. What works against those like Levi who try to educate democratic citizens about recurrent danger is the flourishing of insular individuality and the proliferation of an infinite set of problems and

27. One need only think about the crimes that have captured our attention. Often, they involve few victims, but rivet our attention with strange or unusual circumstances.

28. See Frederic D. Homer, *Character,* for an extended discussion of the bizarre in modern society.

29. Does this clash with Levi's ideas about the benefits of a nonprogressive society? Perhaps if progressivism disappeared altogether, but there is little chance that would happen.

solutions. How do we teach people John Stuart Mill's lesson that we must keep ideas vital for the future through intelligent discussion, especially when most ideas may not be on the plate long in a democratic society?

Perhaps our protection is that vital ideas are remembered whenever a threat is serious; the free flow of information allows for the refreshing of memory, or genuine learning for the first time. Those like Levi give evidence to the fact that there are serious patterns, like genocide, that are continuously repeated. Levi's naturalistic studies of man suggest that we can identify recurring patterns. Isaiah Berlin expresses the same idea in the following way: "Incompatible these ends may be; but their variety cannot be unlimited, for the nature of men, however various and subject to change, must possess some generic character if it is to be called human at all."[30] Beneath the pessimism usually lies the glimmer of hope, however tenuous, but cannot minimize how discouraged Levi got at times about educating whole new generations to the lessons of Auschwitz.

The previous section has sketched out the difficulties in getting people in a progressive democracy to listen to any one story, and even if they do, getting them to remember the lessons and not "weigh anchor" on the truth. This third and final section, given this backdrop of difficulties, shows how Levi perseveres to educate people to the Holocaust. His efforts have to be seen once again against the backdrop of his optimistic pessimism; he knew educating people to the Holocaust was a losing battle, but one that had to be fought. First, we will address his motives for telling and retelling the story: compulsion, guilt, and reason. Second, we will examine the persuasive styles he uses to tell his story—scientific narrative, moral narrative, and accusation—and assess their effectiveness in working against the forces of forgetting.

Compulsion is a common motive for Holocaust survivors, as evidenced by the recurring dream Levi says is common among the prisoners of Auschwitz. In the dream, he or another prisoner is talking to someone at home about what is happening in Auschwitz, and the person he is addressing turns away and ignores him. Levi needs to be a witness: "I wrote because I felt the need to write. If you ask me to go further and find out what produced this need, I can't answer. I've had the feeling that for me the act of writing was equivalent to lying down on Freud's couch. I felt such an overpowering need to talk about it that I talked out loud. Back

30. Berlin, *The Crooked Timber,* 80.

then, in the concentration camp, I often had a dream: I dreamed that I'd returned, come home to my family, told them about it, and nobody listened."[31]

In *Moments of Reprieve,* Levi acknowledges the psychologist's insight that survivors fall into two groups, "those who repress their past *en bloc,* and those whose memory of the offense persists, as though carved in stone, prevailing over all previous or subsequent experiences."[32] Levi is clearly in the latter group.

A second motivation is the felt moral obligation to those who died; they must not be forgotten. In *Moments of Reprieve,* he describes this in a most moving manner: "A great number of human figures especially stood out against that tragic background: friends, people I'd traveled with, even adversaries—begging me one after another to help them survive and enjoy the ambiguous perennial existence of literary characters."[33]

Elie Wiesel, with characteristic ruthless honesty, indicates that this imperative, this obligation, is a burden as well, and can distort thoughts about the Lagers: "For the camp survivor life is a battle not only for the dead but also against them. Locked in the grip of the dead, he fears that by freeing himself, he is abandoning them. Hence the near-impossibility of loving, or believing in humanity."[34] Levi, in his writings, is almost forced into a Hobbesian view of humanity in deference to the dead. If we suggest that people are basically good, we almost deny the deaths of those who perished in the Holocaust. How, then, would we explain the optimistic view of human nature to those who had died? This restraint on survivors, in this case Levi, must be taken into account when we think overall about his political philosophy and his idea of optimistic pessimism. His ideas on human nature may be influenced by his obligation to the dead of Auschwitz.

The third motive obliging Levi to witness is a pragmatic one: The lessons of Auschwitz can be used to prevent a repeat of the events. It is the tragic call for the virtues of civilization and the push for solidarity so that he can, in some small way, help prevent another recurrence. Levi's dreams, his guilt toward the dead, and his pragmatism give him the direction and energy to overcome his shyness and persist in the tasks of speaking and writing about the Holocaust. Even though he felt increasingly inadequate

31. Camon, *Conversations,* 41–42.
32. Levi, *Moments of Reprieve,* 10–11.
33. Ibid., 10.
34. Wiesel, *All Rivers Run to the Sea,* 298–99.

to the task as the years passed, he persevered despite the public's erosion of memory and the competition of more recent events.

Another way to express the three rhetorical strategies Levi uses to tell the story of the Holocaust—scientific observations, moral narrative, and accusation—is to say that Levi is interested in what happened, why it was wrong, and who is to blame. All three inform his writings, but given his thorough empiricism, the scientific observations serve as the bedrock on which he develops his moral narrative and accusation.

Critics often cite Levi for his detached scientific narrative, and one has to agree with this judgment of the overall mood of his writings. However, this work tries to highlight his commitment to a fuller philosophy of moral narrative and judgment. Levi suggests that we are perpetual judging machines, making it most difficult for us to separate out the different moral narrative strands. Levi's awareness of our propensity to judgment and his scientific detachment allow him to keep the strands separated. He may want to limit accusation, but it has its place, and he knows that knowing and judging both have their place in human discourse as well.

Levi uses the scientific narrative or report throughout his writing. He wrote his first book, *Survival in Auschwitz,* in the manner of a factory report so that he would be believed. The Lager was a laboratory for violence, and it has to be understood in the objective perspective of the scientist. Even though many of his other books eased up from this strict reportage, he never strayed from his careful scrutiny of the facts. For example, in his essay "The Wines of Borgias," Levi criticizes the spin the press put on two major public scares, one of which was the adulteration of Austrian wines. In the essay, Levi uses his knowledge as a chemist to clear up the scientific muddles that reporters investigated superficially and got wrong. Clear and distinct ideas are paramount for Levi.

His books could be used as a model of "field research" in the social sciences. He helps maintain his objectivity by letting the reader know his biases and potential biases.[35] Repeatedly, Levi lets us know that he is not among the best, because the best did not survive, and he is careful to talk about what he knows from firsthand observation, making a clear distinction from secondhand accounts from friends or acquaintances. He let the reader know that he read a great deal about genocide, but he preferred to report on what he knew best, his observations from inside Auschwitz.

35. This is a method I call "valuative empiricism" in Homer, *Character,* 52.

Levi's detached narrative style nevertheless has a powerful effect. We are free to enter into the events, wander about, and come to our own conclusions. Levi appeals to emotion through reason, with no angry, opinionated narrator so obviously in evidence that we react to his or her character rather than the events themselves. Levi's detached "field reports" avoid almost any negative feelings about the narrator.[36] This is not to say that more emotional discourses do not have their place in rounding out the picture of what went on, but clearly Levi's strategy is deliberate and it works. The emotional impact of reading his books is powerful, and we are free to make up our own minds. We do not need a heavy hand reminding us of how we should feel about the horrors. The brute objectivity of the facts will lead most of us in the same direction; that is inevitable.

This is the pragmatic way of telling the story. After hearing the facts, people are asked to make up their own minds about how to deal with the Holocaust. If some people still think that murder and pain should be the way of existence and the other group, hopefully larger, believes that such pain and suffering should be prevented, there is no ultimate way to settle the argument. The first group is "uncivilized," and there is probably no way to reach them. The key to education is to grasp and hold the attention of what James calls the peace party, and to try to educate the young before they have made up their minds about civilization.

Levi was an empiricist first, but he has a moral philosophy, which appears in his writings from the beginning. This philosophy culminates in *The Drowned and the Saved,* his last major work. For Levi, there is enough ambiguity in the world without the writer further muddling it up by unclear and indistinct ideas: "As long as we live we have a responsibility: we must answer for what we write, word by word, and make sure that every word reaches its target." When Levi speaks of morality, his strength, as it is with his empiricism, is in his clarity of expression.[37] For instance, the moral in each of his essays and short stories is rarely ambiguous; we know where the author stands on the issue. However, he is not preachy and judg-

36. For example, I have used his books for years in my courses, and students are rarely inflamed by what he says and often note that he does not intrude on his own works. A bit later we will see that despite this objective reportage, some blaming of the victim does inevitably occur.

37. Levi, *Other People's Trades,* 174–75, 169–75. Levi states that clarity and responsibility "are preferences of mine, not standards."

mental. He walks a fine line in his fiction and essays between fable and sermon. His ambiguity is expressed in the tragic situations of life where it is difficult to decide which direction to incline. Ordinarily, he moves to the position of optimistic pessimism, but rarely with a heavy touch. He is not neutral to the world; we must try to render at least a tentative judgment. There are enough people who see a confusing world, and their only response to it is, "Whatever."

His central moral question is: Why should we care about anyone but ourselves? We are ill-constituted, self-regarding beings with a thin veneer of caring for others, which can be stripped away quickly in any adverse situation. As a consequence of our nature, we bring pain and death upon ourselves and others. Here, he urges us to join together in a civilization that does not expect very much of its citizens, where there is not much talk of the good, but where at least the citizens can try to come to some agreement on the bad. This is the basis for his hedonism. He keys his thoughts on educating people so that they will accept responsibility for pain and death and try to minimize these human misfortunes. In short, his moral philosophy rests on his idea that we are ill-constituted beings who should proceed as optimistic pessimists in a civilized liberal political system.

The agony of deciding between self-interest and the interests of the group remains to be discussed. Does the pendulum swing toward the individual or collective judgment? In his essay "The Struggle for Life," Levi expresses keen awareness of the tension in a free society between freedom and responsibility, and he points out that being judged can be humiliating. Yet to evade making judgments is dangerous: "We might likewise observe that while it is disagreeable to be judged, and it is humiliating and debilitating to be continually *sub judice,* to expect to elude all judgment is unnatural and dangerous." Although he doesn't mention Nietzsche in this essay, he seems to be criticizing him for extolling the callous and massive assertion of will (as interpreted by the Nazis). On the other hand, he acknowledges the Nietzschean agony of being judged, and he puts us on notice that receiving judgment is neither pleasant, nor should it simply be received uncritically: "It is certainly difficult to establish case by case which judges can be accepted and which 'recused,' but to recuse all judges is not only presumptuous but useless. Useless because every turn in life, every human encounter, involves a judgment delivered or received, so it is a good idea to get used to receiving and delivering judgments when one is young, when it is easier to contract habits."[38] Making and receiving judgments are among the agonies and responsibilities of living.

Levi's reasons for submitting, at least occasionally, to the facts brought forth by others is the hubris in thinking that he—or anyone else—is always right; there is much damage that a person, convinced of his immortality and infallibility, can do. Still, we should not accept the judgments of others simply on the basis of authority. We should listen to others and if the facts, which are merciless in rendering their judgments, are true, we must submit to them; "facts are obstinate and pitiless judges."[39] However, in our arrogance we may not accept facts that go against our inclinations; we are not fully masters of our house. This is why we must at least listen to others while privileging our own reason as the final arbiter. The facts given to us by others are at least a compass to aid in the preliminary calculations of the direction we shall proceed:

> One must be cautious in accepting an external judgment, but must nevertheless accept at least one: this cannot be avoided, since nobody can judge himself (anyone who does so, consciously or not, merely reproduces the external judgment that emotionally appears the most correct, whether positive or negative) and since living without one's actions being judged means renouncing a retrospective insight that is precious, thus exposing oneself and one's neighbor to serious risks: it is the same as piloting a boat without a compass, or wanting to maintain a constant temperature without consulting a thermometer.[40]

In other words, we ought to understand ourselves as social beings rather than conceptualizing ourselves as purely autonomous beings. Within our own psyche, unconsciously, we deal with the conflicting views of accepted identifications on one side, and rejected identifications on the other. We should consciously sift through the available information, and no matter how much another person's facts may contradict our position, we must put all the information under the scrutiny of our own reason. This manner of educating people will, in Levi's view, "produce truly free and responsible citizens."[41]

Here is a key to Levi's theory of action and tragic liberalism. He agonizes over the responsibilities to the group and the importance of freedom

38. Levi, "The Struggle for Life," in *"Mirror,"* 99.
39. Ibid.
40. Ibid.
41. Ibid.

and finally comes down decisively on the side of freedom, because he realizes the dire consequences of giving up final authority to the group. The arbiter is the individual, but the individual should be informed. He is wary of the "Nietzschean" intoxication possible in making choices. In sum, he delivers us to the stance of an "educated free being." For the individual to be the arbiter means he must engage his circumstances on his own terms after having relativized himself in terms of the other.[42] Others' opinions of us and of our beliefs must be incorporated into ourselves, and we must objectify them to ourselves in order to come to decisions as informed free beings. Levi hopes that this receptive, self-critical human being will freely choose his arguments for civilized liberalism.

The first two strategies of persuasion, scientific detachment and moral philosophy, are meant to appeal to reason. When carrying out moral objectives in foreign policy, such as intervention in genocide or the potential genocide of a people, the third method of persuasion, guilt, can be very potent. We only need think about the effectiveness of guilt as a weapon in the American civil rights movement. Guilt is most effective in convincing those who hold to an unarticulated philosophy, and for moving people from thought to action. "Do not be a hypocrite" is the cry: Carry your ideas into action.

Convincing people to participate in helping others through guilt is quite effective, but it affects different people in different ways. In James's terms, it is effective on the peace party because it closes the gap between theory and praxis. Levi, however, understands that guilt is wasted upon the guilty. He found that it was the victims, those who would not have committed the crimes in the first place, who suffered from guilt at the end of the Holocaust. Guilt works better on the innocent than the guilty.

A big part of education is the learning of constructive guilt. If not impressed in childhood, it often cannot be taught later. Even Nietzsche, who spent much of his life urging people to take their life into their own hands, admitted at his weakest moments that conscience in society may be even more powerful and become an instinct, a dominating instinct.[43] To shore up this "instinct," the peace party may have to be reminded of its responsibility with the judicious use of guilt.

42. As a friend so astutely pointed out, this is the link between Primo Levi and the person of character in Homer, *Character*—perhaps the unwitting reason for choosing Levi as the subject for study.

43. See Nietzsche, *Genealogy of Morals,* 160, and *Human, All Too Human.*

Of course, guilt has an inevitable backlash. When responsibility is used to educate oppressors or potential oppressors, guilt, the glue of responsibility, unfortunately takes a holiday from the mind of the oppressor. Those angered by arguments of conscience, oppressors or potential oppressors, will often retaliate with personal attacks on those who urge them to moral action.

Levi rarely uses guilt to ask his audience to close the gap between theory and practice.[44] Once the application of guilt occurs, especially to an unsympathetic audience, the accused change the topic to "collective guilt" and its inherent unfairness, and the battle becomes very heated and personal. Levi's scientific discourse and moral philosophy mean practically that he avoided the hostile responses of those forced to consider their own complicity at the urging of the speaker. When they read Levi, they may come to the conclusion that they are in fact guilty of something, but that self-judgment will appear as their own. Here, he uses a light touch and avoids the hostile responses of those whom he might have personally accused. Besides the empirical contention he marshals above, guilt may not be an effective way to educate about the Holocaust, but there is a philosophical reason as well. Levi doesn't use guilt as a weapon because it clashes with his idea of civilized decency and his conception of human nobility. He is certainly to be praised highly for this—he keeps his standards and evinces his character consistently.

When his audiences asked him questions, they often insinuated that Levi in particular, or the Jews in general, are at least partly responsible for what happened. In other words, they try to make Levi feel guilty.[45] Ironically then, one way in which he has to deal with guilt is to explain why the Jews are not guilty. Why didn't the Jews leave Europe before the Nazis came, escape from the Lagers, or rebel in the Lagers? Levi answers the questions patiently. The ordinary citizens were not trained in heroic freedom, nor did their literature contain much about it. Even those who were trained in resistance, for instance, Russian Army soldiers, had an impossible time escaping or rebelling against the systematic Lagers. In addition, Levi believes it is a bad idea for anyone to judge people with the morality

44. We might wonder why this is so and speculate that Levi saw the pernicious hold guilt can have on our psyches, which would run counter to his virtue of free choice, but that would only be a guess.

45. From my own experience, just bringing up the subject of the Holocaust manifests a profound uneasiness in an unsympathetic audience. In these circumstances, some members of the audience try to make the speaker pay for their discomfort.

spective of a tragic liberal. What light does Levi's civilized liberalism shed on contemporary politics? Is any light cast upon the problems that vex modern democratic thought, the problems generated by power, progress, knowledge, and memory? First, is human nature or modernism the source of abuses of power? Can virtue temper power in any political system? Can the overwhelming propensity for hierarchy and the continuous scrambling for personal advantage be overcome to some degree by civilized conduct? Second, is the idea of progress necessary, or even useful, for modernism? Can the concept of progress be replaced by Levi's optimistic pessimism? Can Levi be a modernist even though he is an optimistic pessimist? Is it possible to have a tragic modernism? Third, is the pursuit of knowledge in a modern political system the beginnings of the system's undoing? Fourth, is the lack of historical memory a problem if we wish to sustain liberal democracies? What difficulties does defective memory provide for Levi when he tries to educate people to a civilized liberalism?

Nationalism is at the center of Levi's discussions about power. In Levi's writings, sources of conflict are often attributed to national character flaws, like the Germans and their penchant for order, or the Americans and their incessant tinkering with the natural order through technology, and their perfection of the techniques of selling technology to others. In Auschwitz, approximately 95 percent of the prisoners who entered the gates were Jewish, but national origin made a large difference among the prisoners. For Levi, the major sociological characteristic that accounted for differences in behavior was their nationality; they were Italians, Hungarians, Greeks, Germans, Poles, and all the other nationalities present.

Levi knows all the large and petty differences that divide humans, whether religious conflicts or class conflicts. In his extensive writings on the Lager, he found many differences among people, however slight, to be the source of conflict and division for himself. Often he participated in such dislikes and came to regret it afterwards. For instance, he expressed his profound contempt for the *musselmans* at the bottom in the Lager, for they could provide nothing for the living Hobbesians. Why get attached to them, for they were not going to live long anyway? There was no charity, nor was this some kind of hospice. Beneath their anger lay the fear that they could become *musselmans* themselves. Another source of friction was that newcomers, *zugang,* were ridiculed by those who had been in Auschwitz for a few months. Levi passed through both phases, from one who was taken advantage of to one of veteran status. The lower the numbers of their tattoo, the longer they had survived, hence the more prestige they had. In addition, the prominants in the Lager also sneered at those without "privilege." Finally, in the last ten days in Auschwitz, a social system developed among the eleven survivors of Levi's barracks. He incurred pains of guilt, because of necessity it had to be an exclusive and not an inclusive group. They could not let everyone into their heated barracks, for example. To feed all of the survivors and keep them all warm would mean that everyone would perish. They regretted drawing the boundary around themselves, but nonetheless they did so to survive. Levi recognized the many dimensions upon which individuals could separate one group from another, and he felt that these were constitutive of being human. Unless people are educated, they tend to look with mistrust upon the stranger and find all sorts of ways to differentiate themselves from others. Divisions between humans for Levi, as we shall see, normally occur not as a result of modernism, but in spite of modernism.

The most important difference for Levi remained nationalism, a division among people that so characterized Europe of his time and unleashed some of the most virulent poisons in the twentieth century. Nationalism is a great source of pain. In Levi's politics less attention is paid to the influence of political and economic systems, for he rivets his attention to nationalism. Levi took criticism in his own country, Italy, because he did not take into account the class politics so crucial to Marxists and socialists. In his experience, class conflict, in contrast to the damage caused by nationalism, must have looked like a mere artifact.

Levi's careful examination of both democracy and nationalism shows that the picture must not be oversimplified. For instance, the Holocaust occurred because diabolical men followed through on a terrible plan and did so with little opposition. The inoculation of education might stem such murderous adventures in the future, but Levi knows that even if there is substantial opposition instead of meek quiescence, this world has few heroes.

On the other hand, the easy triumph of nationalism is not assured. The unusual combination of a murderous leader and badly educated subjects is potentially more deadly when the leader gives steady attendance to means to achieve his ends. Levi's fellow countryman Machiavelli is an idealist in believing that a leader can carry out systematic plans for the consolidation of personal and collective power against great forces. In some ways, the "real" in Machiavelli's Italy, political fragmentation, is far from his ideal, which is the consolidation of power over all of Italy in the hands of a prince. Just as the training of a leader for achieving the good rarely translates into the successful practice of statesmanship, so it takes a rare discipline for a leader to carry through Machiavellian plans with emotional detachment and devotion to instrumental reason. As Levi suggests, only a rare confluence of forces causes the development of an effective mass murderer.

The relationship between nationalism and democracy is problematic because of the fragility of democracies. Eric Hobsbawm believes that democracy is a rarity because of its difficulties in dealing with the diverse and hostile ethnic composition of most countries. On the other hand, the lack of democratic institutions in a country provides no guarantees for a minority. The experience of the former Yugoslovia shows us that power elites can hold people of significant differences together, and yet, at a later time, lead murderous purges of minorities.[1]

Levi understands the complexities of democracy, nationalism, and their interrelationship, but he resents the arguments for a causal relationship between modern democracy and virulent nationalism. The subtle argument that nationalism, fascism, and their facsimiles arise in a dialectic with modernism casts the latter in an extremely unfavorable light. The first variant of the dialectic is that an ideology of terror arose as a reaction to the Enlightenment and its virtues. Edmund Burke predicted that a radical restructuring of France in terms of the stark ideals of the Enlightenment and the Revolution would end in tyranny. Many others condemn revolution as bringing in the same kind of tyranny they profess to conquer. However, when we speak of this dialectic, we must not forget that many transitions are peaceful.[2]

In a second form of the dialectic, we can point out that hateful ideologies arise in contrast and opposition to modern democratic societies. As Isaiah Berlin remarks, Joseph de Maistre, an antimodern predating much of modernism, expressed his murderous sensibilities in systematic form. Berlin sees Maistre putting his philosophy in opposition to modernism when he calls for the return to a Church-dominated social order. The executioner is his ideal for enforcing the laws. Maistre's reactionary views are put forth as an alternative to modernism, just as fascism much later is put forth as an alternative to the Enlightenment and modernism. He takes the Church as his model, and clearly his bloody scheme is in response to

---

1. Hobsbawm, *The Age of Extremes: A History of the World, 1914–1991*, passim.
2. Burke and Thomas Paine, "*Reflections on the Revolution in France*" and "*The Rights of Man*," 75.

what he sees as the enlightenment challenges to the Church—liberty, equality, and "scientific progress." Democratic regimes throw modernism in sharp relief with its alternatives of nationalism and irrationalism, but Berlin makes no claims that the Enlightenment "caused" the rise of nationalism and fascism. He does not speak of some dialectic inherent in modernism that calls forth violent and terrible opposition. History is populated with terrible models responding to all sorts of political systems.[3]

Even if it were true that modernism bred virulent enemies of liberty, equality, and technology, Levi can see no other way of being. What is the alternative to civilization? Would we turn back the clock because we believe that tyranny is more modest in its intentions when it arises out of states where there are no thoughts of popular sovereignty? Would we roll back a modern agenda because a potential great leader might get angry and mobilize his forces? Should we not inflame an inquisitor or tyrant by creating a modern society that could drive him to a fury?

We could argue that increasing mechanical and behavioral technology applied to human situations makes mass murder more of a possibility in modern times. We could cobble together Levi's idea that it takes a free society to come up with innovative ideas and to carry them to fruition, and deduce, therefore, that if modernism had not occurred there would not have been the possibility of mass destruction. But as Levi suggests, we can't put the genie back in the bottle, nor can we turn the clock back on such innovation. We have to live with the increasing means of power in the hands of ill-constituted beings. Short of being bombed back into the Stone Age, education is the only way of turning back the godlets of modernity.

A third possible form of the dialectic within modernism is the battle of individualism with collectivism. Democratic society can become mass society without any real restraints against the mobilization of the masses. A murderous campaign can be carried out by a strong leader who has not been convinced by the herd mentality of democratic regimes and proceeds to write and deliver his own table of values. Amitai Etzioni, in his writings about communitarian virtues, indicates that there should be a balance between autonomy and order in a democratic society, because the inevitable result of tilting too far one way is anarchy, and of tilting too far the other way is an autocratic society.[4] Levi recognizes that tyranny arises on dem-

3. Berlin, *The Crooked Timber of Humanity*, 91–174.
4. Etzioni, *The New Golden Rule: Community and Morality in a Democratic Society*, 34, 57.

ocratic soil, but he resists any idea that it is inevitable or encouraged more in modern societies: "It took place in the teeth of all forecasts; it happened in Europe; incredibly, it happened that an entire civilized people, just issued from the fervid cultural flowering of Weimar, followed a buffoon whose figure today inspires laughter, and yet Adolf [*sic*] Hitler was obeyed and his praises were sung right up to the catastrophe. It happened, therefore it can happen again: this is the core of what we have to say."[5]

Modern civilization is no absolute guarantee against mass violence, and Levi notes that since World War II, there have been plenty of violent tendencies in democracies as well as in the Communist bloc; he was a vociferous opponent of the Vietnam War. There is no automatic dialectic between nationalism and modernism, however: "'Violence,' 'useful' or 'useless,' is there before our eyes: it snakes either through sporadic and private episodes, or government lawlessness, both in what we call the first and second worlds." What he refuses to do is privilege the third world as the innocent or long-suffering victim. In fact, in the third world, without democracy, fewer checks against violence exist: "In the Third World it [violence] is endemic or epidemic. It only awaits its new buffoon (there is no dearth of candidates) to organize it, legalize it, declare it necessary and mandatory and so contaminate the world" (*Drowned*, 199–200).

Finally, no inevitable historical sequence arises out of the dialectic between democracy and autocracy. Just as we can argue that fascism in Germany arose out of the Weimar republic, so we can argue that democracy grew from the ruins of Hitler's Germany. One of the safest predictions a being can make is that a system will inevitably fail whether in a few years or over hundreds of years. All systems are overcome, but in his optimistic pessimism, Levi believes that the establishment of democracy is our best hope to stave off carnage. At least in a democracy a dialogue can be reinforced that educates us against our natural suspiciousness and divisiveness, which often manifests itself with respect to our hatred of other religions, nationalities, and classes: "Few countries can be considered immune to a future tide of violence generated by intolerance, lust for power, economic difficulties, religious or political fanaticism, and racialist attritions." As always, our defense is our reason: "It is therefore necessary to sharpen our senses, distrust the prophets, the enchanters, those who speak and write 'beautiful words' unsupported by intelligent reasons" (*Drowned*, 200).

---

5. Levi, *The Drowned and the Saved*, 199. Future references will be cited parenthetically in the text.

Ill-constituted beings are found within every political arrangement. The penchant for autocracy and fear of strangers, coupled with the ability and willingness of the few to carry these tendencies to the extreme, have their roots in human nature and may be found in all regimes. Free discussion and inculcated attitudes of civilization are our only hopes against the acid tendencies of our nature. This is the optimistic pessimism that permeates Levi's writings.

We can turn our full attention to the idea of progress, having looked at the relationship between modernism and autocratic power. Levi is an optimistic pessimist, which is where he parts with most modernists. We must push to make progress, but our striving remains in the shadow of our ill-constituted beings and our victories tend to be temporary. For example, in his most personal quest, the prevention of future genocide, Levi realizes that mass murder happens all too frequently and of course has occurred since the Holocaust. We will explore his tragic perspective in more detail and see if Levi's optimistic pessimism blunts some of the usual criticisms of modernism.

For Levi, the tragic civilized modernist, belief in progress can cause severe difficulties in a political system. There are real dangers to the overselling of the government's ability to deliver progress. Civilization dictates that we try to make life better for the less fortunate. The modest political arrangements that Levi depends on, the social contract drawn up in his last ten days in Auschwitz, and the need for political education to support civilization, might prevent the worst. Government can help alleviate the worst of material circumstances, but whether for the rich or for the poor, politics cannot deliver the good life.

Politics is thus oversold as the deliverer of the good. As Levi suggests, we can never be completely happy or unhappy, and often we blame government if personal happiness does not come to fruition. The hierarchy of troubles keeps throwing up additional concerns. Survivors are in a good position to understand the limitations of government; government can lead through modest exchange relationships to the alleviation of pain, but it is not clear what the good is, other than the alleviation of pain. From the tragic perspective of life as finite beings, Levi is faced with agonizing choices over new troubles that were submerged during the Holocaust, and he cannot rely on politics (the modern limited government perspective) to make his life good.

Government should be limited in how it can inflict itself on the rights of citizens, and it is also limited in how much it can deliver to the people. This is the contemporary paradox of wanting to be left alone by government and at the same time relying upon it to make our lives better. This is the progressive impossibility. We want the achievement of the good life through politics, and while politics can provide some good, it cannot provide all for all. Basically, government should provide people with the minimum so that they can function on their own. In these issues, he seems more comfortable with John Locke's view of limited government, and not as comfortable with the quest for the good life, which is so central to the classical philosophers. Allan Bloom, for instance, wonders if we have given up the quest for the good life.[6] Levi argues that we must flee from the bad life first. Levi sees democracy as the adjudicator of pain: We must make smaller sacrifices on the way to freeing ourselves from more severe pain.

In speaking of the social contract in the last ten days at Auschwitz, Levi describes how little it took for his comrades in Ka-Be to be satisfied with their new political arrangements. With the backdrop of Auschwitz, civilization never looked so good. Now, as Levi senses, many people look at Holocaust survivors as irrelevant, because in ordinary life they have moved beyond scarcity to the point where they are miserable in their own free ways. Often they don't comprehend the reasons for their misery, and the convenient scapegoat is the political system. In contrast, the survivors seem grateful for so little. What seems inverted, perhaps perverted, is that today we want more from government than it has to give in the way of positive good, and the government gives less to those trapped in scarcity, those who rely on government to alleviate pain.

There is a tendency to dismiss the idea that some people are beneath social sufficiency, and it is easy to argue that they are in that condition of their own doing. After all, in a free society they should have made it. Levi warns that we need to educate people to help those who are poor and miserable. We must be reminded, even if we don't want to hear: Some people are poor and miserable, living beneath the social contract, who need help out of their worst miseries. Our ill-constituted souls must be trained to virtue against our initial inclinations, trained to treat the most unfortunate as human beings.

What accentuates malaise? Does a working democratic life create conditions conducive to boredom and dissatisfaction with life? Does it create this ennui that a democratic politics is asked to fix, but is not in a position

---

6. Bloom, *The Closing of the American Mind*, 372–82.

to do anything about? Perhaps Harold Lasswell best sees politics as a canvas on which citizens paint their aspirations. He expresses this as the projection of private motives on public objects and their being rationalized in terms of public interests. If the canvas of democratic political life doesn't deliver on their good, people project their needs into politics and often call for more dramatic activities. If this is true, then the crisis of rising expectations from the anticipation of progress, as opposed to Levi's minimal expectations from the state, can have real negative consequences for the contemporary situation.[7]

Nietzsche and other critics of modernism emphasize the unthinking aspects of the bourgeoisie. Perhaps the decisive factor is that modernism lacks excitement; the bourgeoisie is boring (and they should know they are bored) and lacking in the heroism of other eras. Levi sees that our hands are full with the troubles of everyday life, which provide all the excitement we need. He knows what "excitement" in the hands of the irresponsible can mean. Expressed in a slightly different fashion, Ortega y Gasset suggests that "live dangerously" is an improvident maxim. Life is dangerous enough without inviting the compounding of our troubles. For Levi, consolidating our inner resources in the day-to-day fight to curb our atavistic tendencies is tough enough. Abstract excitement is hopefully traded in for the everyday alleviation of pain.

William James points to the gulf between those who are educated to decreasing violence, the peace party, and those who thrive on the excitement of war, the war-regime. James's view suggests that we cannot persuade the war party, as Levi submits, simply through education. James is more pessimistic. We must find the moral equivalents of war and channel those atavistic feelings into activities that are safe substitutions for war. James's idea resembles the philosophy of the Eastern martial arts by arguing that we take the individual's direction of force and use it to neutralize him, or make it work against him. Where Levi makes a strong point with education is that the peace party can more easily be talked out of their position and must continually be educated. The war-regime, in contrast, will more easily tear through the veneer of civilization and take advantage of the smallest weakness or lack of will on the part of the peace party.[8]

Democratic theorists know that we need opposition to prevailing virtues

7. Lasswell, *Psychopathology and Politics,* 75–76.
8. Levi does not use James's concept of the war-regime, but he has many names for those individuals ready to provoke violence. Many of theme have appeared in this text.

not only to subvert boredom and to prevent adventure into destructive heroism, but also to sharpen democratic ideas. John Stuart Mill recognized that if public ideas are held casually and left unchallenged, they become habitual, stale, and cliché. Levi knows we are quick to recognize and act on our differences with others, and these differences should be ironed out through democratic processes. Peaceful rivalry sharpens wits.

Levi also knows that democracies can carry on nationalist campaigns against their own citizens or against other nations. Democracies also are failures if dissident minorities are suppressed in the name of peace. Like Madison, Levi gives up the idea of the good as eternal peace in exchange for arrangements for managing conflict. There is to be no Augustinian quest for permanent peace. As Augustine suggested, the end of war is peace, but as we have come to understand, democracies attempt to counteract ambition with ambition in various institutional arrangements. Democracies fail if people take over who are exponents of progress and view success as the complete elimination of conflict.

For Levi, the ideas of the free and "naïve exchange" provide cohesiveness in political systems. Of course, this exchange is fragile and does not inevitably lead to progress. For instance, the opposite of naïve exchange, the "perfection of exchange," does not lead to progress either, but worse, to human estrangement.[9] When all of these mechanisms of exchange become rationalized-perfected, democracy tends to self-destruct, for utility has simply become advantage with no room for an induction of feeling. We have been warned since Adam Smith that certain virtues must accompany capitalism. In practice, however, the market mechanism tends to displace all other virtues, such as trust and good will.

If we have perfected the naïve exchange that Levi so cherished, it takes on a mean, exploitative edge. Naïve exchange, which can be the basis of commerce, conveys the friendliness that may carry over to other transactions with the same person and openness to exchange in general. We can find naïve exchange in the contrast between Cesare and Mordo. Cesare takes the market seriously, but he does not reduce it to Mordo's bare-bones pure exchange. Exchange was exchange and friendship was friendship, a far cry from Aristotle's friendship, which combined induction of feelings with exchange and pleasure. Pleasure and induction of feelings interfered with business for Mordo.

---

9. Levi leaves the opening for a concept of reflective exchange, which is an understanding of exchange as part of a full reflection on the role of all virtues in our lives.

Adam Smith first worried about the impersonality of the market and the possibility that affairs would not be conducted in the context of other virtues. Frederick Jackson Taylor took what looked like a weakness on Smith's part, his concern with virtues other than the bottom line, and gave us the theory of cold, perfected exchange. Many have criticized societies that have moved in the direction of Taylor away from humanity and toward efficiency. From the examples of Mordo and Cesare, we can see that Levi lamented this perfection of the market. Trade, just like his own profession, could embody many virtues, but Mordo's perfection of trade was chilling.

In Levi's ideal of his profession, there is the need to sell a product while being fair to others involved in the transaction. A professional also should have decent relations with those he works with, the bosses he works for, and those who buy what he has to sell. Central to the vocation of the chemist is the autonomy he needs to bring forth discovery. Work is central to Levi's existence, and this work should embody many virtues and not be totally in the service of perfected exchange. Levi is lucky to find an interstitial area in modern industrial society where can cultivate his skills in a job that allows for a good deal of autonomy. Although he never expresses it this way, his idea of exchange is close to Alexis de Tocqueville's idea of self-interest rightly understood. One's own welfare is primary, but in a liberal society room should exist for some generosity toward others. The person acting under the principle of self-interest rightly understood aims lower than martyrdom and higher than perfected exchange, a working medium that has useful possibilities for a modern society.

Levi understands very well the idea of exchange, its importance, and how markets arose first in abject circumstances. In the Lager there were no virtues other than survival, and with no trade there was little chance of survival. With the liberation of the camps and the understanding of the interconnectedness of individuals, civilization began anew. The crassness of the modern perfection of exchange is the return to a survival mentality with respect to economics and politics, the narrowing of virtue when it is not even necessary. Finally, he even recognizes tragic aspects of work, for it may simply be the veil that keeps us from thinking about the abyss. At this deeper level, Levi suspects that even with autonomous work and naïve exchange, there is no necessary progress.

Another area in which humans try to achieve perfection is toolmaking, and here again we cannot call this progress. Levi agrees with many others in thinking that what we build may lead to a variety of consequences for humans—good, bad, and indifferent. Science has flourished in modern

regimes, and it has become a cliché to state that our scientific achievements outrun our wisdom in using them. For Levi, there is no turning back the clock on science and technology. Shortly before he died in 1948, Martin Ryle, a radar specialist born in England, tried to halt science. He "formulated his drastic proposal: 'stop science now,' let us stop all scientific research, even the research that is called 'basic.' Since we cannot foresee the outcomes of our research and the uses to which it will be put, let us stop the discoveries through research." Levi calls Ryle's proposals "extremist and utopian." What Ryle neglects is how central to our nature the toolmaker really is: "We are what we are: each one of us, even the peasant, even the most modest artisan, is a researcher, has always been that."[10]

Again, Levi is the tragic optimist. We have a built-in tendency toward tool making, we arrange ourselves in hierarchies, we make tools in the service of others, and they are used for evil purposes. Levi again recommends education as the only possibility for an intractable problem. It is the best we can do, given our proclivities to build, and often in the service of others: "It would please me (and it seems to me neither impossible nor absurd) if in all scientific departments one point were insisted on uncompromisingly: what you will do when you exercise your profession can be useful, neutral, or harmful to mankind. Do not fall in love with suspect problems. Within the limits that you will be granted, try to know the end to which your work is directed."[11]

Levi knows that weighing ends is difficult, but nonetheless it must be done: "Don't hide behind the hypocrisy of neutral science: you are educated enough to be able to evaluate whether from the egg you are hatching will issue a dove or a cobra or a chimera or perhaps nothing at all." He can't see abandoning basic research, even though the risks are high, because to do so would be to betray our nature and our highest selves: "As for basic research, it can and must continue: if we were to abandon it, we would betray our nature and our nobility as 'thinking reeds' and the human species would no longer have any reason to exist."[12] Here is the highest embodiment of tragedy in humans: Our greatest achievements, the good, can lead to our destruction, for we are ill-constituted beings. Ironically, of course, work, given Levi's darkest suspicions, may not even be the good, but just the veil over the abyss.

10. Levi, "Hatching the Cobra," in *"The Mirror Maker,"* 175.
11. Ibid.
12. Ibid., 176.

He is not willing to concede that our achievements are a third force, culture, detached from our hands. This is pure pessimism, often used to sever responsibility for the most terrible acts. Revisionist German historians have begun to rationalize the Holocaust as an imitation of "'Asiatic' practice comprised of slaughter, mass deportation, ruthless exile to hostile regions, torture, and the separation of families. Our single innovation was purely technological: we invented the gas chamber."[13] The revisionist logic is simply a more sophisticated variant of "they made me do it." We must be made to understand our responsibility in terms of the development of technology and its subsequent use. We must be educated and habituated to intelligent use, definitely an Aristotlean analysis of virtues.

In sum, we know from Levi that the seductions of power are almost irresistible, and that the belief in progress—optimistic optimism—is one of the components of modernism that must undergo modification. At times, power and progress form a scary, unshakable alliance. Power and belief in progress shield us from a useful finitude: "Like Rumkowski, we too are so dazzled by power and money as to forget our essential fragility, forget that all of us are in the ghetto, that the ghetto is fenced in, that beyond the fence stand the lords of death, and not far away the train is waiting."[14]

We have now examined Levi's understanding of power and nationalism's effects, as well as the tension between progress and optimistic pessimism. We turn here to another of Levi's defenses of modernism, his spirited affirmation of the free flow of knowledge in the modern world. The first section will ask if the dissemination of knowledge inevitably leads to the destruction of modernism and straight to the gates of terror. The second section will show that in a democratic society, the free flow of information is so plentiful and diffuse that we must ask if the information glut causes the crucial ideas of civilization, pain, and danger to be lost in the surfeit. Finally, given all of the above-mentioned restraints, we will see what Levi found to be the most effective ways to teach about civilization and pain in a democratic society. Citizens of nations need to be inoculated against complicity with those who preach and perform cruel acts and murder on a mass scale. To be successful, Levi had to wage a war against the loss of memory.

13. Levi, "The Hard Sellers," in *"The Mirror Maker,"* 163.
14. Levi, *Moments of Reprieve*, 172.

of another time—a time, for instance, in which people were not schooled in resistance, nor had a background in understanding genocide.

Levi recurred to facts, which showed the virtual impossibility of people in such abject conditions fighting back. They didn't know where they were; they were wearing the garb of prisoners; the surrounding populace was hostile; and, most important, the prisoners were exhausted, starving. In such a miserable state, it was a miracle that any rebellion at all took place: "[O]nly at first glance does it seem paradoxical that people who rebel are those who suffer the least. Even outside the camps, struggles are rarely waged by *Lumpenproletariat*. People in rags do not revolt."[46]

Parrying guilt is necessary for Levi, but delivering it was carefully, judiciously, and infrequently done. He makes clear who the enemy was and how they should not be allowed to get away with what they did. He knows accusations will not make the perpetrators feel guilty, but those who excuse the behaviors of monsters can, and should, be made to feel guilty.

Throughout his writings, Levi makes clear who the perpetrators are and how they should be punished, but his anger comes through more clearly in his poetry than his prose. The poems speak for themselves. For example, in "For Adolph Eichmann," Levi's passion is clear:

> Oh son of death, we do not wish you death.
> May you live longer than anyone ever lived.
> May you live sleepless five million nights,
> And may you be visited each night by the suffering of everyone
>   who saw,
> Shutting behind him, the door that blocked the way back,
> Saw it grow dark around him, the air full with death.[47]

Or in his rephrasing of the common prayer in the poem "Shema," where he asks those of us who are comfortable in our own homes to

> Consider whether this is a man,
> Who labors in the mud
> Who knows no peace
> Who fights for a crust of bread
> Who dies at a yes or no.

46. Levi, *Reawakening*, 203.
47. Levi, "For Adolph Eichmann," in *Collected Poems*, 24.

He goes on to condemn those who continue to live in blissful security knowing what they now know:

> Consider that this has been:
> I commend these words to you.
> Engrave them on your hearts
> When you are in your house, when you walk on your way,
> When you go to bed, when you rise.
> Repeat them to your children.
> Or may your house crumble,
> Disease render you powerless,
> Your offspring avert their faces from you.[48]

In the poem, the enemy is those of us who forget the lessons of the Holocaust, and we are made to feel guilty. The poems, originally composed for a few friends, are a catharsis for him, but they do not take away from his primary mode of expression—as a civilized man trying to persuade by fact and moral philosophy.

He feels anger and hatred, but he doesn't want these sentiments to get in the way of objective analysis, which he believes is the major tool for persuasion: "I believe in reason and discussion as supreme instruments of progress, and therefore I repress hatred even within myself: I prefer justice."[49] Civilization must be brought to bear against the toughest aggressive forces. Civilization must be re-established primarily through education, not through the affixing of blame.

Throughout his writing he is not willing to turn the other cheek, and he argues that the civilized should not show mercy to the perpetrators. His books do not draw an indictment, but he does want to make sure that the perpetrators get punished now and in the future. Earlier, we discussed how many in the Lager fell in the "gray zone" and are less to blame than the Germans who were ultimately in charge. Levi suggests with his interpretation of Dostoyevsky's story in which an old woman receives absolution for giving a stranger an onion—a point made on Yom Kippur as well—that the survivors or others among the living cannot give forgiveness. Those who can give forgiveness are dead. He is extremely firm on this point.[50]

48. Levi, "Shema," in ibid., 9.
49. Levi, *Reawakening*, 196.
50. With respect to the position of blaming the enemy, we have today the radical embodiment of those ideas in the works of Daniel Goldhagen's *Hitler's Willing Executioners*

Levi used the three strategies to try to prevent the events of the Holocause from happening again, and he urges us to care about those we might not have the human inclination to care about. Perhaps Levi's greatest strength is that his writing is fresh and rich and he rarely repeats himself. He had a facility that Nikos Kazantzakis saw in his friend Alexis Zorba. Primo Levi saw everything as if anew, and he imparted this world to his readers. In a world that rushes through everyone's messages, the reader hesitates and browses through Levi's insights, so unique and thoughtful. He continually gives life to that which we have an inclination to forget.

Did Levi finally give up his quest to tell the story of the Holocaust? Some commentators argue that he was very discouraged at the end of his life. As the years passed, he did suggest that it was more difficult to get through to his young audiences. Yet, until the day of his death, he continued making plans and talking and writing about his experiences. As an optimistic pessimist, he knew that he was working against our basic inclinations in a protracted but losing battle. Genocide had occurred again, and again, and surely not for the last time. Science may give us a rough calculation of the dangers we face and the slim chance that we can stop the tide of nature and history, but ultimately, as James points out, deciding a course of action is not prescribed by science. It does not tell us when to persist and when to quit. If we have little chance of affecting events, but the consequences of those events are dire, we must keep up the fight against all odds.

Levi and John Dewey seem to share the same optimism against overwhelming odds. In *I Believe,* Dewey talks about how we can fight against overwhelming odds through group solidarity. More important for us here, Dewey felt that if individuals took new steps forward, even if hardly noticed, they could effect major change later on. He gave as an example the merchant who pitched his tent in front of a castle and whose small halting trade, followed by other merchants with their tents, led to the demise of the castle and the rise of towns. Levi also saw the ripples that events could put into history and that still reverberate. As mentioned previously, Levi spoke of how different history would be if Cleopatra's nose had been longer than it was. With respect to the Nazis, Levi lamented the fact that their evil continues to reverberate and poison the world: "In actuality, many signs lead us to think of a genealogy of today's violence that branch-

---

and Alan Dershowitz's *Chutzpah.* They are outspoken about the enemy and suggest that for centuries Jews ducked enemies to appease them. It didn't work with the Nazis. Levi never shirks from talking of the enemy in his writings, but he prefers us to come to our own conclusions.

es out precisely from the violence that was dominant in Hitler's Germany" (*Drowned*, 200).

On the positive side, the ripples of the testimony from Holocaust survivors will continue to find ways to inoculate future generations. Like Plato, whose *Republic* is an educational treatise on how to achieve the good life through politics, Levi's work can be seen as a detailed report on the education that must be provided in defense of civilized modernism.

Conclusion

12

Levi's Death

But we [the survivors] were denied the screen of willed ignorance. . . . The ocean of pain, past and present, surrounded us, and
its level rose from year to year until it almost submerged us. It was
not possible for us [to close our eyes to the pain] nor did we want
to become islands; the just among us . . . felt remorse, shame, and
pain for the misdeeds that others and not they had committed, and
in which they felt involved, because they sensed that what had happened around them and in their presence, and in them, was irrev-
ocable. Never again could it be cleansed.

—*The Drowned and the Saved*

Go away. I haven't dispossessed anyone,
Haven't usurped anyone's bread.
No one died in my place. No one.
Go back into your mist.
It's not my fault if I live and breathe,
Eat, drink, sleep and put on clothes.

—"The Survivor"

How to measure another's sufferings against one's own?

—*Other People's Trades*

The need to comment on Primo Levi's death and his views on suicide was
reinforced in a communication I had with a graduate school friend, George
Balch. I told him I was writing about Primo Levi. I said I was gathering
his ideas into a political philosophy and that Levi's ideas would be useful

255

in instructing us how to live in a "slightly inhospitable" world. He answered, "Correct my ignorance as needed, but didn't Primo Levi commit suicide? If so, how do you construe him as a useful source on 'how to live in a slightly inhospitable world?'" An anonymous journalist expressed roughly the same sentiments in the *New Yorker:* "The efficacy of all his words had somehow been canceled by his death—that his hope, or faith, was no longer usable by the rest of us."[1] In response, it is important to make the case that Levi's death makes sense in terms of being integral to his life, and that death is not the occasion that discounts everything he wrote and did. If his death diminishes the way he lived his life, why not just read his straightforward accounts of the Lager and discard his philosophy?

Levi biographer Mirna Cicioni described Levi's death matter-of-factly: "On the morning of Saturday 11 April 1987 Italian television announced that Primo Levi had fallen to his death down the stairwell from the third-floor landing of his home." Although generally assumed that he took his own life, one line in defense of Levi is to claim that his fall was accidental. Diego Gambetta in a *New York Times* article, "Primo Levi's Plunge: A Case against Suicide," writes, "The most pressing question, however, is not why Levi committed suicide but whether he committed it at all. Indeed the possibility of an accident has never been seriously examined even though there is no conclusive proof that Levi killed himself."[2] A close reading of this article and Cicioni's and Myriam Anissimov's biographies help clarify the questions surrounding his death by carefully examining his motives for and against suicide, as well as examining the physical possibilities of suicide or accident. We will leave it to his biographers to clear up any speculation as to whether or not he took his own life, but there will always be doubts, one way or another, as to the cause of his death. If it was an accident then, of course, the criticisms mentioned above do not apply. However, even if his death was intentional, it does not detract from his life.

What makes his death, particularly by suicide, a betrayal to some is that he came through the worst, a Hobbesian nightmare, and survived to preach an optimistic philosophy. An optimistic Levi taking his own life makes no sense in terms of his life or ideas. It is also an apparent betray-

---

1. *New Yorker,* 11 May 1987, 32.
2. Cicioni, *Primo Levi: Bridges of Knowledge,* 170; Gambetta, "Primo Levi's Plunge: A Case against Suicide," 7 August 1999, A15.

al because in some sense, the Nazis had the last word. Levi never overcame the foot on his chest no matter how hard he tried. We will answer.

Levi had many difficulties at the end of his life, and many Holocaust survivors took their own lives, including, for example, Jean Améry and Jerzy Kosinski. Their deaths and his troubles could serve as reasons for excusing Levi's death. I would prefer to argue that taking his own life is consistent with his ideas. Levi's life difficulties in particular, and the lives of survivors in general, are not excuses for Levi, but part of his equation of life and death.

Suicide is not contradictory to the way that Levi thought and lived. To explain, we will first highlight the agonic forces of life and death and see them in the larger context of his overall philosophy of optimistic pessimism. We initially confronted this in his story *"Force Majeure,"* where his protagonist faces the rest of life with the prospect that he may not overcome the force of a major tragedy. His need to respond to adversity comes up against the agonies of existence. We will also address his hedonism and a deliberate calculation that may be made to end one's own life. Second, we will ask if those beneath life at the end are subject to a different kind of circumstance, one in which the rational calculation of pleasures and pains gives way to will and guile, only to ultimately fail in the face of an overwhelming mood.

Most individuals have a strong will to live, coupled with an inordinate fear of death. Therefore, death is an evil, and we make great efforts to survive. Because we are ill-constituted beings, life is replete with pain; ultimately, life is a losing proposition in terms of pleasure and pain. His pessimism is modified by his optimism, which fortifies our will to survive and overcome the difficulties of this world. However, when the evil or pain overwhelms the good or pleasure, optimism is overridden, and at that time we may consider taking our own life.

Life is not "sacred" for Levi, because it is not consecrated by God, and there is no solace for him in thoughts of an afterlife. Suicide is no "sin." Also, as we have shown, the decision about our own life should not be in the hands of others. Our life and death belong to us and nobody else. Suicide is a utilitarian calculation that often takes place where there is a chance for thought and where the optimism that leavens pessimism is crushed by pain.

Levi clarifies his thoughts on the pulls of optimism and pessimism in his short stories. In "Westward," Walter, one of the protagonists, bluntly expresses the core of Levi's pessimism: "We are wrong [as beings], and we know it, but we find it more agreeable to keep our eyes shut. Life does not have a purpose; pain always prevails over joy; we are all sentenced to death, and the day of one's execution has not been revealed; we are condemned to watch the end of those dearest to us; there are compensations, but they are few."[3]

Levi's pessimism is modified by his mood of optimism, which is fueled by our vital will to live. In "The Hard Sellers," the story where the bureaucrats choose a man to go into the world, Levi reiterates that the will to live is within all creatures. With no contradiction from the others, one of the managers says: "The born, all the born, with very few exceptions, cling to life with a tenacity that surprises even us propagandists, and which is the best praise of life itself."[4] Walter and the other protagonist in "Westward," Anna, question why lemmings kill themselves in a mass suicide and why the Arunde tribe also has a very high rate of suicide. Anna says at one point early in the story, "We are alive because we want to live. It is a characteristic property of living substance; I want to live, I have no doubt. Life is better than death: that seems an axiom to me" (129).

Walter rejoins: "You have never had any doubts? Be honest!" Walter and Anna also see the provisional social reasons that impel us to persist in our agonic life even though we have seen the abyss. Anna says, "Some find a defense in religion, some in altruism, some in obtuseness, some in vice; some are able to distract themselves uninterruptedly." Walter continues: "[T]he most common and also the least ignoble defense is the one that exploits our essential ignorance of tomorrow." Here Walter seems to be expressing Levi's small change optimism (128, 129).[5]

In "Westward," Levi also personifies the battle between optimism and pessimism, pleasure and pain, which takes place in the more abstract debates between Walter and Ann. He takes us to the Amazon and the fictive Arunde tribe. Their ethos is Levi's, one of pleasure and pain, devoid of metaphysical convictions: "The elder confirmed that the Arunde had since time immemorial lacked metaphysical convictions: alone among all their neighbors they had neither churches nor priests nor witch doctors, and did not expect succor from the heavens nor the earth nor from the lower

---

3. Levi, "Westward," in *"The Sixth Day" and Other Tales*, 129. Future references to this story will be cited parenthetically in the text.
4. Levi, "The Hard Sellers," in *"Sixth,"* 157.
5. Anna has doubts, which we shall deal with shortly. They are important in explaining the attitude of those beneath life.

depths." He goes on to say, "Each of them was taught from infancy to evaluate life exclusively in terms of pleasure and pain, factoring in, of course, also the pleasures and pains the behavior of each individual caused his fellow men." When the balance sheet was permanently negative, the member of the tribe went before the council of elders, and if the person's judgment was affirmed, he went off to die. The tiniest seeds of a grain used to make flat bread are given to the person, seeds usually sifted out of the flour. They have a "drugging and toxic effect," and "he lives on bread made from unsifted seed, and in a few days, or a few weeks, as he may choose, he reaches a state of agreeable stupor, which is followed by definitive rest" (132, 133). The contending forces expressed in optimistic pessimism fight it out within the psyches of the individual members of the Arunde tribe. If life gets too oppressive, then they can deliberately choose, with the approval of the council, to take their own life.

Levi's optimistic pessimism clearly allows for the deliberate calculation of the pleasures and pains of life. Also, given our fear of death, our will to live, and if we have it, our optimism, we will put up with a great deal of pain. This is why most choose to live, even through severe pain. The deliberate choice to kill oneself is not a crime or a sin, nor can we from the outside judge what the balance of pains is for another human being. Like the Arunde council, we can guess at the other's pain, but only imperfectly.

If Levi's death was a suicide, we are right to ask if it was a choice born of deliberation. He left no notes, and his choice of method seems spontaneous rather than deliberate: "Primo Levi had fallen to his death down the stairwell from the third-floor landing of his home."[6] In the Lager, it was difficult to think about suicide, but in normal life there is time to contemplate it for a long time and then do it on impulse. Doestoyevski describes the mechanism of rumination followed by impulse in *The House of the Dead,* in which a prisoner faces his tormentor in a lineup day after day and one day simply kills him.

What is the final trigger to a long rumination about suicide? We have certain dispositions or inclinations, and as William James suggests, we may think of will as what happens when we finally incline in one direction against other thoughts. James suggests that we may have very strong impulses in one direction, but we can cultivate a doubt on the fringes until reinforcements are called in to the mind. Perhaps inclined to suicide on that day, Levi did not hear the small voice urging him not to, or heard the

---

6. Cicioni, *Primo Levi,* 170.

faint voice but did not cultivate it. Did his small change optimism finally
fail him? We will never know. However, if death did come through suicide,
it would be consistent with his utilitarian thinking and not take away from
his life and work.

Levi thought about suicide in a second way. In "Westward," he once
again qualifies a generalization about human behavior to show the richness
and complexity of human life. As a result of some prodding, Anna reminds
Walter of her doubts about the constancy of the vital will to live. She describes what her state of mind was like for the few months after their child
Mary was born: "That hold. That void. That feeling . . . useless, with all
around me useless, drowned in a sea of uselessness. Alone also in the midst
of a crowd: buried alive amidst everybody else buried alive" (128). As suggested earlier, this vital life force, which is lost in this instance, is Levi's
ground for our practicality and the reason death is a tragedy psychologically for us. Anna has described the plausible opening for suicide to take
place; vitality is lost. At these times, suicide might not be a deliberative act.

She thought of death when she was buried in a timeless void of uselessness, when she felt lost in the crowd. For her, there was no more future;
she was beneath life. This is beyond the Hobbesian Zen state in the Lager
Levi often found himself in, in which he was conscious of going along with
orders. She was in a state similar to the *musselmans* of the Lager. Walter
argues that the gulf between the normal spirited fear of death buoyed by
optimism is unbridgeable: "Now I also wanted to tell you that between a
person who possesses the love of life and a person who has lost it there exists no common language. The same event is described by both in two ways
that have nothing in common: one person draws joy from it, the other tor-
ment, each draws from it the confirmation of his own vision of the world"
(129).

Those so beneath life will draw their own conclusions about their chances
with life. Their circumstances seem awful, and the universe seems static.
One who uses optimism to counter the adversities of existence may be a
gulf away from the *musselmans* who lose that optimism and is on his way
to oblivion. There may be no way to prepare oneself for the final mood,
for it belongs to a different realm of discourse. At some point, for the *musselmans,* the event which usually comes to prove that there is good, small
change optimism, may not happen, and the doubts about suicide, which
are on the fringes of the mind, may not get reinforced. If there are circumstances where nothing good can be thought of, suicide becomes soli-

tary in the mind: "Or is it raining, windy and you have the usual hunger, and then you think that if you really had to, if you really felt nothing in your heart but suffering and tedium—as sometimes happens, when you really seem to lie on the bottom—well, even in that case, at any moment you want you could always go and touch the electric wire-fence, or throw yourself under the shunting trains, and then it would stop raining."[7]

Death came soon enough to the *musselmans* in the Lager, but it was unlikely to be a deliberate act. Levi suggests that suicide needs time for deliberation. In ordinary life there is such time for deliberation and those beneath life have often deliberated on it prior to being in the *musselmans* state. When beneath life, they may take their own life when it does not "stop raining." Levi did suffer from bouts of "depression" after Auschwitz, and this may account for his vivid descriptions of living beneath life: "I've had a few attacks of depression. I'm not sure if they go back to that experience [Auschwitz], because they come with different labels, from one to the next. It may seem strange to you, but I went through one just recently, [the interviews took place within a year of his death] a stupid fit of depression, for very little reason: I had a small operation on my foot, and this made me think that I'd suddenly got old. It took two months for the wound to heal."[8]

In the Lager, Levi saw the *musselmans* and feared their end, even hated them for giving in, a possible projection of his own fears. As he did not know the way into the corrosive mood, either in the Lager or later in his depressions, so, perhaps, he did not know the way back.

Suicide may be a rational calculation of pain and pleasure where the pain is overwhelming and there is no relief in sight. The final act may be deliberate or it may appear relatively spontaneous, but it may be the last act in a long chain of deliberation. Or it could be hatched in the *musselmans'* state beneath life, a state in which no small change goods appear, no prospects of the good are evidenced, and no countervailing fringe thoughts are grasped and cultivated. Levi's writings account for both possibilities, one based on rational calculation of pains and pleasures and the other made in a state not accessible to the "normal" person, a state beneath life based on pleasures and pain but in the full shadow of hopelessness. Levi accounted for these reasons for suicide, and neither of them, if true of him, will detract from his life.

7. Levi, *Survival in Auschwitz*, 131.
8. Ferdinando Camon, *Conversations with Primo Levi*, 63.

There is one more consideration in deciding about the relationship between his life and his death. Pain is subjective, and it is difficult to judge
in advance just how much we could take over our lifetimes or in times of
acute crisis before we would take our own life. We sit here thinking about
Primo Levi, much as Levi's judges in the Arunde tribe judge those who
come before them. We try to see if life was severe enough for Levi to make
the utilitarian decision in favor of death. It is difficult, if not impossible,
to know how much pain he had endured and to comprehend the horrors
he saw. In order to try and understand, we need to return where we began
and remember his short story *"Force Majeure."* As well as the pains of
everyday existence, Levi had to overcome the scars of *force majeure*. When
the prisoners were liberated from the camps, pain was replaced by anguish: "Anguish is known to everyone, even children, and everyone knows
that it is often blank, undifferentiated."[9] The differentiation begins to take
place retrospectively when he speaks of the various types of shame that do
not go away over the years. As psychologists have discovered, even if we
are so self-aware as to distinguish the multiple faces of anguish, this self-
awareness does not automatically make the attendant pain disappear. In
the aftermath of Auschwitz, the survivors suffered more than the perpetrators; the "sick points" burned in their soul never disappeared.

The pain of guilt may be worse than the prospect of death.[10] Death can
look like a reasonable alternative next to a life of extreme pain, a theme
Levi develops in his powerful poem about Adolph Eichmann. In the poem,
Levi indicates that there is a worse penalty for wrongdoing in this life than
death. Worse is when we are confronted every day by our guilt. Eichmann's
punishment should be that for the rest of eternity he has to face each individual killed on his orders. Death is too good for him.

Levi reminds us how difficult it is to live an ordinary life, and how we
must optimistically fight the good but losing battle. To ordinary life we can
add on the horrors he saw and had to personally live with. As we read his
works, it is impossible not to read them as survival manuals. We calculate
our chances and guess at the strength of our moral and physical resolve.
By any measure, despite his modest protestations about luck, Levi's intelligence and will are extraordinary. His life is an inspiration, not a failure,
regardless of how he died.[11]

9. Levi, *The Drowned and the Saved*, 71.
10. Remember that Levi uses shame and guilt as synonyms.
11. Many survivors took their own lives, and if Levi is correct, under the heel of *force
majeure*.

Finally, we must take heed of Levi's own words about speculating on the death of one who may have taken his or her own life. We can try to understand what motivates humans to behave the way they do, but it is a daunting task: "Améry's suicide, which took place in Salzburg in 1978, like other suicides admits of a cloud of explanations."[12]

Reading Levi's original works is like finding a treasure left in the ashes of a terrible time, and this book is an urgent plea to those who have not already done so—read Levi's original works. The purpose of this modest volume is to cast the eye of the reader in a slightly different direction to see Levi's work as the mature life philosophy of a cunning amateur. He reminds us of the lesson that regardless of circumstances and vocation, we can live an intelligent life. In particular, this volume is an answer to the question first posed: First me, second me and why you? It is a political philosophy that arises out of the worst of circumstances to make its claim on the intelligence of those of us who may be troubled by modern civilization, but who are loathe to blame that civilization for the worst that has happened. We are tragic beings, and civilization is our faintly beating pulse against the strong currents of our nature.

12. Levi, *Drowned*, 136.

Bibliography

Anissimov, Myriam. *Primo Levi: Tragedy of an Optimist*. Woodstock, N.Y.: Overlook Press, 1999.

Aristotle. *Politics*. Trans. C. D. C. Reeve. Indianapolis, Ind.: Hackett Publishing, 1998.

Bartov, Omer. "The Penultimate Horror." *New Republic*, 13 Oct. 1997, 48–53.

Bauman, Zygmunt. *Modernity and the Holocaust*. Ithaca, N.Y.: Cornell University Press, 1989.

Becker, Ernest. *Escape from Evil*. New York: The Free Press, 1975.

Bellamy, Edward. *Looking Backward, 2000–1887*. New York: Houghton Mifflin, 1931.

Bentham, Jeremy. *An Introduction to the Principles of Morals and Legislation*. Oxford: Clarendon Press, 1907.

Berlin, Isaiah. *The Crooked Timber of Humanity*. New York: Vintage Books, 1990.

———. "On Political Judgment." *New York Review of Books*, 3 Oct. 1996, 26–30.

———. *The Proper Study of Mankind*. New York: Farrar, Straus and Giroux, 1998.

Bloom, Allan. *The Closing of the American Mind*. New York: Touchstone Books, 1987.

———. *Giants and Dwarfs: Essays, 1960–1990*. New York: Touchstone Books, 1990.

Buber, Martin. *The Tales of Rabbi Nachman*. New York: Avon Books, 1956.

Burke, Edmund. "Reflections on the Revolution in France." In Edmund Burke and Thomas Paine, *"Reflections on the Revolution in France" and "The Rights of Man."* Garden City, N.J.: Doubleday, 1961.

265

Camon, Ferdinando. *Conversations with Primo Levi.* Marlboro, Vt.: The Marlboro Press, 1989.

Canetti, Elias. *Crowds and Power.* New York: The Noonday Press, 1991.

Cicioni, Mirna. *Primo Levi: Bridges of Knowledge.* Oxford: Berg, 1995.

Cooke, Jacob E., ed. *The Federalist.* Cleveland, Ohio: Meridian Books, 1961.

Darwin, Charles. *The Origin of Species & The Descent of Man.* New York: Modern Library, 1983.

Dawidowicz, Lucy. *The War against the Jews, 1933–1945.* New York: Bantam Books, 1975.

Deak, Istvan. "Memories of Hell." *New York Review of Books,* 26 June 1997, 38–43.

Defoe, Daniel. *Robinson Crusoe.* New York: Rand McNally, 1916.

Dershowitz, Alan. *Chutzpah.* Boston, Mass.: Little Brown, 1991.

Descartes, René. *Discourse on Method and Meditations on First Philosophy.* Indianapolis, Ind.: Hackett, 1980.

Dewey, John. *Experience and Nature.* New York: Dover Publications, 1958.

Dostoyevsky, Fyodor. *The Brothers Karamazov.* New York: Vintage Books, 1991.

———. *Memoirs from the House of the Dead.* London: Oxford, 1956.

Doyle, Arthur Conan. *Tales of Terror and Mystery.* Middlesex, Eng.: Penguin Books, 1979.

Durrell, Lawrence. *Reflections on Marine Venus.* New York: Marlowe and Co., 1996.

Eidelberg, Ludwig. *Encyclopedia of Psychoanalysis.* New York: The Free Press, 1968.

Emerson, Ralph Waldo. *Emerson's Complete Works: Riverside Edition.* Boston, Mass.: Houghton, Mifflin, 1892.

Etzioni, Amitai. *The New Golden Rule: Community and Morality in a Democratic Society.* New York: Basic Books, 1966.

Fanon, Franz. *The Wretched of the Earth.* New York: Grove Press, 1968.

Foucault, Michel. *Discipline and Punish.* New York: Vintage Books, 1979.

———. *Madness and Civilization.* New York: Vintage Books, 1965.

Freud, Anna. *The Ego and Mechanisms of Defense.* Madison, Conn.: International Universities Press, 1966.

Freud, Sigmund. *Character and Culture.* New York: Collier Books, 1963.

———. *Civilization and Its Discontents.* New York: W. W. Norton, 1961.

Friedlander, Saul. *Nazi Germany and the Jews*. Vol. 1, *The Years of Persecution, 1933–1939*. New York: HarperCollins, 1997.

Gambetta, Diego. "Primo Levi's Plunge: A Case against Suicide." *New York Times,* 7 Aug. 1999, A15.

Goldhagen, Daniel Jonah. *Hitler's Willing Executioners*. New York: Vintage Books, 1996.

Gould, Stephen J. *The Panda's Thumb*. New York: W. W. Norton, 1980.

Groddeck, Georg. *The Book of the It*. London: Vision Press, 1979.

———. *The Meaning of Illness*. New York: International Universities Press, 1977.

Hegel, Georg Wilhelm Friedrich. *Reason in History*. New York: Liberal Arts Library, 1953.

Heller, Joseph. *Catch-22*. New York: Dell Publishing, 1955.

———. *Picture This*. New York: Ballantine Books, 1989.

Hilberg, Raul. *The Destruction of the European Jews*. New York: Holmes and Meier, 1985.

Hobbes, Thomas. *Leviathan*. Edited and introduced by Edwin Curley. Indianapolis, Ind.: Hackett, 1994.

Hobsbawm, Eric. *An Age of Extremes: A History of the World, 1914–1991*. New York: Vintage Books, 1994.

Hoffer, Eric. *The True Believer*. New York: Harper and Row, 1951.

Homer, Frederic D. *Character: An Individualistic Theory of Politics*. Burke, Va.: Chatelaine Press, 1996.

———. *Guns and Garlic: Myths and Realities of Organized Crime*. West Lafayette, Ind.: Purdue University Press, 1974.

———. *The Interpretation of Illness*. West Lafayette, Ind.: Purdue University Press, 1988.

Howe, Irving. *A World More Attractive: A View of Modern Literature and Politics*. New York: Horizon Press, 1963.

Hume, David. *An Enquiry Concerning Human Understanding*. Indianapolis, Ind.: Hackett, 1977.

Huxley, Aldous. *Brave New World*. New York: Harper and Row, 1946.

James, William. *"Pragmatism" and Other Essays*. New York: Washington Square Press, 1963.

———. *Psychology: The Briefer Course*. Ed. Gordon Allport. Bloomington, Ind.: University of Notre Dame Press, 1985.

———. *The Writings of William James*. Chicago: University of Chicago Press, 1997.

Kafka, Franz. *The Trial*. New York: Alfred A. Knopf, 1937.

Kaufmann, Walter, ed. and trans. *The Portable Nietzsche*. Middlesex, Eng.: Penguin Books, 1968.

Kazantzakis, Nikos. *Freedom or Death*. New York: Ballantine Books, 1955.

————. *Report to Greco*. New York: Touchstone Books, 1965.

Kolakowski, Leszek. *"The Key to Heaven" and "Conversations with the Devil."* New York: Grove Press, 1972.

Kosinski, Jerzy. *The Painted Bird*. New York: Bantam Books, 1988.

Kundera, Milan. *The Art of the Novel*. New York: The Grove Press, 1988.

Lacan, Jacques. *Ecrits: A Selection*. Trans. A. Sheridan. New York: Norton, 1977.

Lasswell, Harold. *Psychopathology and Politics*. New York: Viking Press, 1962.

Leopardi, Giacomo. *Essays and Dialogues*. Trans. Charles Edwards. London: Trubner and Sons, 1882.

Levi, Primo. *Collected Poems*. London: Faber and Faber, 1988.

————. *The Drowned and the Saved*. New York: Vintage Books, 1989.

————. *If Not Now, When?* New York: Penguin Books, 1986.

————. *"The Mirror Maker": Stories and Essays by Primo Levi*. New York: Schocken Books, 1989.

————. *Moments of Reprieve*. New York: Penguin Books, 1979.

————. *The Monkey's Wrench*. New York: Penguin Books, 1986.

————. *Other People's Trades*. New York: Summit Books, 1989.

————. *The Periodic Table*. New York: Schocken Books, 1984.

————. *The Reawakening*. New York: Collier Books, 1987.

————. *"The Sixth Day" and Other Tales*. New York: Summit Books, 1990.

————. *Survival in Auschwitz*. New York: Collier Books, 1993.

Levine, Donald N., ed. *Georg Simmel: On Individuality and Social Forms*. Chicago: University of Chicago Press, 1971.

Locke, John. *Second Treatise of Government*. Indianapolis, Ind.: Hackett Publishing, 1980.

Lukacs, John. *The Hitler of History*. New York: Knopf, 1997.

Machiavelli, Niccolo. *"The Prince" and "The Discourses."* New York: Modern Library, 1950.

MacIntyre, Alasdair. *After Virtue*. Bloomington, Ind.: University of Notre Dame Press, 1984.

Marcel, Gabriel. *The Philosophy of Existentialism*. London: Havrill Press, 1954.

May, Rollo. *Love and Will*. New York: W. W. Norton, 1969.

Mill, John Stuart. *"Utilitarianism," "On Liberty," "Considerations on Representative Government."* Ed. Geraint Williams. London: J. M. Dent, 1972.

More, Sir Thomas. *Utopia*. New York: W. W. Norton, 1992.

Nelson, Brian R. *Western Political Thought*. Englewood Cliffs, N.J.: Prentice Hall, 1996.

Nietzsche, Friedrich. *Human All Too Human*. Lincoln: University of Nebraska Press, 1986.

———. *"On the Genealogy of Morals" and "Ecce Homo."* New York: Random House, 1967.

Novick, Peter. *The Holocaust in American Life*. New York: Houghton Mifflin, 1999.

Nozick, Robert. *The Examined Life*. New York: Touchstone Books, 1989.

Ortega y Gasset, José. *"The Dehumanization of Art" and "Notes on the Novel."* Trans. Helene Weyl. Princeton: Princeton University Press, 1948.

———. *The Modern Theme*. New York: Harper and Row, 1961.

Orwell, George. *1984*. New York: Signet Books, 1962.

Phillips, Adam. *The Beast in the Nursery*. New York: Pantheon Books, 1998.

———. *Monogamy*. New York: Random House, 1996.

———. *On Kissing, Tickling and Being Bored*. London: Faber and Faber, 1993.

Plato. *The Republic of Plato*. Trans. Allan Bloom. New York: Basic Books, 1988.

Rawls, John. *A Theory of Justice*. Cambridge, Mass.: Harvard University Press, 1971.

Regge, Tulle. *Dialogo*. Princeton, N.J.: Princeton University Press, 1989.

Rorty, Richard. *Philosophy and the Mirror of Nature*. Princeton, N.J.: Princeton University Press, 1979.

Rousseau, Jean-Jacques. *Émile; or, On Education*. Introduced, translated and with notes by Allan Bloom. New York: Basic Books, 1979.

———. *The Social Contract*. Middlesex, Eng.: Penguin Books, 1968.

Royce, Josiah. *The Spirit of Modern Philosophy*. New York: Dover Publications, 1983.

Rubenstein, Richard L. *The Cunning of History*. New York: Harper, 1978.

Rudolph, Anthony. *At an Uncertain Hour: Primo Levi's War against Oblivion*. London: Menard Press, 1990.

Russell, Bertrand. *"In Praise of Idleness" and Other Essays*. New York: Simon and Schuster, 1972.

Samenow, Stanton. *Inside the Criminal Mind*. New York: Random House, 1984.

Schopenhauer, Arthur. *Essays and Aphorisms*. New York: Penguin Books, 1970.

———. *The World as Will and Representation*. Vols. 1 and 2. New York: Dover, 1966.

Schumpeter, Joseph. *Capitalism, Socialism, and Democracy*. New York: Harper Torchbooks, 1950.

Schwartz-Bart, Andre. *The Last of the Just*. New York: MFJ Books, 1996.

Secord, Paul, and Carl W. Backman. *Social Psychology*. New York: McGraw-Hill, 1968.

Simmel, Georg. *The Philosophy of Money*. London: Routledge and Kegan Paul, 1978.

Singer, Isaac Bashevis. *The Penitent*. New York: Ballantine Books, 1985.

———. *"The Spinoza of Market Street" and Other Stories*. New York: Bard Books, 1961.

Spiegelman, Art. *Maus*. New York: Pantheon Books, 1986.

Sykes, Gresham, and David Matza. "Techniques of Neutralization: A Theory of Delinquency." *American Sociological Review* 45 (Dec. 1957), 664–90.

Tarrow, Susan, ed. *Reason and Light: Essays on Primo Levi.*. Ithaca, N.Y.: Center for International Studies, Cornell University, 1990.

Tavris, Carol. *Anger*. New York: Simon and Schuster, 1989.

Taylor, Frederick Jackson. *Principles of Scientific Management*. New York: Harper and Brothers, 1934.

Timerman, Jacobo. *Prisoner without a Name, Cell without a Number*. New York: Vintage Books, 1981.

Tocqueville, Alexis de. *Democracy in America*. Vols. 1 and 2. New York: Vintage Books, 1945.

Weber, Max. *Economy and Society*. New York: Bedminster Press, 1968.

———. *From Max Weber: Essays in Sociology*. Ed. H. H. Gerth and C. Wright Mills. New York: Oxford University Press, 1958.

Weinstein, Michael A. *Culture/Flesh: Explorations of Postcivilized Modernity*. Lanham, Mass.: Rowman and Littlefield, 1995.

———. *Finite Perfection: Reflections on Virtue*. Amherst: University of Massachusetts Press, 1985.

Whitehead, Alfred North. *Adventures of Ideas*. New York: The Free Press, 1967.

———. *Modes of Thought*. New York: The Free Press, 1968.

———. *Science and the Modern World*. New York: Macmillan, 1925.

Wiener, Philip, ed. *Leibniz: Selections*. New York: Charles Scribners Sons, 1951.

Wiesel, Elie. *All Rivers Run to the Sea: Memoirs*. New York: Schocken Books, 1995.

———. *Night*. New York: Hill and Wang, 1960.

Wiesenthal, Simon. *The Murderers among Us*. New York: McGraw-Hill, 1960.

———. *The Sunflower: On the Possibilities and Limits of Forgiveness*. New York: Schocken Books, 1976.

Wilson, James Q. *The Moral Sense*. New York: The Free Press, 1993.

Wood, Garth. *The Myth of Neurosis*. New York: Harper and Row, 1986.

Wood, James. "Essences Rising." *New Republic,* 16 June 1997, 41–45.

Index